AF539585

TO PLEASE EVERY TASTE

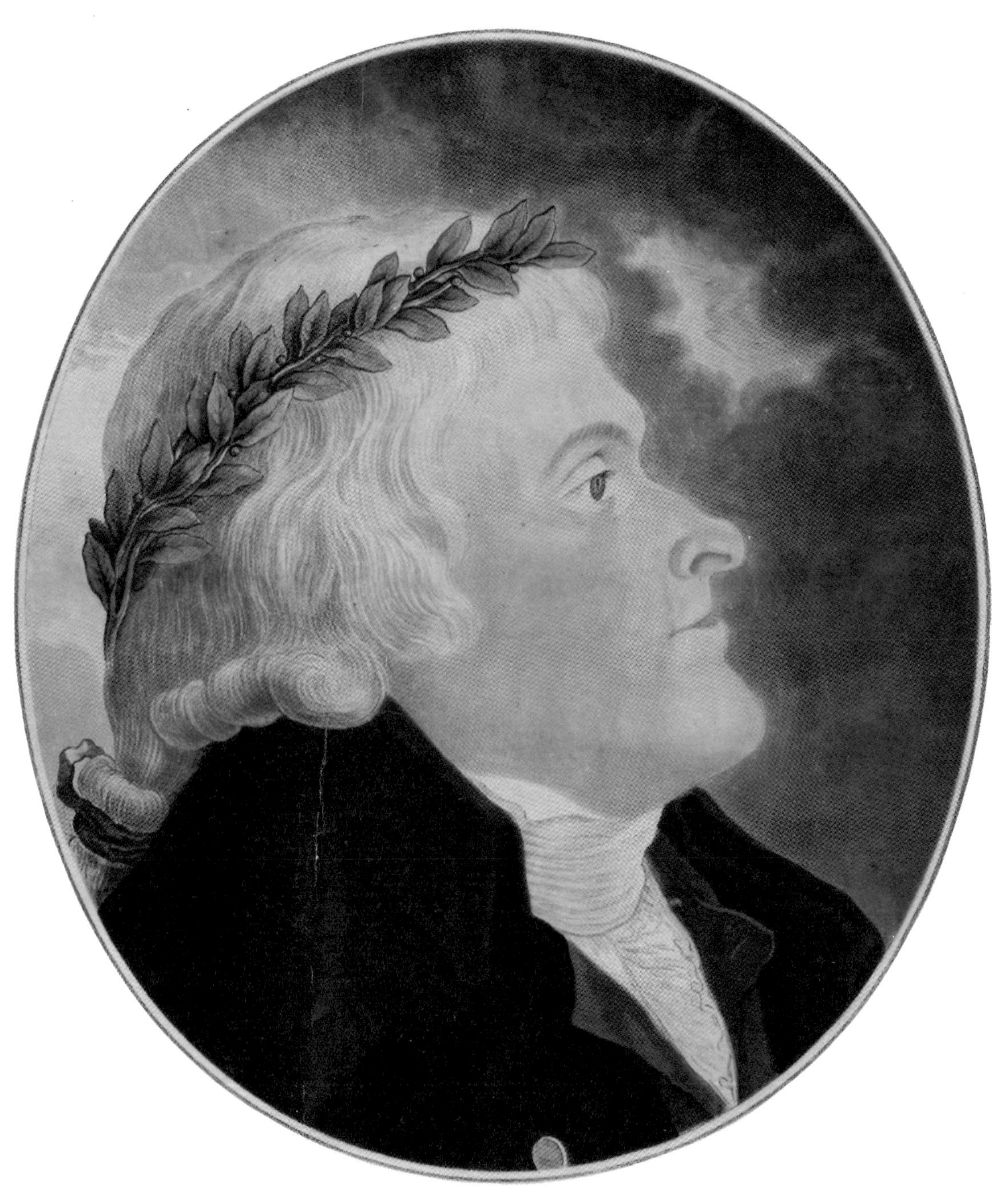

TO PLEASE EVERY TASTE

Eighteenth-Century Prints from the Winterthur Museum

E. McSherry Fowble

ART SERVICES INTERNATIONAL
ALEXANDRIA, VIRGINIA 1991

Frick Art Museum
Pittsburgh, Pennsylvania

Terra Museum of American Art
Chicago, Illinois

Fine Arts Museum, Cheekwood
Nashville, Tennessee

Fraunces Tavern Museum
New York, New York

Museums at Stony Brook
Stony Brook, New York

The exhibition is organized and circulated by Art Services International, Alexandria, Virginia.

Library of Congress Cataloging-in-Publication Data

Fowble, E. McSherry, 1933—
To please every taste: eighteenth-century prints from the Winterthur Museum/E. McSherry Fowble
p. cm.
Exhibit catalog.
Includes bibliographical references.
ISBN 0-88397-098-8
1. Prints, American—Exhibitions. 2. Prints—18th century United States—Exhibitions. 3. United States in Art—Exhibitions. 4. Henry Francis du Pont Winterthur Museum—Exhibitions. I. Henry Francis du Pont Winterthur Museum. II. Title.
NE506.F6 1991
769'.974'07474—dc20 91-2960
CIP

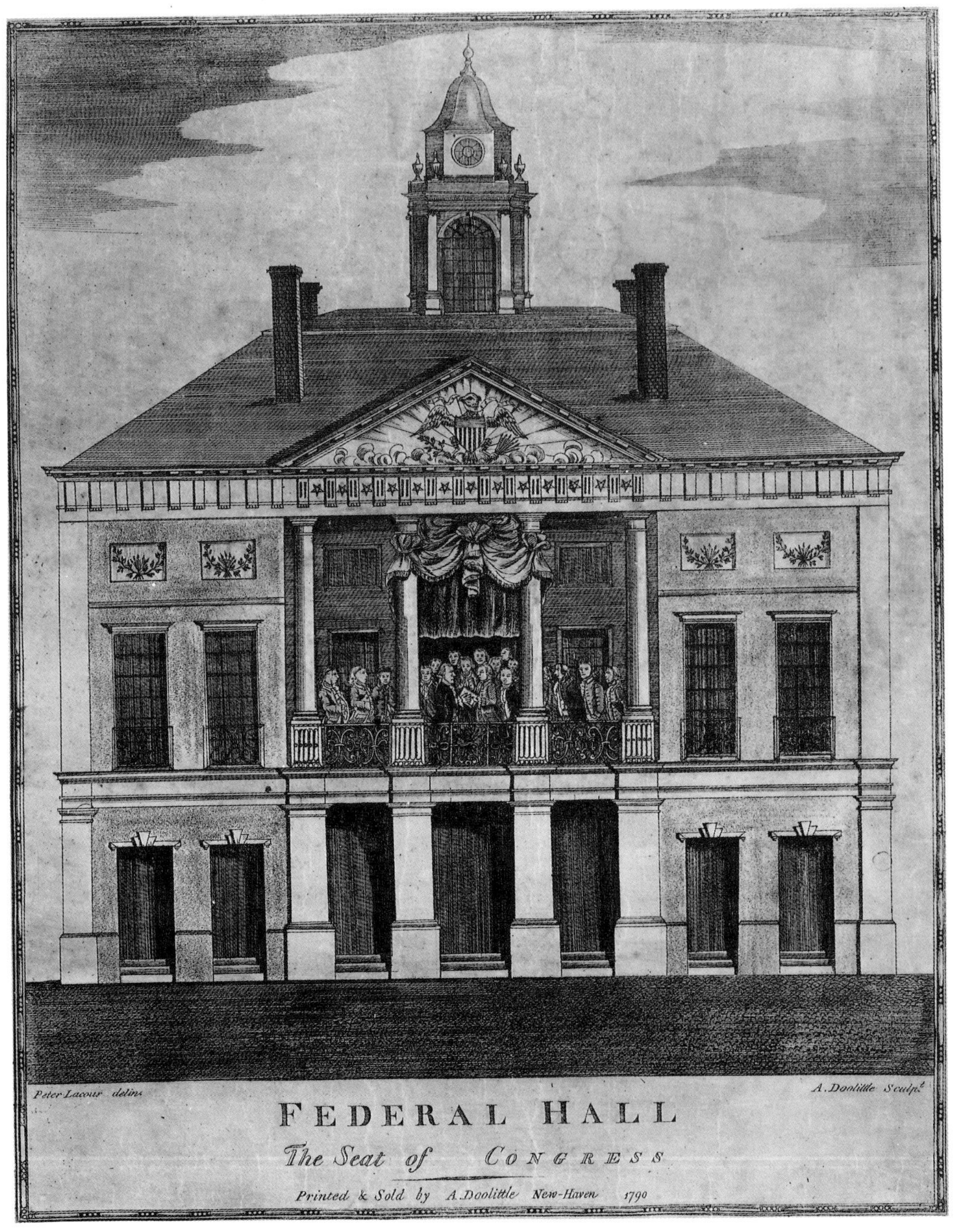

Federal Hall (cat. no. 14)

CONTENTS

Acknowledgments 6

Preface 8

To Please Every Taste 11

Notes to the Catalogue 37

Catalogue of Works 39

Selected Bibliography 211

ACKNOWLEDGMENTS

It is a great pleasure for Art Services International to present this handsome exhibition of eighteenth-century prints from the Henry Francis du Pont Winterthur Museum. Long renowned for its exceptional holdings in early American furnishings and works of art, Winterthur has never before allowed an exhibition of objects derived solely from its impressive holdings to tour. Naturally, we at Art Services International are honored to be endowed with such trust in bringing these exceptional documents of American history to audiences throughout the country.

Americans today often forget that the earliest settlers in colonial times considered themselves Englishmen and Europeans merely transplanted to foreign shores. They retained the customs, attitudes, and preferences instilled in their native lands, including the decoration of their homes with prints and maps. As the demand for etchings and engravings grew in the prospering colonies, artists, printmakers, and publishers crisscrossed the Atlantic to offer their talents and works. Prints from eighteenth-century America dealt with such various subjects as the expansion and development of territories, the changing relationship between the colonies and England, and the evolving tastes in fashion and home decoration. All these subjects and more are found within this exhibition.

We are grateful to Dr. Thomas A. Graves, Jr., Director and Chief Executive Officer of the Winterthur Museum, for his endorsement of this project and his generosity in lending such a superb selection of works. With great pleasure we also send our personal thanks to Charles F. Hummel, Deputy Director of Collections, for his confidence, which we value so highly, and his continued support.

A special acknowledgment is extended to E. McSherry Fowble, Curator and in Charge of Graphics and Paintings at Winterthur and Guest Curator of this exhibition. Without her vision and dedication, this presentation would not have taken place. In addition to selecting the works and writing the catalogue text, she responded patiently and with consistent good humor to our various requests for information. Her efforts to bring this project to fruition cannot be overstated, and we offer her our highest praise.

Our sincere appreciation extends as well to the institutions that collaborated with Art Services International to present these works to American audiences. Their enthusiasm and thoughtful support of this exhibition have made our work all the easier. We would like to thank in particular DeCourcy E. McIntosh and Alan Fausel of the Frick Art Museum in Pittsburgh; Harold O'Connell and Scott Atkinson of the Terra Museum of American Art in Chicago; David Ribar of the Fine Arts Museum, Cheekwood in Nashville; William S. Ayres and Lauren Kaminsky of the Fraunces Tavern Museum in New York City; and Dr. Judith O'Sullivan and Amy McKune of the Museums at Stony Brook in New York. To these directors and curators, we extend our warmest regards.

The production of this catalogue was skillfully overseen by our editor, Nancy Eickel, and the book's sensitive design is the work of Grafik Communications, Ltd. Together, they produced a stately catalogue that merits our gratitude.

Once again, it is through the efforts and talents of the staff of ASI, notably Marcene Edmiston, Donna Elliott, Margaret Frazier, and Sally Thomas, that this examination of prints from early America has been possible, and we extend to them our deep appreciation.

Lynn Kahler Berg
Director

Joseph W. Saunders
Chief Executive Officer

PREFACE

October 1991 marks the fortieth anniversary of the opening of Winterthur to the public. In the years since 1951, Winterthur's premier collection of decorative arts made or used in America between 1640 and 1860 has been brought before an ever-widening audience through expanded tour programs, lecture series, conferences, seminars, institutes, research and publication, and three graduate programs that offer degrees in early American material culture and the conservation of art objects.

Over 89,000 objects, including furniture, textiles, paintings and prints, glass, copper and brass, iron, silver, pewter, needlework, porcelain and earthenware, architecture, and wallpapers, are on display at Winterthur. To encourage and facilitate study and analysis of these objects, Winterthur instituted in 1952 a series of catalogues of the special collections, beginning with Joseph Downs' American Furniture. *More than thirty-six catalogues and fourteen conference reports have been published to date. Individual catalogues on the glass, silver, copper and brass, New England furniture, and Windsor furniture in the Winterthur collections are forthcoming. Since 1977, Winterthur has also loaned objects from its collections to exhibitions that have been seen throughout the United States, Canada, and Europe, and which have significantly advanced our understanding of the decorative arts.*

Two Centuries of Prints in America, 1680-1880: A Selective Catalogue of the Winterthur Museum Collection, *by E. McSherry Fowble, Curator and in Charge of Graphics and Paintings at Winterthur, was published in December 1987. In the spring of 1988, we were pleased when Lynn Kahler Berg and Joseph W. Saunders of Art Services International expressed interest in working with us to prepare a traveling exhibition from our collection of maps and prints. That October, Lynn Kahler Berg, Joseph Saunders, Charles F. Hummel, Philip D. Zimmerman, and E. McSherry Fowble met to review a selection of objects. It was decided at that meeting to focus the exhibition on prints, because they particularly reflect the times and the tastes of eighteenth-century Americans.* To Please Every Taste *includes many of the great graphic treasures from the Winterthur collections. This is a visual history in microcosm of the period of colonial growth, revolution, and an emerging national image. To emphasize the point that many of these prints were used as household furnishings, some are traveling in original frames. Others are accompanied by ceramics and furniture that added to the enjoyment and enlightenment eighteenth-century Americans found in the printed image.*

It is a significant achievement for Winterthur that this exhibition, the first of its kind made up entirely of objects from the Winterthur collection, will begin its journey in our fortieth anniversary year. Through the encouragement and support of Art Services International, this traveling exhibition will be seen in institutions throughout the United States. I am especially pleased that in this way we are able to share our treasures with broader audiences.

Dr. Thomas A. Graves, Jr.
Director and Chief Executive Officer
Winterthur Museum

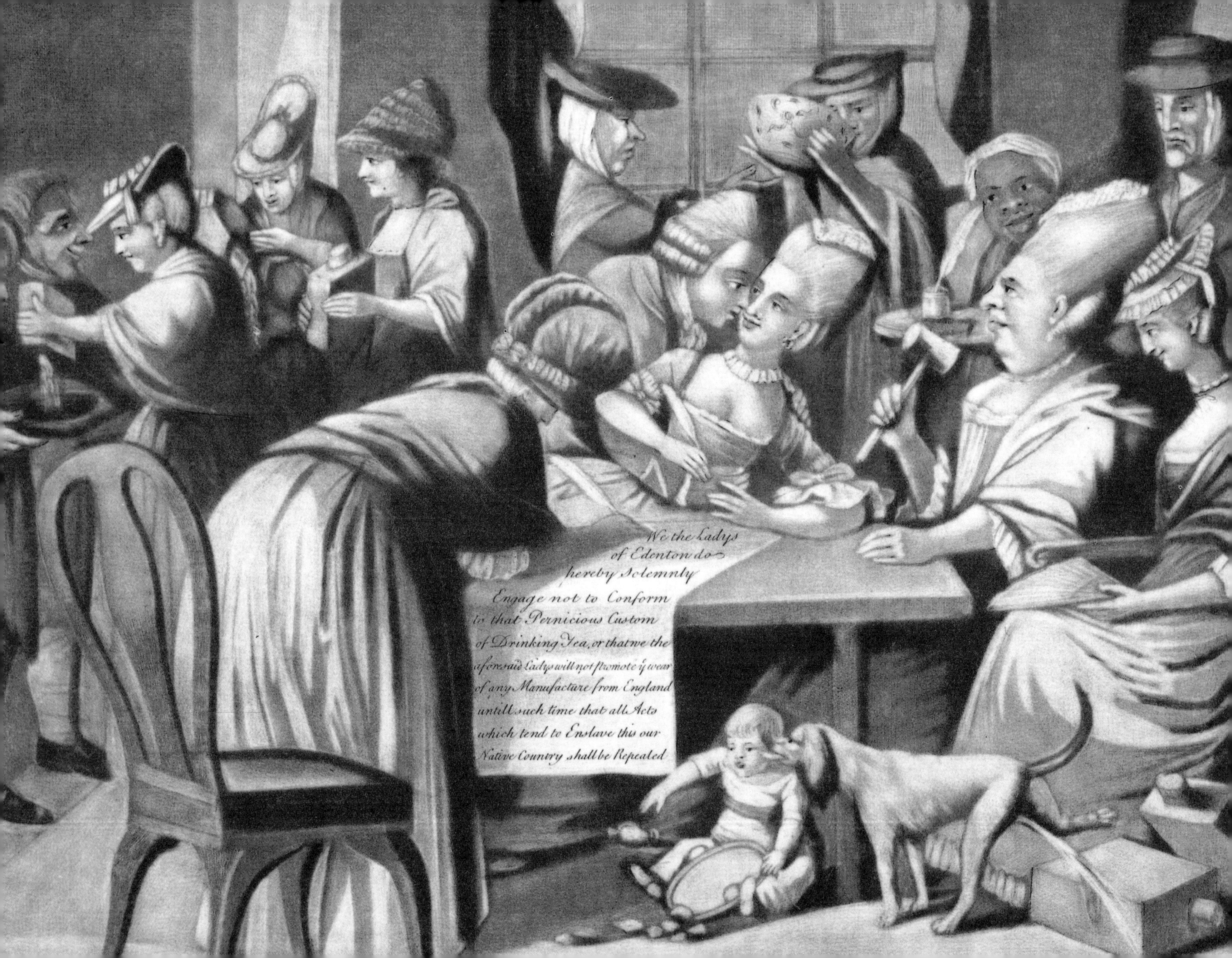
We the Ladys
of Edenton do
hereby Solemnly
Engage not to Conform
to that Pernicious Custom
of Drinking Tea, or that we the
aforesaid Ladys will not promote ÿ wear
of any Manufacture from England
untill such time that all Acts
which tend to Enslave this our
Native Country shall be Repealed

TO PLEASE EVERY TASTE

The eighteenth century was a golden time for engravings. Before the end of the century most of the hand-executed techniques for printing from copperplate, wood, or stone were in place. Professionals specifically skilled in translating images from original art to a printing surface were finally recognized by artists as associates, if not as full equals. In England and America the number of printsellers or publishers increased from a relative few as the popular demands for a wide variety of subjects at modest prices and a current inventory developed and matured. The small number of studied collectors of the seventeenth and early eighteenth centuries were joined by a growing number of casual collectors and occasional impulse buyers. Print shops became print galleries, where the serious collector could compare and augment his holdings and where the newly initiated could spend an afternoon browsing.

To understand the business of printmaking and printselling in eighteenth-century America requires some understanding of later seventeenth- and eighteenth-century printmaking and selling in England, on which the American print trade was so dependent. The American colonists were largely Englishmen abroad. Their understanding and taste for art was what they brought with them, imported, or saw practiced by the artisans or limners who continued to arrive throughout the seventeenth century.[1] Englishmen leaving to settle in Virginia and Plymouth in the first quarter of the seventeenth century probably knew of printed images on paper from an occasional book illustration, a map, or one of the cheap prints hawked by street vendors in their home towns or ports of departure. Although it lagged far behind developments in England

[1] See Jonathan Fairbanks, "Portrait Painting in Seventeenth Century Boston: Its History, Methods, and Materials," in *New England Begins: The Seventeenth Century*, 3 vols. (Boston: Museum of Fine Arts, 1982), 3:413-79.

Left: Detail of *A Society of Patriotic Ladies* (cat. no. 48)

in some respects, the rise of printmaking and printselling in America—reinforced by a scattered but steady influx of English engravers and entrepreneurs, and a ready supply of maps and pictures from abroad—followed the English model throughout the last years of the seventeenth and all the eighteenth century.

TECHNIQUES: EARLY DEVELOPMENTS AND PRACTITIONERS

At the beginning of the seventeenth century, printmaking in England was closely aligned with the book trade. Many of the leading names working for publishers of engraved images in England were foreign: the Van de Passe family from Utrecht, Marcus Gheeraets from Bruge, and Francis Delaram and Martin Drueshout (1601-1652) from the Netherlands.[2] Wenceslas Hollar (1607-1677) first came to England from Bohemia to work in 1636. Perhaps more than any other engraver, Hollar brought variety in subjects to a trade that concentrated on portraits. He copied great paintings from the collection of his patron, Thomas Howard, earl of Arundel and Sussex. He engraved architectural subjects, fashionable ladies, genre, cityscapes and landscapes, and natural studies. Hollar's output was prodigious, and his work was found in some of the most important illustrated publications of the late seventeenth century. His contemporary, Englishman Francis Barlow (ca. 1626-ca. 1704), a draftsman and etcher, focused on animals, both natural and fantastic, and on fables and genre.

By the time Hollar arrived in England there was a well-developed business in mapmaking, led by John

[2] Crispin Van de Passe executed English subjects from his studio in Utrecht. His sons Willem (ca. 1599-ca. 1637) and Simon (ca. 1595-ca. 1647) worked in England. See Stephen Calloway, *English Prints for the Collector* (Guilford and London: Lutterworth Press, and Woodstock, Vt.: Overlook Press, 1981), 16-21, and Richard T. Godfrey, *Printmaking in Britain* (New York: New York University Press, 1978), 16-17.

Speed (1553-1629) and others, which flourished in an era of exploration, colonization, and wars. But "heads," from small images bound as frontispieces in octavo editions to more ambitious portraits of kings, nobility, and gentry, continued to dominate engravers' productions through the end of the seventeenth century and well into the next.[3]

The first to practice printmaking in the colonies did not execute an image until 1670, and in keeping with the preponderance of English production this earliest of American prints was a portrait.[4] John Foster (1648-1681), who was born in Boston and graduated from Harvard College in 1667, would have known of prints from the books he studied. In or about 1670, he prepared a portrait of Richard Mather (1596-1669), which measured 5 15/16 by 5 15/16 inches (15.1 by 15.1 cm).

Historically in Western countries, the initial technique used for reproducing multiple images on paper continued to be block printing or woodcut, whether employed for Foster's portrait of Mather (the first print produced in Massachusetts), the late fifteenth-century productions of William Caxton (ca. 1422-1491), which were the earliest prints executed in England (ca. 1481), or the first playing cards printed in Europe (ca. 1400).[5]

Technically grouped as a relief process, woodcut is compatible with the printing of text on a letter-press. If necessary, woodcut can be printed by hand, without benefit of a machine. It requires only the most basic of equipment to prepare the design: a knife or gouge and a flat, planed piece of plank

3 Calloway, *English Prints for the Collector,* 30; Godfrey, *Printmaking in Britain,* 26.

4 See Richard B. Holman, "Seventeenth-Century American Prints," in *Prints in and of America to 1850,* ed. John D. Morse (Charlottesville: University Press of Virginia for the Henry Francis du Pont Winterthur Museum, 1970), 25-30. Mr. Holman discusses in detail the extant versions of Foster's printed portrait of Richard Mather and the validity of its traditionally assigned date of 1670, as well as its probability of being issued as a frontispiece to the pamphlet *The Life and Death of that Reverend Man of God, Mr. Richard Mather,* printed by Cambridge Press in Massachusetts.

5 For a discussion of seventeenth-century prints in America and specifically the technique of woodcut in America see Holman, "Seventeenth-Century American Prints," 23-52.

wood. After the image is drawn on the wood, all that is not part of the design is cut away, leaving the drawing intact and in relief. In the hands of practiced and skilled artisans, a woodcut is capable of transferring an exceptionally detailed image in outline. Its flexibility in rendering tonal variations is limited, however, in large measure due to the basic characteristics of the wood.

In Europe, England, and America, woodcut was soon replaced by techniques that allowed finer detail and wider tonalities in reproducing the image. It regained popularity as a principal printmaking method in the late eighteenth century when, in the hands of English engraver Thomas Bewick (1753-1828), the use of a burin on end-grain blocks of boxwood and other dense, evenly textured hardwoods made it possible to execute fine intersecting lines and patterns intricate in detail and tone.

Printmaking in the eighteenth century was dominated by the intaglio process, whereby the image to be reproduced was tooled or etched into a metal plate. As in England, the first of the intaglio processes to be used in America was line engraving. In 1702, Thomas Emmes (working in Boston in the late seventeenth to the early eighteenth century) used a burin to cut a linear image of Increase Mather (1639-1723) in the surface of a copperplate.[6] Cutting into metal presented problems that the makers of woodcuts, who could use broad planes of flat printing surface for color, did not have to address.

Engraving in line required greater manual control in that the entire design was made up of lines of varying widths laid in close patterns to reproduce tone and form. Mastery of the technique required long

[6] Wendy J. Shadwell, *American Printmaking: The First 150 Years* (Washington, D C.: Smithsonian Institution Press for The Museum of Graphic Arts, 1971), 17-18, cat. no. 6.

practice. By the seventeenth century, some of the tedium of the process of line engraving was eliminated through the substitution of an intermediary process of etching the basic design.

Etching was described in *Traicte des manières de graver* by Abraham Bosse in 1645, and it was delineated in some detail in *Ars Pictoria* by Alexander Browne (ac. 1667-1690), when it was published in London in 1675.[7] The first step in etching was the application of a suitable protective ground to a polished copperplate. Several grounds were suggested, but basically each was a mixture of varnish or resin, wax, and coloring agent. The design was scratched through this coating, and the plate was washed with a dilute acid solution until the acid had removed any exposed metal to a satisfactory depth. Scratching through the protective coating required little strength and could be executed as swiftly and as spontaneously as drawing with a pencil. With etching completed, the copperplate was cleaned of the coating. Engravers then worked over the design with burins to sharpen lines and to add the subtle details that are expressive of line engraving. Using etching as part of the line technique reduced the time needed to execute the copperplate, and in the long run helped reduce the cost of the print to the public.

On the Continent line engraving remained the preferred method of printmaking from the fifteenth century until the second half of the eighteenth century, and long-established guild systems and ateliers preserved and pursued the medium's excellence. Among the earliest line engravers in England and America were silver and goldsmiths, who were accomplished in using the burin to execute cyphers, coats

[7] Alexander Browne, *Ars Pictoria: Or An Academy Treating of Drawing, Painting, Limning, Etching. To which are added XXI Copper Plates Expressing the Choicest, Neatest, and Most Exact Grounds and Rules of Symmetry, Collected out of the most Eminent Italian, German and Netherland Authors*, 2nd ed., corrected and enlarged (London: Arthur Tooker and William Battersby, 1675), 97-110.

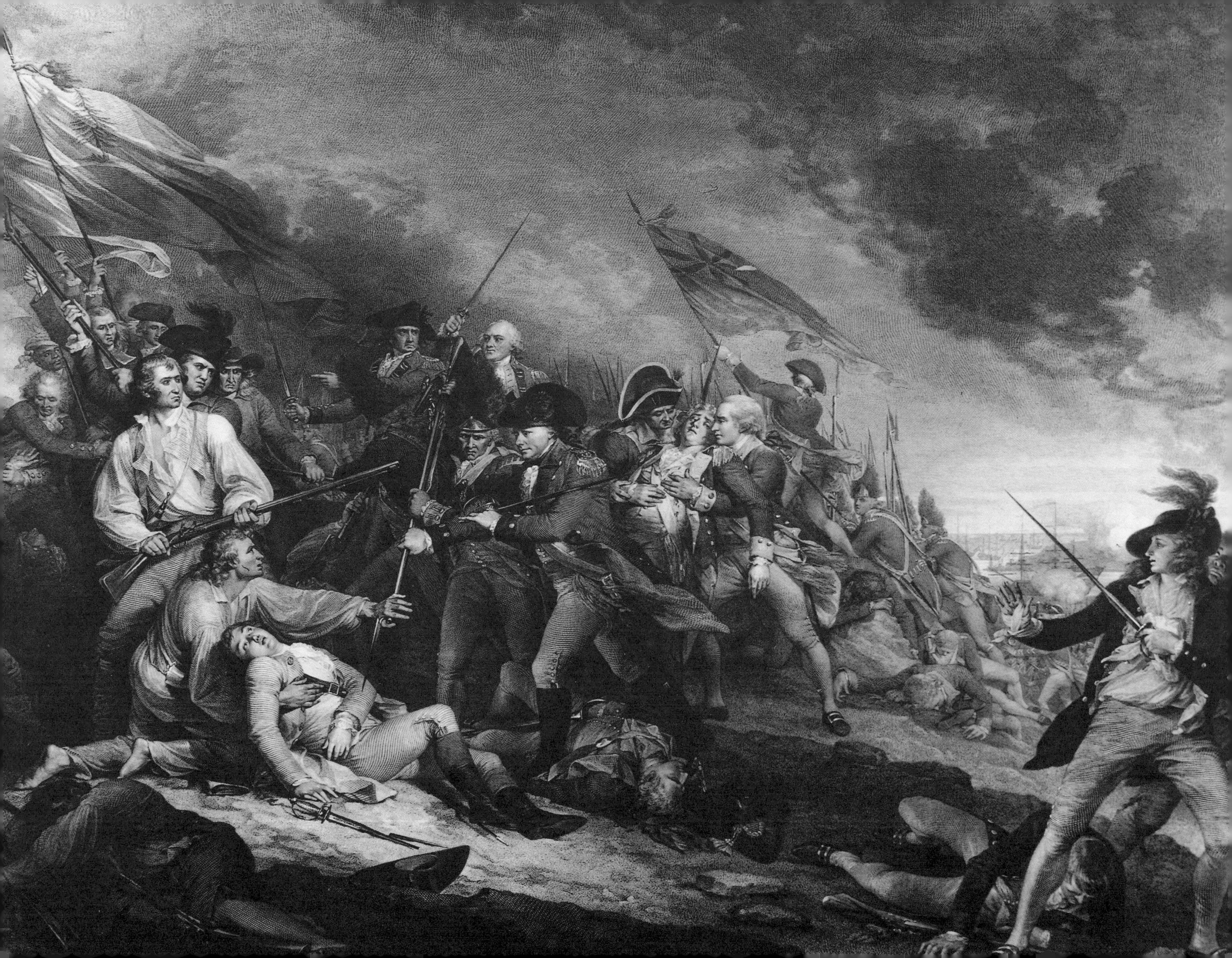

of arms, inscriptions, mottos, and other designs on metal objects. William Hogarth (1697-1764), whose first essay as a printmaker was an engraver's trade card in 1720, and Simon Gribelin (1661-1733),[8] were among a number of English engravers trained first to work on silver or gold forms. American silversmiths Nathaniel Hurd (cat. no. 25) and Paul Revere (cat. nos. 42, 43) likewise produced engravings of significance. Amos Doolittle (cat. nos. 14, 35, 49) was trained as a silversmith, but others who practiced the line technique, such as Thomas Johnston (cat. no. 7), James Smither (cat. nos. 12, 54), and Charles Willson Peale (cat. no. 13), seemed to have learned it through brief experiences with trained engravers.

In 1642, Ludwig von Siegen (b. 1609, last known work 1657) of Bavaria executed a portrait that depended upon subtle tones rather than lines for its image.[9] His method, also an intaglio technique, utilized a toothed, wheel-like instrument called a roulette that, when pressed into the copperplate, left a series of small pits, with the displaced metal raised around the perimeter of each. Initially, the inventor used the roulette to work locally, as one might use crayon to develop a drawing. In the aggregate these depressions and the surrounding raised metal held an enormous amount of ink, which in printing produced very rich black tones. As an improvement to the method of execution, Prince Rupert (1619-1682) in the court of Charles II introduced the rocker, which he intended to be used to work over the entire surface of the copperplate to lay on a deep, uniformly textured base. Then using either a scraper or a burnisher, the engraver created an image by working from the deepest tones to the white of the paper by depressing

[8] Simon Gribelin was best known to the American market through a set of engravings that he made after Raphael's *Cartoons,* issued first in 1707, and his illustrations for Shaftesbury's *Characteristics,* an essay on taste and arts that was published in 1712 and consulted by American native artists such as Robert Feke.

[9] Portrait of the *Landgravine of Hesse Cassel.* See John Evelyn, *Sculptura: or Historie of Calcographie* (London, 1662) for discussion of the invention of this technique and its introduction into England as well as for a detailed discussion of printmaking techniques practiced at that time. A more detailed description of the mezzotint technique is found in Browne, *Ars Pictoria.*

Left: Detail of *The Battle of Bunker's Hill* (cat. no. 58)

the toothed surface accordingly. With the help of John Evelyn (1620-1706), Rupert brought the technique of mezzotint engraving to England.

Lacking a firmly positioned guild of line engravers (like that which existed on the Continent) to resist the introduction of this experimental process, England in the last quarter of the seventeenth century became the principal center for mezzotint engraving. It was a technique particularly adaptable to the copying of portrait paintings, with their wide variety of tones and textures. Its arrival coincided with the rise of English portraiture under Peter Lely (1618-1680) and Godfrey Kneller (1646/9-1723). Trained line engravers from France and the Low Countries emigrated to England to join native engravers in the practice of mezzotint engraving. Their work and that of the eighteenth-century mezzotint engravers to follow replicated the mode of English portraiture and popularized the painters' works throughout Britain and North America. Collecting "heads"—engraved portraits of famous personages—took on new meaning, and getting one's portrait scraped was a decided honor. Mezzotint was first practiced in America by Peter Pelham (cat. no. 22), whose portrait of the Reverend Cotton Mather was published in Boston in 1728. Pelham was followed in the technique almost immediately by William Burgis (ac. 1716/8-1731), whose landscape of the *View of the LightHouse* at Boston was finished in 1729.

The interest in landscape prints that began in seventeenth-century England did much to sustain a general appreciation of etching as a line technique throughout the rising popularity of mezzotint. With tenures under several German print publishers, Hollar had developed into a skilled topographical draftsman and etcher when he arrived in England. His first published work, a double view of *Greenwich* of 1637, set the format and may have established the style for long views of cities that continued in favor to the middle of the eighteenth century, as evidenced in the grand perspectives of Boston, New York, Charlestown (cat. no. 5), and Philadelphia (cat. no. 6). Between 1707 and 1726, Johannes Kip (1653-1722) published in *Britannia Illustrata* etchings of important English palaces, country houses, and buildings with surrounding gardens, forests, and fields, and through it popularized the bird's-eye view. By the mid-eighteenth century, John Boydell (1719-1804), trained as an etcher and engraver, and newly established as a publisher, was executing romantic views of English country houses, gardens, and surrounding lands (cat. no. 68). Beginning in the 1760s he joined with several other London publishers in undertaking the publication of twenty-eight views of North American cities, which were issued in sets and/or bound and titled *Scenographia Americana* (cat. nos. 10, 11).

While some printmakers combined etching and colored woodcuts to reproduce wash drawings by topographical artists, a group led by Paul Sandby (1730-1809) in England popularized the technique of aquatint as it would be applied to landscape and cityscape prints until the middle of the nineteenth century. A variant of etching, aquatint is also an intaglio process. Even though J. B. Le Prince (1734-1781) may have found inspiration in a technique in limited use in the seventeenth century, the development and basic formulation of the method of aquatint is credited to him. Jean Claude Richard, Abbé de Saint Non (1727-1791) demonstrated aquatint to Benjamin Franklin in Paris in 1778 (cat. no. 56).

In preparation for etching in aquatint, an etcher grounds a copperplate with a dusting of granular resin, which when heated adheres to the plate and leaves channels of exposed metal between each grain. Working over a lightly scratched or etched outline, the engraver begins by applying a protective varnish to all areas that are to remain absolutely white or without color in the final printing. He next emerses the plate in an acid bath just until the lightest tone is etched. After he removes and dries the plate, a second coat of varnish is applied to protect the lightest tones of the design from further biting. In stopping out areas from the lightest to the darkest or most deeply etched tones, an etcher may repeat the process a dozen or more times, depending on the subtlety of tonal transitions desired. Before the etching is complete, he might strengthen the design with additional etched lines for definition. The plate is then cleaned of the layers of varnish and prepared for printing. Black and white proofs have a granular quality in the image, but with the application of transparent watercolor washes, they readily approximate a watercolor drawing.

Stipple engraving can be either an engraved or an etched process. Traditional line engravers made limited use of the burin in a flicking action or with minute, quick movements that created delicate tonal transitions, most often seen in the faces and hands of portrait subjects. Working through an overall protective varnish coat with an etcher's needle or burin, an engraver can employ an acid bath to establish the desired depth of design. In essence, stipple designs are built dot by dot, and depending on the size of the plate it can take from a few days to years to complete the project.

The French used stipple in connection with color printing[10] and the British for both color printing and for small book illustrations at the end of the century. Except for limited essays in the context of line etching or engraving, Americans were late to employ this technique as a method of picturemaking. Edward Savage's *The Washington Family* (cat. no. 38) was not published until 1798. Other engravers working in the United States, such as English-born William Rollinson (1762-1842) and David Edwin (1776-1841), used stipple very successfully in connection with American book publishing in the early nineteenth century.

The invention of lithography belongs to the eighteenth century, although its commercial practice in England and the United States dates from the nineteenth. In 1798, Alois (or Alöys) Senefelder (1771-1834) perfected a process for printing which he referred to as chemical printing. He had discovered that if he made a drawing using a greasy substance like ink or crayon on a freshly surfaced Bavarian limestone and kept the stone saturated with water, a print of the design could be pulled by simply applying an even scraping pressure to the reverse of a sheet of paper laid over the image. Any draftsman could work directly on the stone without the engraver as intermediary. So could an artist, and either engraver or artist could work as spontaneously as if he or she were drawing on a sheet of paper. Senefelder further developed a method for chemically setting the design into the pores of the stone. In 1800, he applied for a patent for

[10] Color was applied locally to the plate, *en poupee,* using a small pounce or wad of material. When all the colors had been applied, the plate was warmed and printed. Between each impression it was thoroughly cleaned and re-inked. Accomplished printers managed only a few impressions in a workday, but the final result was an image that successfully effected a pastel or crayon painting.

the process in England, and thereafter the art of reproducing images in quantity and at the cheapest prices was forever changed.

PUBLISHERS, ENGRAVERS, AND ARTISTS

From the beginning of its history in Europe, printmaking was appreciated principally for its capacity to produce the same image many times over. Some artist-engravers were fascinated with understanding and extending the limits of the technology, but for the most part engravers were artisans skilled in reproducing others' designs, and they were in the regular employ of publishers who directed the content and the quality of their work. In the European ateliers of the sixteenth and seventeenth centuries, emphasis rested on mastery of the technique to the limits of exquisite detail. Relatively few engravers were known by name, and most worked invisibly through the ranks of the guild system.

Late to venture into the business of printmaking, English publishers and printmakers labored to catch up with their foreign competitors, and in the process their activities attracted many competent engravers from abroad. Until the end of the seventeenth century and the use of mezzotint in the reproduction of paintings in England, few engravers were recognized in their own right and most remained dependent on their publishers. Surprisingly fewer took on students or assistants to carry their style forward, although some such as Alexander Browne did publish descriptions of printmaking techniques. A small number of English engravers became their own publishers,[11] and in so doing some became publishers for other printmakers. Before the 1750s, few were able to compete successfully even on the London market with the highly admired European productions.

As an engraver and publisher, William Hogarth proved to be a notable exception from his earliest published works of 1721-24. Apprenticed to a decorative engraver of silver, Hogarth determined that he would follow a wider path as an artist and engraver. He produced a uniquely British art form and one that both mirrored a scene and moralized on lost virtues. Using a combination of social satire and contemporary reporting, Hogarth executed images that were both amusing and profound. His work, which appealed to a broad audience, touched upon the lives of rich and poor alike, and his engravings were issued in single sheets or in sets as short stories in four, six, or eight episodes. Acting as his own publisher he faced competition from his imitators, and early in his career he secured copyright protection for engravers through an act passed in Parliament in 1735. Hogarth's success as a designer of engraved pictures extended far past his lifetime. His plates were printed until they were well worn, only to be re-engraved by others and published again. Beyond his own success, Hogarth proved to artists and publishers alike the value in translating contemporary art, other than portraiture, to print. Doing so had not only extended his reputation, but sales of his prints from the copperplate well exceeded the profits realized from the sale of a single painting.[12]

The publisher John Boydell, described as a colossus astride the eighteenth-century English print

[11] George Vertue (1684-1756), an engraver and antiquarian, published one hundred fifty heads in a volume celebrating the most illustrious personages of England. Between 1732 and 1736, Arthur Pond (ca. 1705-1758) in association with Charles Knapton produced imitations of works by Salvatore Rosa, Claude de Lorraine, Parmigianimo, Carracci, and Guercino in English collections. A number of these were included in the collection of John Smibert, the British artist who worked in Boston in the 1730s.

[12] For a discussion of Hogarth's time see Derek Jarrett, *England in the Age of Hogarth* (New Haven and London: Yale University Press, 1974). For a discussion of Hogarth's career as artist, engraver, and publisher see Ronald Paulson, *Hogarth's Graphic Works,* rev. ed., 2 vols. (New Haven and London: Yale University Press, 1970), 1:3-84.

[13] Calloway, *English Prints for the Collector,* 53. See also Sven H. A. Bruntjen, *John Boydell, 1719-1804: A Study of Art Patronage and Publishing in Georgian London* (New York and London: Garland Publishing, Inc., 1985).

market, built upon Hogarth's idea.[13] Of average ability as an engraver, Boydell turned to publishing the work of other artists and engravers in the mid-eighteenth century. His first great success came with the employment of William Woollett (1737-1782) to engrave Richard Wilson's (1713/4-1782) brooding landscape with the mythological subject of *The Destruction of the Children of Niobe* (1760). Boydell continued to encourage the best of English painters to submit their work to the engraver, for the benefit of art and a profit for all. Among the earliest to respond was the American painter Benjamin West (cat. no. 55). Woollett's engraving after *The Death of General Wolfe* gained wide recognition of West's work and secured for the artist the title of historical painter to King George III. Shortly afterwards Woollett was given the title of historical engraver to His Majesty.

At last English engravers were finding an appreciative market at home as well as in Paris and other European capitals. Known not only by name, they were eagerly sought by artists anxious to have their paintings copied. Even so, engravers were excluded from the inner circles of art. Indeed, engraving had not been considered an original artistic expression by founding members of the Royal Academy in 1768, and it was recognized only on second thought when associate memberships were instituted in 1769. Interestingly, however, painter-members such as Thomas Gainsborough (1727-1788) did apply their talents to engraving with some measure of success.

For numbers of English engravers, as for their American contemporaries, life was not one important undertaking after another. Many found it necessary to engage in the more mundane activities of the jobbing engraver, executing cards and bill heads, reworking worn plates, and copying earlier popular publications (see Bowles' sets of flowers, cat. nos. 69, 70, 71). The celebrated Wenceslas Hollar ended his career doing whatever incidental work publishers sent his way. And William Woollett, although later honored by the king, began his career with the ordinary job work of engraving cards, labels, and the like. Whatever the financial uncertainties of the business of printmaking in the colonies, American engravers as independent artists and most often as their own entrepreneurs were spared the humiliating treatment that many of their English contemporaries suffered under the management of harsh publishers determined to extract the greatest possible profit.

It is believed that Hogarth himself wrote in 1734 in support of the Engraver's Act of 1735.

> There are only twelve printshops in London and Westminster, "and these are in the Power and Direction of a very few, who are the Richest." The print seller insists upon an extravagantly large percentage of the profits ("near double what a Bookseller ever demands for publishing a Book"), and, moreover, if the print is a popular success, he increases his personal profits by having one of his hacks make a cheap copy. These copies are then "imposed upon the Incurious for the Originals, or at least are industriously dispatched to all Parts of the Country, where the Original is never suffer'd to appear."[14]

[14] *The Case of Designers, Engravers, Etchers, &c. stated in a letter to a Member of Parliament,* 7 pp. (n.d.), Victoria and Albert Museum Library, as referred to in Paulson, *Hogarth's Graphic Works,* 1:5-6.

PRINTSELLERS AND COLLECTORS IN PURSUIT OF TASTE AND ELEGANCE

Whether in England or America, the printed image in the eighteenth century was produced to sell in quantity and to make a profit for the publisher and, as the century progressed, increasingly for the engraver and the artist. To accomplish this, printmakers and publishers required a market beyond the book publisher, the bibliophile, or the itinerant street vendor. They needed to attract a regular audience that was encouraged to collect separate sheet engravings as a mark of taste, intellectual curiosity, and worldliness. To do this successfully, publishers had to provide an inventory that would entice customers, and furnish a place where their latest offerings could be enjoyed in a pleasant atmosphere of culture and refinement. Hogarth complained that in London few printmakers, particularly the engravers, had the appropriate quarters for displaying their work to potential customers. Instead, they had to depend upon the established shops to keep their offerings before a regular clientele, which put them even further under the control of the shop proprietors, that is, the publishers. Early in his career, Boydell found it profitable to take rooms at the business place of a London stationer, but he soon realized that he needed his own establishment if he was to profit as an engraver and publisher.[15]

The best of London printshops in the second quarter of the eighteenth century had display rooms on the ground floor, with adjacent quarters sometimes on upper floors for the printing and coloring of impressions. On one or both sides of the street-level entrance were display windows made of rows of small

[15] Bruntjen, *John Boydell,* 9, 14.

panes or lights into which the proprietor fitted the latest of his inventory. Here, the fashionable and those hoping to be noticed as such gathered to peruse. By the third quarter of the century printsellers were using scenes outside their shops as subjects of their own presses, preserving a precise record of the manner in which they displayed prints for the amusement of the passerby and, hopefully, the customer. To insure their success, print publishers had to extend themselves beyond their respective locations to reach a distant public through aggressive merchandizing, which included advertising and catalogue orders.

From the outset print publishers in eighteenth-century America followed a practice long held in Europe and England of pre-publication subscription.[16] With designs in hand, publishers first brought the project before the public through newspaper advertisements that addressed persons of discriminating tastes who would appreciate an opportunity to secure the first and finest impressions with a small deposit. In America, where it was generally necessary and preferred to send ambitious undertakings to England or Europe for engraving, such deposits generated working capital for the undertaker of the project. Subscription lists, when published, served as an inducement for others of cultivated tastes to join a select group. Frequently, however, several years elapsed between the initial announcement of a subscription and the receipt of the finished product, a condition that on more than one occasion proved costly to the publisher.

In America, booksellers continued to be a source for the latest maps and occasional engravings in separate sheets. They were joined by newspaper printers who, from time to time working with a local artist,

[16] See advertisement of William Burgis in the *New England Courant* for November 5/12, 1722, and the advertisement of Michael De Bruls in the *Boston Evening Post* for December 27, 1762, as quoted in George Francis Dow, *The Arts & Crafts in New England, 1704-1775: Gleanings from Boston Newspapers* (Topsfield, Mass.: Wayside Press, 1927), 15-16, 6-8.

would open their rooms to display new works proposed for subscription or engravings recently arrived from London. For the curious and the casual buyer of printed pictures in America during the eighteenth century, there were local vendors or auctions,[17] an itinerant hawker, or direct order from one of the major London print publishers.

Artists and drawing masters, coming from abroad to practice their craft in America, brought and kept on hand large collections of engravings for reference and as models for their students. In time their collections were offered for sale to gentlemen of taste and to amateurs intent upon improving their familiarity with great European art. Among the earliest of these collections were ones belonging to William Dering, who was working in Virginia, and John Smibert (1688-1751) in Boston.[18] While the specifics of Dering's collection of two hundred engravings is not given, the extent of Smibert's holdings was described in the 1735 sale of his personal collection of "valuable PRINTS, engraved by the best Hands, after the finest Pictures in Italy, France, Holland, and England, done by Raphael, Michael Angelo, Poussin, Rubens, and other the greatest Masters containing a great Variety of Subjects, as History, etc, most of the Prints very rare, and not to be met with, except in private Collections. . . ."[19]

While a dozen or so enterprises were dedicated to the publication and sale of prints in London in the 1730s, it would be several years before American customers were to enjoy the equivalent of a London print shop in the colonies. William Price (1684-1771, ac. 1721) of Boston may have been the first in America

[17] See Dow, *Arts & Crafts in New England,* 14, as quoted from the *Boston News-Letter* for April 28/ May 5, 1712, and the *Boston Gazette* for April 4/11, 1720.

[18] Dering's personal belongings included two hundred engravings. See Thomas Thorne, "Eighteenth Century Painting in the South," *Antiques* 59, no. 3 (March 1951), 204-206. Smibert offered prints he had received from Arthur Pond at his Color Shop as well as mezzotint portraits. In 1734 and 1735 he advertised in the *Boston News-Letter* the sale of "Frames of several sorts, the best Metzotints, Italian, French, Dutch and English Prints, in Frames and Glasses, or without, by Wholesale or Retail," as quoted in Dow, *Arts & Crafts in New England,* xx.

[19] Advertisement of John Smibert, *Boston News-Letter,* May 15/22, 1735, as quoted in Dow, *Arts & Crafts in New England,* 7.

Right: Detail of *An East Perspective View of the City of Philadelphia* (cat. no. 9)

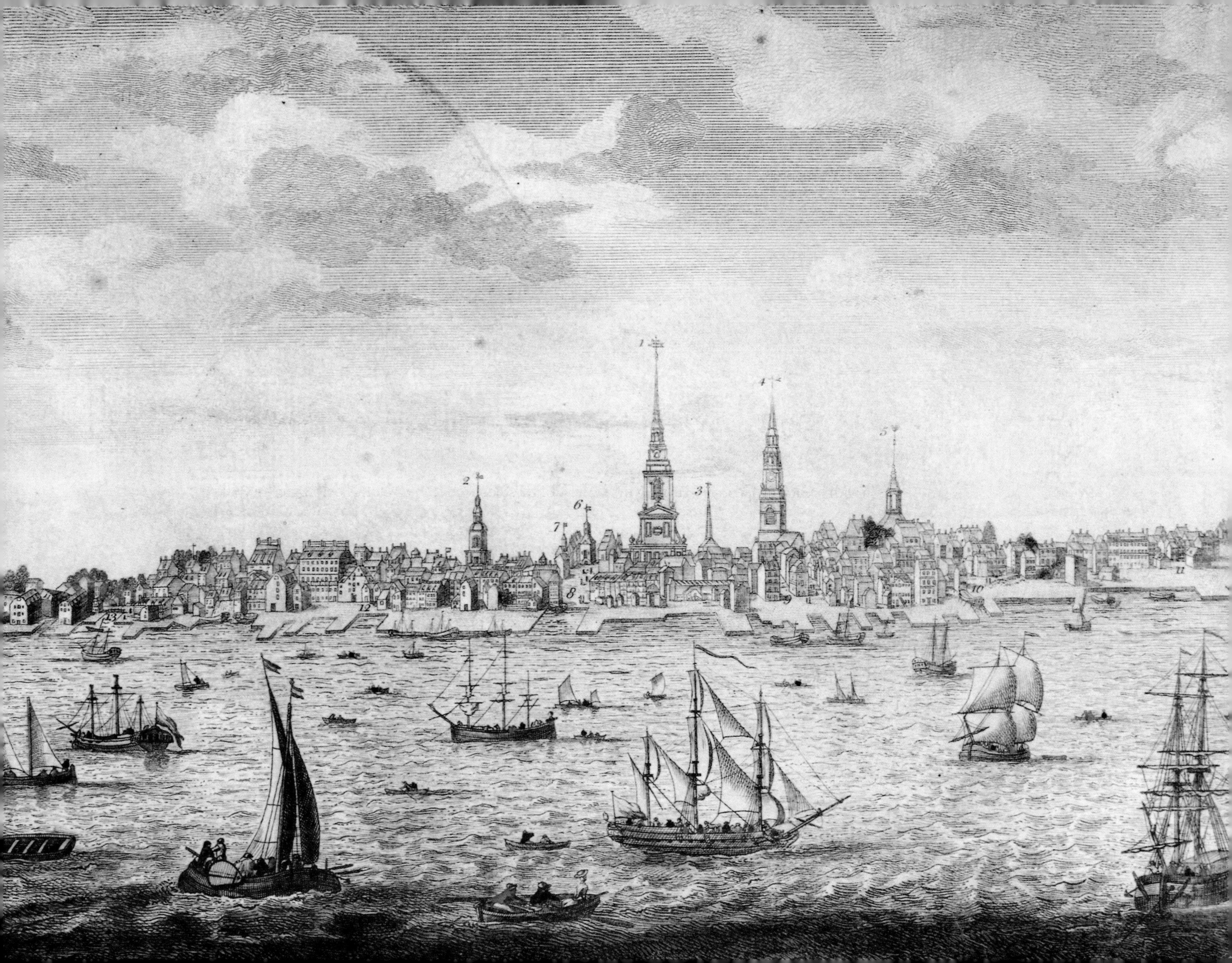
1
4
5
2
3
6
7
8
9
10
11
12
13

to advertise himself as a printseller, although he was a cabinetmaker by trade whose inventory by the 1740s included looking glasses, children's toys, musical instruments, tea tables, china, and perspective glasses.[20] In New York the artist and japanner Gerardus Duyckinck II (1723-1797) sold artists' supplies, maps and charts of many sizes, and engraved and mezzotint prints in his Universal Store.[21] Print shops, either as fashionable departments conducted in a tradesman's business or as small enterprises attached to a printing profession, had been established in larger American cities by the 1760s. Some offered service to outlying areas through vendors who were encouraged to buy in quantity at wholesale prices. America's first full-service print shop, offering equivalent services of such enterprises in London, was established in Philadelphia. Robert and Thomas Kennedy (w. 1761-1771) first advertised their looking glass and print store in Philadelphia in 1768.[22] The Kennedys promised their customers pictures "in the present English taste, neatly ornamented with carved and gilt corners and sidepieces, from Forty-two to Three and Six-pence a piece" and "prints very saleable and cheap for country chapmen." Even earlier, in December of 1761, Robert Kennedy offered the services of a copperplate printer and press to accommodate customers with specific commissions.[23]

Gleanings from newspapers of the day, inventories, and personal and business papers of Americans indicate that a variety of printed pictures, to be enjoyed for decoration, imitation, or simple amusement, were available to American customers for most of the eighteenth century. Although such descriptions as

[20] In 1722, Price advertised his place of business as a picture shop next to the Town House in Boston. See Emma Forbes Waite, "William Price of Boston: Map Maker, Merchant, Churchman," in *Old-Time New England* 46, no. 2 (October-December 1955): 52-56. See E. McSherry Fowble, *Two Centuries of Prints in America 1680-1880: A Selective Catalogue of the Winterthur Museum Collection* (Charlottesville: University Press of Virginia for the Henry Francis du Pont Winterthur Museum, 1987), 68-69.

[21] See advertisement of Gerardus Duyckinck in the *New-York Journal or the General Advertiser,* as quoted in Rita Susswein Gottesman, *The Arts and Crafts in New York 1726-1776: Advertisements and News Items from New York City Newspapers* (New York: New York Historical Society, 1938), 25.

[22] Fowble, *Two Centuries of Prints in America,* 10-13. The advertisement of Robert and Thomas Kennedy appeared in the *Pennsylvania Chronicle* on December 12, 1768, as quoted in Alfred Coxe Prime, *Arts and Crafts in Philadelphia, Maryland, and South Carolina 1721-1785: Gleanings from Newspapers* (Topsfield, Mass.: Walpole Society, 1929), 33.

[23] From the *Pennsylvania Packet,* November 4, 1771 (supplement), "Robert Kennedy at West's Head, in Second-street, near

"newest fashion" or "latest issue" appear in personal papers on occasion, the emphasis in newspaper advertisements was almost *always* put upon the engravings as representing the latest English taste or being equal in quality to any English offering. From Boston to Charleston, a certain similarity in language is found in the description of recent imports or general inventory, a similarity that undoubtedly had as its basis the catalogues of English printsellers of the period. While surprisingly few of these catalogues remain for ready reference, those that do (whether published by John Bowles or Robert Sayer and John Bennett) bear strong resemblance to shop inventories advertised in American newspapers. Consistently listed in eighteenth-century newspaper advertisements as being available to the American market are maps and charts; landscapes, prospects, views of country seats, and gardens; portraits of kings and queens, and ladies of quality and beauty; views of recent battles and portraits of those who distinguished themselves in them; humorous and droll subjects, including genre, sporting and hunting pieces, social and political satire, and most particularly the works of William Hogarth; as well as a wide variety of sets and series, views for the perspective glass, and small prints for children.

From the early years of the century, printsellers in Boston and New York followed the practice of their contemporaries in England in suggesting just where prints might be used successfully as household furniture. Often quoted are references to the use of prints on the walls of dining rooms, in halls, and on staircases.[24] Indeed, in Boston in April of 1720, an advertisement for a public vendue suggested that

Walnut street, philadelphia, Has imported in the *Britannia,* Capt. Falconer from London, a large collection of beautiful Pictures and Prints, on the most interesting and pleasing subjects, done from the most Capital Paintings of the greatest masters that England, France or Italy hath ever produced. Said Kennedy frames, carves, gilds and glazes all kinds of Paintings and Pictures in the most elegant and newest fashions, varnishes maps &c. and carries on the copper-plate printing in the best manner, as usual. Those who choose to furnish their houses or cabinet of curiosities, with the finest of pictures and prints, or crown glass for pictures of all sizes, clock faces, cabinet work or ship lights, &c. will be served with the utmost care and expedition," as quoted in Prime, *Arts and Crafts in Philadelphia, 1721-1785,* 221.

[24] Advertisement of Gerardus Duyckinck from the *New-York Weekly Journal* for March 19, 1750, "To Be Sold by Gerardus Duyckinck, of the Dock, between the Old Slip, and Coentjes Market. A very fine Assortment of Glass Pictures, Paintings on Glass, prospects, History, Sea Skips and Land Skips & large Assortment of Entry and Stair Case Pieces ready framed, With the Maps of the World: And in four parts. London all on Rollers, Prints of Sundry Sorts, Do. ready Coloured for Jappanning...," as quoted in Gottesman, *Arts and Crafts in New York,* 130.

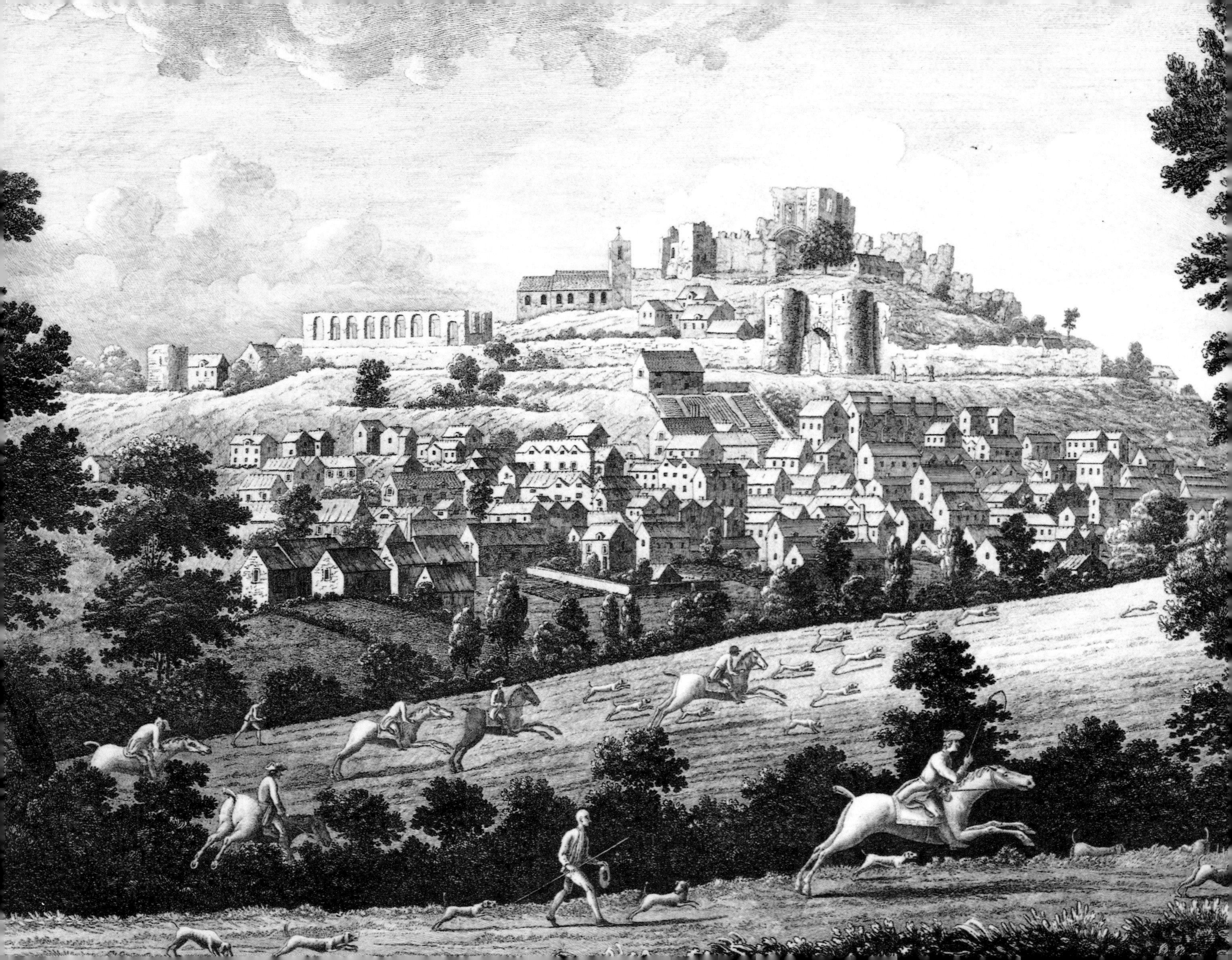

the pictures offered would be "fit for any Gentleman's Dining room,"[25] interestingly at a time when dining rooms, *per se*, were not generally designated rooms in American houses.

Just how many colonial customers depended upon the printsellers' attempts to serve as interior decorators cannot be guessed.[26] John Cadwalader of Philadelphia undoubtedly was impressed with Robert Kennedy and may have heeded that printseller's advertisement in the *Pennsylvania Chronicle* for December 12, 1768, which included the note: "Such as want any thing extraordinary in the print way, are requested to send their orders soon that they may be had in next spring." Cadwalader bought eleven pictures for a total of £6 6*d*. in 1769 and subsequently a lot of pictures framed by Kennedy that amounted to £71 16*s*.[27] Included in the lot were among the most recent English publications, many to be found in the catalogues of Robert Sayer.[28]

Earlier in 1753, the inventory taken by William Clayton and Moore Thurman of the household goods of John Coxe of New Jersey listed six pictures of *The Harlot's Progress* after Hogarth, twelve "Heads" or portraits of philosophers, four maps, a portrait of "Princess Louise," and two mezzotints as well as thirteen miscellaneous pictures.[29] It is curious to note that just two years after this inventory was taken, one Alexander Hamilton received on the ship *Carolina*, recently arrived from London, a

> variety of pictures, vis. sciences painted on glass, scenes, months, seasons, cartoons, hunting pieces, Roman antiquaries, parts of the day by Hogarth, roast beef of old England, distressed

[25] From the *Boston Gazette* for April 4/11, 1720, "On Wednesday the 20th Currant, will be sold at Publick Vendue at the Crown Coffee-House on the Long Wharff, a Collection of choice Pictures, fit for any Gentleman's Dining-room or Stair-case, to be seen at Mr. Shores in Queen Street, from Wednesday next to the time of Sale, between the hours of 9 and 12, and 3 to 6," as quoted in Dow, *Arts & Crafts in New England,* 14.

[26] Joan D. Dolmetsch, "Prints in Colonial America: Supply and Demand in the Mid-Eighteenth Century," in *Prints in and of America to 1850,* ed. John D. Morse (Charlottesville: University Press of Virginia for the Henry Francis du Pont Winterthur Museum, 1970), 53-74.

[27] Nicholas B. Wainwright, *Colonial Grandeur in Philadelphia: The House and Furniture of General John Cadwalader* (Philadelphia: Historical Society of Pennsylvania, 1964), 49-50.

Left: Detail of *A North View of Denbigh Castle* (cat. no. 68)

poet, and enraged musician, humours of a fair, march to Finchly, midnight conversation, India settlements, Vandeval's green sea-pieces, industry and idleness, judgement of Hercules, Paul before Feliz, in the Dutch taste, sleepy congregation, the lottery and several other humorous pieces by Hogarth, large India pictures, setts of maps of the world and quarters and many other goods, not here mentioned.[30]

Spelling and capitalization aside, a remarkable similarity exists in the lists of prints advertised by American printsellers for most of the eighteenth century to those descriptions found in the catalogues of Bowles, Sayer and Bennett, and other large printselling establishments in England. Daybooks and business papers of Americans engaged in the picture trade document that many conducted direct business with Sayer and others.[31]

In spite of the hostilities of war, Americans continued to buy the latest issues from London and abroad, particularly those works that cut incisively through the rhetoric to the matters that freemen held dear, whether in England, on the Continent, or in the colonies. To these works were added homegrown essays in printmaking, many being satirical adaptations of English productions. Some appeared in single sheet; others were bound in monthly magazines published in Boston and Philadelphia. Engravers and artists arriving from England and the Continent undertook the publication of subjects designed to reflect a new spirit of sacrifice, freedom, and independence that was wholly American, although their prototypes

[28] Robert Sayer and John Bennett were business partners from 1770 to 1784. Sayer operated as printseller and publisher from 1751 to 1770 and again from 1787 to 1794, when he retired and his inventory of plates was acquired by the firm of Laurie and Whittle. As was typical of London printsellers, the firm kept old copperplates from which they continued to issue impressions and at the same time added new titles on a regular basis. For an example of their catalogues see *Sayer & Bennetts Catalogue of Prints for 1775*, reprint of *Sayer and Bennett's Enlarged Catalogue of New and Valuable Prints in Sets, or Single. . . in Great Variety. . . Where Gentlemen for Furniture, Merchants for Exportation, and Shopkeepers to sell again, May be supplied with the greatest Assortment, on the most reasonable Terms. For 1775* (London: Holland Press, 1970).

[29] Inventory of John Coxe, taken June 25, 1753; total value £425.14.7. Winterthur Library, Downs Manuscript Collection, 55 x 17.1.

[30] Advertisement of Alexander Hamilton, *Pennsylvania Gazette*, no. 1375, May 1, 1755.

[31] Dolmetsch, "Colonial Prints: Supply and Demand," 59.

were distinctively European.

In the waning years of the eighteenth century, numbers of artists and engravers, encouraged by the growing appetite for pictures in America, came from England and the Continent to find a market for their talents. None came with a more ambitious scheme than the English print publisher Tristram Bampfylde Freeman (cat. no. 37), who advertised that he was prepared to initiate in Philadelphia a print publishing business to equal that of any in London. He found a financial backer in John Nicholson (1757-1800), opened a print shop and gallery in Philadelphia, and set about establishing a network of satellite shops in cities to the south and north. Perhaps his scheme grew too quickly. Certainly Freeman's money source failed when Nicholson found himself overextended. Nevertheless, Freeman should be remembered for being among the earliest to recognize an ever-widening market for printed pictures in the United States. In the course of the eighteenth century, Americans, from the very wealthy to tradesmen and widows of moderate means, had come to delight in collecting printed pictures as household furniture and to viewing them as enlightening, entertaining images to be enjoyed and shared in a wide community of friends and contemporaries at home and abroad.

NOTES TO THE CATALOGUE

Titles
The presence of bold type signifies the use of a shortened or popular title; otherwise titles are transcribed in upper and lower case as on the print. Italics and peculiar typefaces have not been reproduced. Superior letters have been brought to line; other abbreviations are transcribed as they appear. All spelling variants have been transcribed without the designation of *sic*. Missing titles, when known, are supplied in brackets.

Measurements
All measurements are provided in centimeters, height before width. Overall dimensions of the object, visible platemarks, and images, including the border or neat line, are given in order. In instances where the object has been trimmed within the platemark or the impression of the platemark is indistinct, the affected measurement is indicated as "trimmed."

Technique
Principal technique is listed first, followed by supporting technique. Incidental use of a technique, such as occasional dry point to reinforce the image, is not noted.

Support
Unless otherwise noted, all images appear on hand-made paper. Principal types cited are laid paper and wove paper. To assist in identifying paper, watermarks and countermarks are recorded where they are sufficiently represented. For additional information on chain intervals or laid lines per centimeter found in the laid papers, see Fowble, *Two Centuries of Prints in America*.

Dates
Birth and death dates of makers, engravers, artists, publishers, and principal portrait subjects are given where available. When two leading authorities assign different dates, both years are given, separated by a slash (e.g., 1718/9). Where dates cannot be ascertained with authority, none are offered and are indicated as such by "n.a." for not available. Known dates of general activity are designated by "ac." for active. Infrequently, an engraver, artist, or publisher may have changed careers or crafts. When working dates can be documented through published sources, such as surviving prints, they are identified by "w."

Accession numbers
These numbers appear as specific identifications of individual objects in the Winterthur collections. Ex coll. information follows where applicable.

References
Citations at the end of each catalogue entry are arranged in the order of their use in the narrative. At the close of certain catalogue entries, standard authorities are cited by author and catalogue designation. Authorities used in this work are:

[British Museum, *Satires*]
British Museum. Department of Prints and Drawings. *Catalogue of Prints and Drawings in the British Museum*. 11 vols. London: Printed by Order of the Trustees, 1870-1954.

[Fielding]
Mantle Fielding. *American Engravers Upon Copper and Steel*. Supplement to David McNeely Stauffer's *American Engravers*. Philadelphia: Privately printed, 1917.

[Hart]
Charles Henry Hart. *Catalogue of the Engraved Portraits of Washington*. New York: Grolier Club, 1904.

[J. C. Smith]
John Chaloner Smith. *British Mezzotinte Portraits: Being a Descriptive Catalogue of those Engravings From the Introduction of the Art to the Early Part of the Present Century*. 4 vols. London: Henry Sotheran & Co., 1884.

[Stauffer]
David McNeely Stauffer. *American Engravers Upon Copper and Steel*. 2 vols. New York: Grolier Club, 1907.

[Stokes and Haskell]
I. N. Phelps Stokes and David C. Haskell. *American Historical Prints, Early Views of American Cities, Etc.* New York: New York Public Library, 1932.

To Please Every Taste represents a small but significant sampling of prints on display with contemporary household furnishings in the Winterthur Museum. This major collection of graphic arts in America is described in further detail in *Two Centuries of Prints in America 1680-1880: A Selective Catalogue of the Winterthur Museum Collection*, published by the University Press of Virginia for the Henry Francis du Pont Winterthur Museum, Inc., 1987.

MAPS

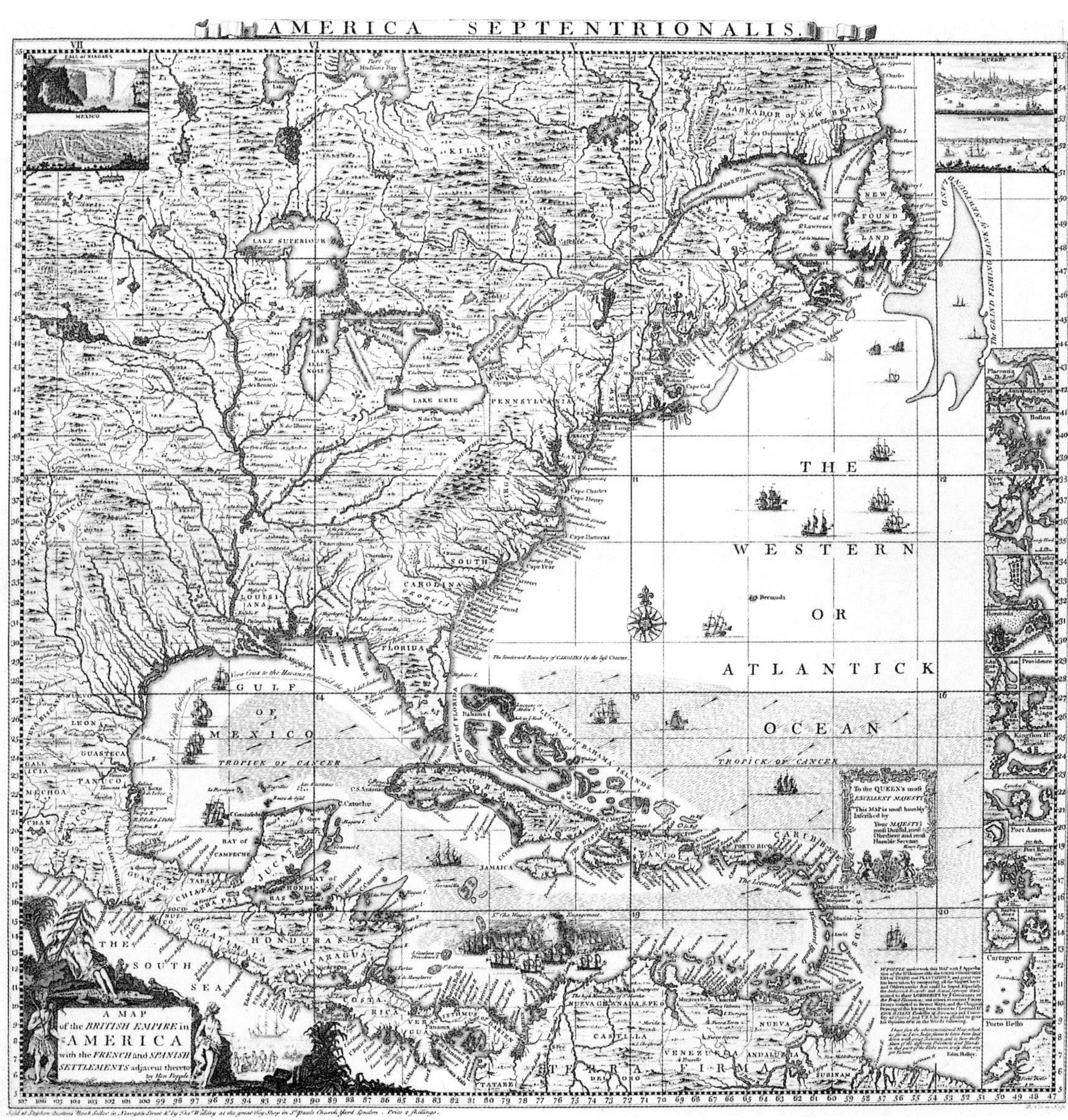

1.

Henry Popple (d. 1743), publisher

AMERICA SEPTENTRIONALIS. A MAP of the BRITISH EMPIRE in AMERICA with the FRENCH and SPANISH SETTLEMENTS adjacent thereto by Hen. Popple. Sold at Stephen Austen's Book Seller in Newgate Street & by Thos. Willdey at the great Toy Shop in St. Pauls Church Yard London. Price 2 shillings.

[Dedication:] To the QUEEN's most EXCELLENT MAJESTY This MAP is most humbly Inscribed by Your MAJESTY's most Dutiful, most Obedient Servant Henry Popple.

London, third state, ca. 1740
Line etching with burin work
Laid paper

Overall size: 77.6 x 56.0 cm
Platemark: 53.8 x 51.5 cm
Image: 50.0 x 49.2 cm

73.288.1

2.

Captain Clement Lempriere (ac. 1731-1733), artist
Bernard Baron (1696-1766), engraver
Henry Popple (d. 1743), publisher

[Title sheet 17]

A MAP of the BRITISH EMPIRE in AMERICA with the FRENCH and SPANISH SETTLEMENTS adjacent thereto.

London, third state, ca. 1740
Line etching and engraving
Laid paper; sheets 15 and 18 of the set with watermark of crowned shield with fleur-de-lis above "L V G" and countermark of "IV," identified in Churchill, no. 406, as a mark introduced by Lubertus van Gerrivink

Overall size (sheet 17):
56.6 x 77.0 cm
Platemark (sheet 17):
50.0 x 69.5 cm
Image (sheet 17):
43.5 x 67.0 cm

73.288.2q, from set of twenty sheets, 73.288.2a-t

By its size alone, Henry Popple's *Map of the British Empire in America,* first published in 1733, dominated the production of eighteenth-century maps of North America. The index sheet, being one twenty-fifth the size of the full scale map, indicates the arrangement of twenty separately printed sheets, which when trimmed and pasted on a support measures 104 by 105 inches (264.2 by 266.7 cm). Customers who had enough wall space or were engaged in a business that required instant access to the whole geography of British North America could purchase a mounted and colored version for £2 12*s*. 6*d*. The customary method of mounting was to paste a map on canvas that was attached at the top to a straight frame and at the bottom to a rod so it could be rolled up when not in use. Maps prepared for permanent display, however, could be pasted to large sheets of cardboard or to a wooden backing.

Cartography for this map was borrowed from several sources and, in final analysis, proved to be inadequate in supporting British claims of disputed territories. Its decorative features, with views of the Falls of Niagara, Mexico City, New York, and Quebec, a naval engagement, and various references to commerce, would recommend it. In the cartouche, America presides as an Indian princess, supported by native figures representing both the potential danger and the fruitfulness of this wild land.

On May 22, 1746, Benjamin Franklin ordered a copy of the Popple map for display to one side of the Pennsylvania Assembly Room door, and a second copy, uncolored and bound, for £1 16*s*. 6*d*, just five shillings more than the cost of an unbound set in black and white.

References: William P. Cumming and Helen Wallis, *A Map of the British Empire in America with the French and Spanish Settlements Adjacent Thereto by Henry Popple* (Lympne Castle, Kent: Harry Margery, 1972); Benjamin Franklin to William Strahan, Philadelphia, May 22, 1746, as quoted in *The Papers of Benjamin Franklin*, ed. Leonard W. Labaree et al., vol. 3, January 1, 1745, through June 30, 1750 (New Haven: Yale University Press, 1961), 77, (original letter in the collection of the American Philosophical Society, Philadelphia).

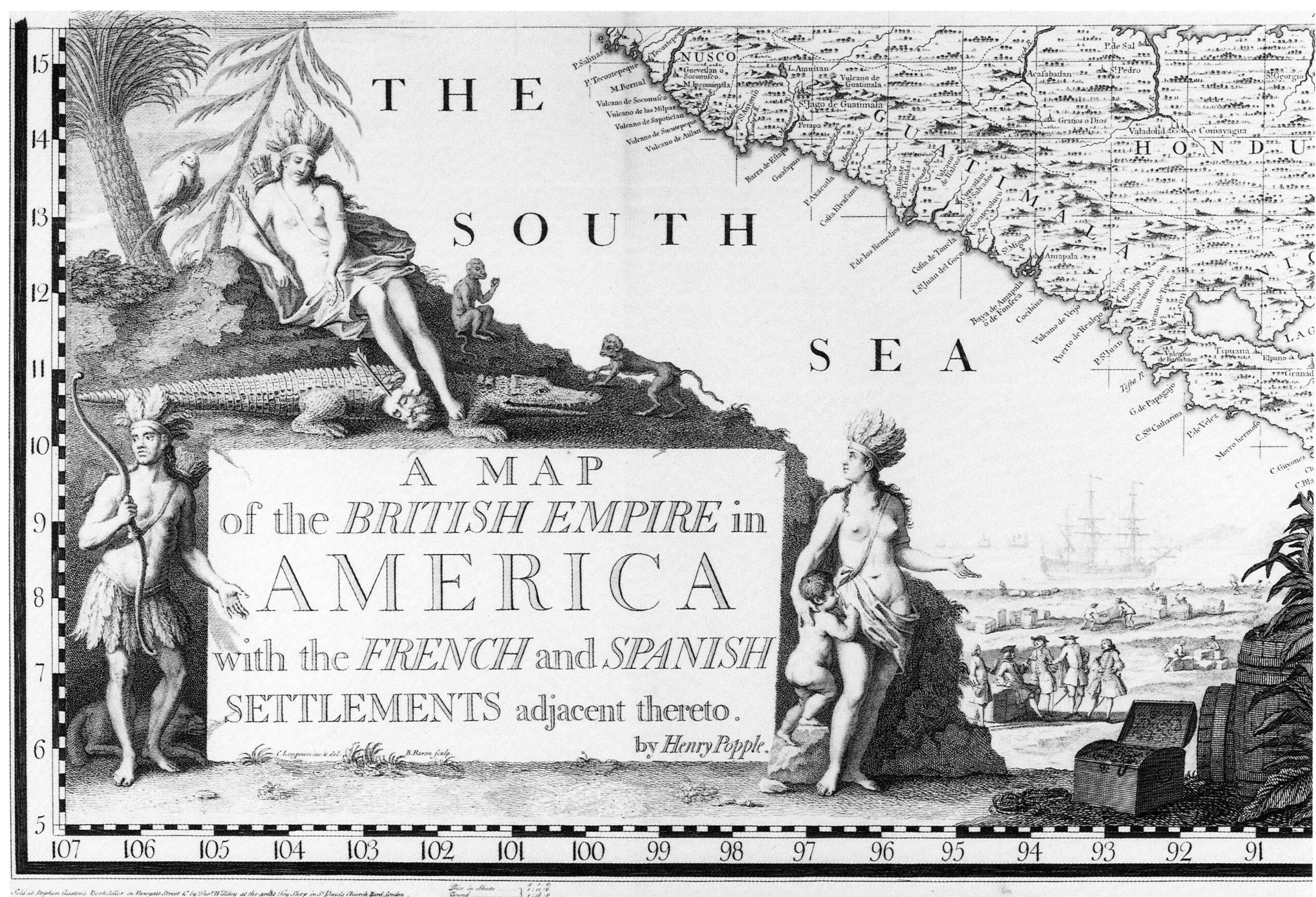
THE SOUTH SEA
A MAP of the BRITISH EMPIRE in AMERICA with the FRENCH and SPANISH SETTLEMENTS adjacent thereto.
by Henry Popple.
HONDU

3.

John Wallis (ac. 1783-1791), publisher

THE UNITED STATES of AMERICA laid down From the best Authorities, Agreeable to the Peace of 1783. Published, April 3d. 1783, by the Proprietor JOHN WALLIS, at his Map-Warehouse, Ludgate Street LONDON

London, 1783
Line etching with burin work, watercolors
Laid paper, watermark of fleur-de-lis in crowned shield above "L V G" (Churchill, no. 406) and countermark of "IV"

Overall size: 52.4 x 59.0 cm
Platemark: 48.4 x 57.4 cm
Image: 45.6 x 54.7 cm

68.517
Ex coll. Charles K. Davis

In 1782, Franklin, John Adams, Henry Laurens, and John Jay met with the British Peace Commissioners in Paris to negotiate a preliminary treaty of peace and to set the boundaries of the new United States of America. The negotiators turned to John Mitchell's mapping of the country, first published in London in 1755. Following this prototype, map publishers in 1783 hastened to be among the first to produce maps recognizing the new nation.

John Wallis' map of the United States of America may be the first to feature the American flag with its thirteen stars and thirteen stripes. On either side of the cartouche are the figures of George Washington, the soldier, supported by Liberty, and Benjamin Franklin, the author of peace, with Minerva as Wisdom and blind Justice behind him.

References: Edmund Berkeley and Dorothy Smith Berkeley, *Dr. John Mitchell: The Man Who Made the Map* (Chapel Hill: University of North Carolina Press, 1958), 73-82; P. Lee Phillips, *A List of Maps of America in the Library of Congress* (Washington, D.C.: Government Printing Office, 1901), 862.

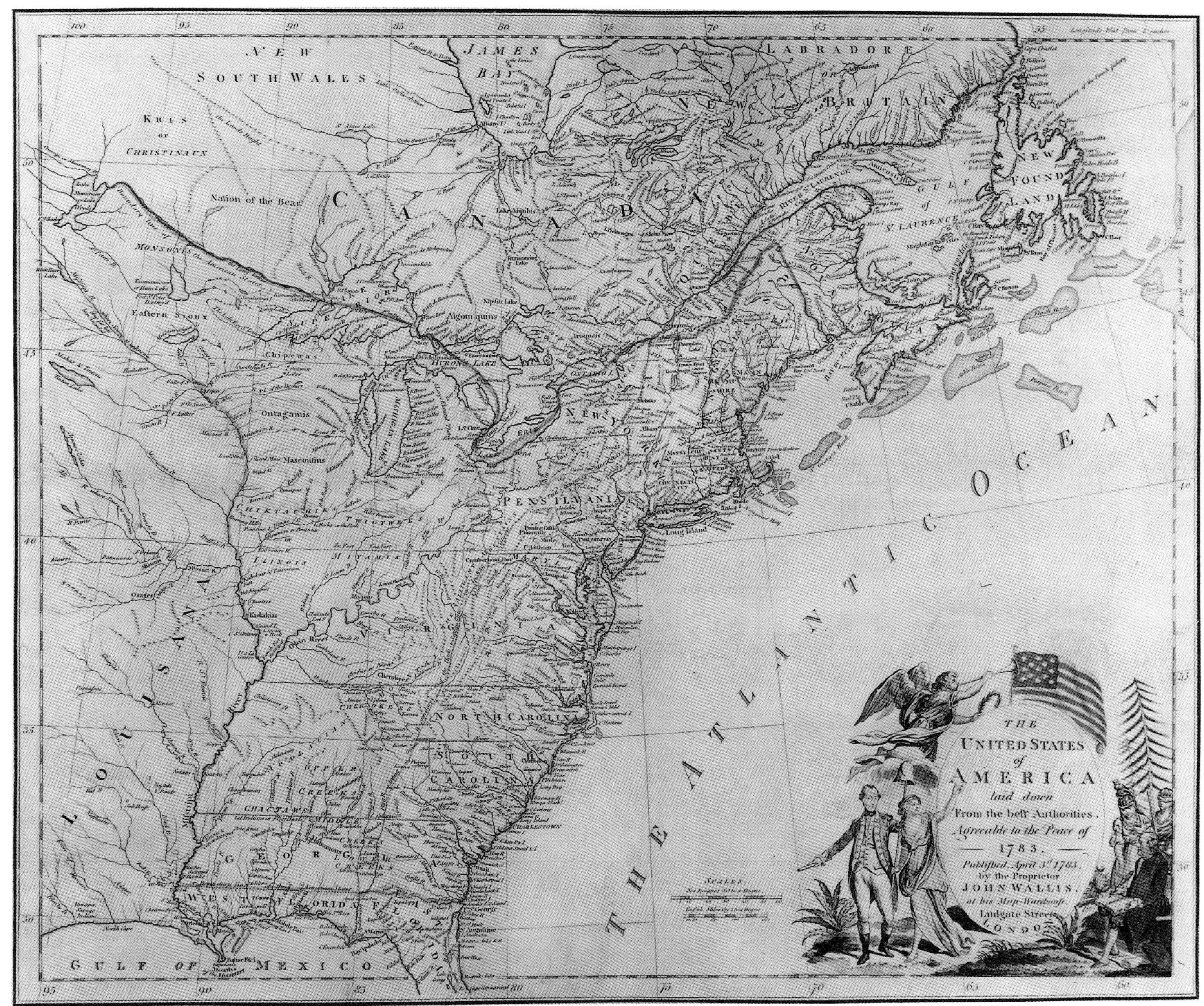
THE
UNITED STATES
of
AMERICA
laid down
From the best Authorities,
Agreeable to the Peace of
1783.
Published, April 3d 1783,
by the Proprietor
JOHN WALLIS,
at his Map-Warehouse,
Ludgate Street,
LONDON.
NEW SOUTH WALES
JAMES BAY
LABRADORE
NEW BRITAIN
KRIS or CHRISTINAUX
Nation of the Bear
CANADA
NEW FOUND LAND
GULF of ST LAURENCE
Eastern Sioux
Chipewas
Outagamis
Mascoutins
Algomquins
Iroquois
HURON LAKE
ONTARIO L.
ERIE
NEW YORK
PENSILVANIA
MARYLAND
VIRGINIA
NORTH CAROLINA
SOUTH CAROLINA
GEORGIA
WEST FLORIDA
EAST FLORIDA
LOUISIANA
ILINOIS
MIYAMIS
TWIGTWEES
CHERKEES
CHACTAWS
UPPER CREEKS
Ohio River
Long Island
CHARLESTOWN
THE ATLANTIC OCEAN
GULF OF MEXICO
SCALES

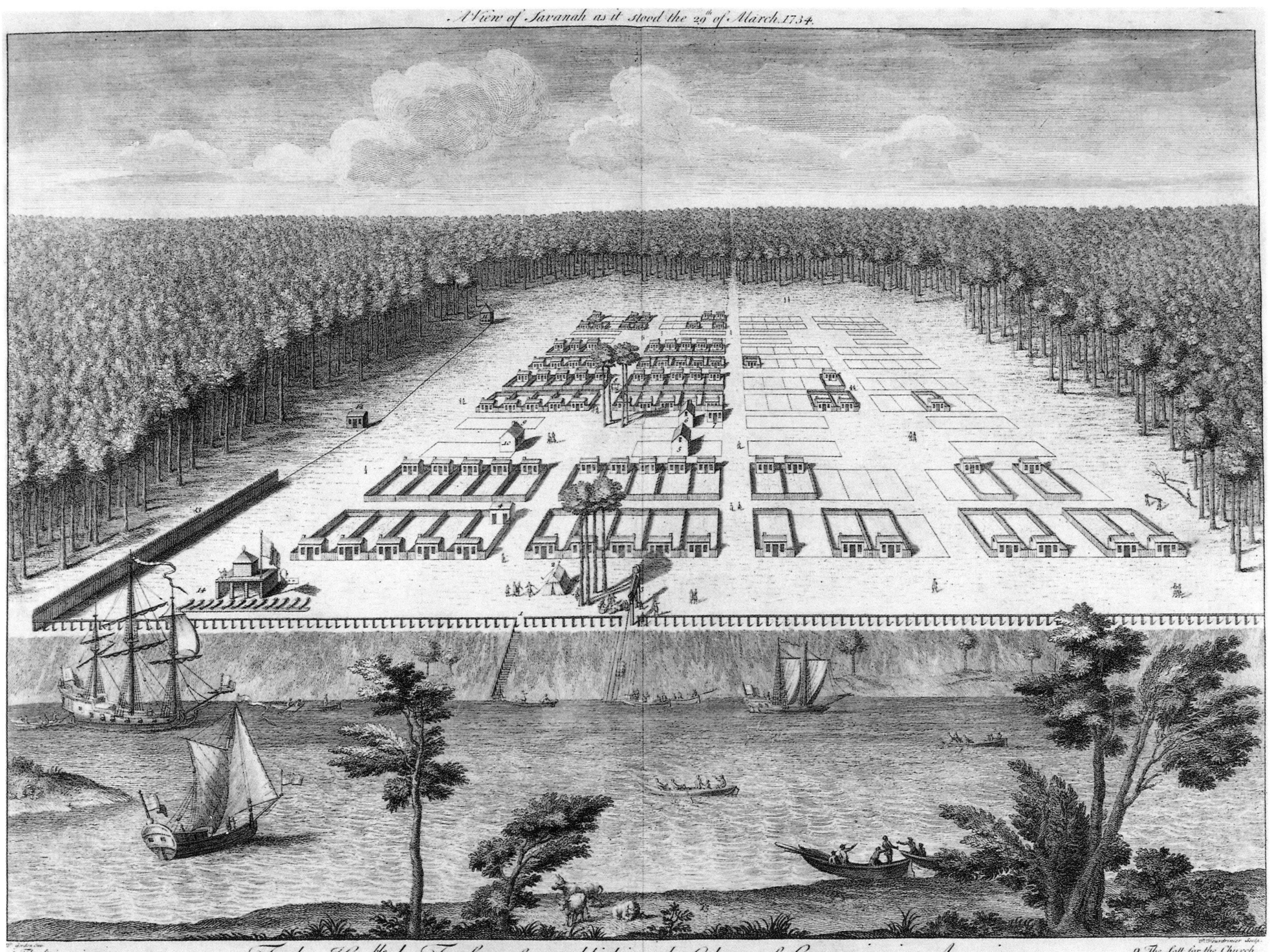

1. The Stairs going up.
2. Mr. Oglethorpe's Tent.
3. The Crane & Bell.
4. The Tabernacle & Court House.
5. The publick Mill.
6. The House for Strangers.
7. The publick Oven.
8. The draw Well.

To the Hon.ble the Trustees for establishing the Colony of Georgia in America
This View of the Town of Savanah is humbly dedicated by their Honours
Obliged and most Obedient Servant:
Peter Gordon.

VUE de Savanah dans la Georgie.

9. The Lott for the Church.
10. The publick Stores.
11. The Fort.
12. The Parsonage House.
13. The Pallisadoes.
14. The Guard House and Battery of Cannon.
15. Hutchinsons Island.

VIEWS AND GENRE, THE CHANGING SCENE

4.

Peter Gordon
(1697-1740), delineator
Pierre Fourdrinier
(ac. 1720-1758), engraver

A View of Savanah as it stood the 29th March. 1734.
P. Gordon Inv. P. Fourdrinier Sculp. To the Honble. the Trustees for establishing the Colony of Georgia in America This View of the Town of Savanah is humbly dedicated by their Honours Obliged and most Obedient Servant. Peter Gordon. VUE de Savanah dans la Georgie. [With fifteen numbered references.]

London, second state, after 1735
Line engraving with etching
Laid paper, watermark of a lily in crowned shield and countermark of "IV"

Overall size: 53.3 x 64.4 cm
Platemark: 46.1 x 58.9 cm
Image: 40.3 x 55.6 cm

61.1699

In 1733, General James Oglethorpe (1696-1785) ordered that the town of Savannah in the colony of Georgia be laid out. The following year his assistant and first bailiff, Peter Gordon, took the plan of the settlement, rendered as a bird's-eye view, to the Trustees in London as part of a progress report.

Gordon's drawing illustrates a town laid out on a grid system, with dwellings in enclosed lots arranged along straight avenues and around four open spaces. Keyed in the drawing are rudimentary accommodations for habitation and government. Stairs (1) in the foreground breach up the embankment from the water to the tent of General Oglethorpe (2) situated in the shade of four very tall, very straight pine trees. Also noted is a crane for lifting supplies. A bell (3), guard house, and the battery of cannon (14) provided security for the community. The public mill, oven, a draw well, public stores, and a house for visitors are shown under construction within the palisade just beyond the guard house.

Pleased with Gordon's sketch, the Trustees paid him sixteen guineas for it and ordered Pierre Fourdrinier, the French engraver, publisher, and mapseller who had been in London since 1720, to prepare it for publication. First issued in 1734, the engraved view provided interested parties with an important picture of the conditions and early process of settlement. The second state differs from the first only in the addition of the French subtitle.

References: Sarah B. Gober Temple and Kenneth Coleman, *Georgia Journeys: Being an Account of the Lives of Georgia's Original Settlers and Many Other Settlers from the Founding of the Colony in 1732 Until the Institutions of Royal Government in 1754* (Athens, Ga.: University of Georgia Press, 1961), 68, as quoted from the *Diary of John Percival, First Earl of Egmont,* 3 vols. (London, 1920-23), 2:36-37; Ronald Vere Tooley, *Tooley's Dictionary of Mapmakers* (Tring Hertfordshire, England: Map Collector Publications, Limited, 1979), 221.

Stokes and Haskell 1734—B-62

5.

Bishop Roberts (d. 1740), delineator
William H. Toms (ac. 1723-1758), engraver

To His Excellency James Glen Esq, Capt. General, Governor, & Commander in Chief in, and over his MAJESTY'S Province of South Carolina, and Vice Admiral within the same. This **Prospect of CHARLES-TOWN** is most humbly inscrib'd by his much Obliged humble Servant B: Roberts.

London, first state, June 9, 1739
Line engraving with etching
Laid paper, watermark of lily in crowned shield and countermark of "IV"

Overall size: 49.8 x 139.5 cm
Left section: 49.7 x 69.7 cm
Right section: 49.8 x 69.8 cm

57.532

Three great prospects or panoramic views of American cities were drawn in the colonies and sent to London for engraving on copperplate between 1720 and 1740. The earliest, a prospect of New York from the south by William Burgis (ac. 1716/8-1731), was engraved on four copperplates in London (1719-21). Burgis' second prospect, a view of Boston, was advertised for subscription late in 1723, and in 1725 impressions from the three plates, which had been engraved in London by John Harris (ac. 1685-d. 1739), were for sale in Boston.

On June 9, 1739, Bishop Roberts' drawing for the *Prospect of CHARLES-TOWN,* engraved by William Henry Toms of London, was published. As those before him, Roberts depended upon pre-publication subscription to initiate the project. Roberts died in Charleston early in 1740, and in February his widow put notice in the *Gazette* reminding subscribers to collect their prints and pay the balance due. Many did not. In August of that year she publicly notified twenty-five delinquent subscribers in the newspaper, and little more than a month later the unclaimed impressions were sold at auction.

Prospects of this size were advertised as suitable for chimney pieces when appropriately framed. (As late as 1771, John Mason in Philadelphia was advertising "harbour prints for chimnies." This may have been in reference to a set of French prints of famous harbors, issued in the 1750s, but it clearly demonstrates the continuing interest in such city views as seen from the water for display on overmantels.) While there is no eighteenth-century pictorial record of a city prospect hanging over the mantel in an American interior, visual evidence of the use of long narrow landscapes above English chimney glasses is still found in the Uppark Baby House (The National Trust, Britain), which was brought to Sussex in 1747 by Sarah Lethieullier when she went there as the bride of Sir Matthew Fetherstonhaugh.

References: Anna Wells Rutledge, "Charleston's First Artistic Couple," *Antiques* 52, no. 2 (August 1947): 100-102; Prime, *Arts and Crafts in Philadelphia, 1721-1785*, 8, 38, 209; Hennig Cohen, *The South Carolina Gazette* (Columbia: University of South Carolina Press, 1953), 164-65.

Stokes and Haskell 1739—B-63

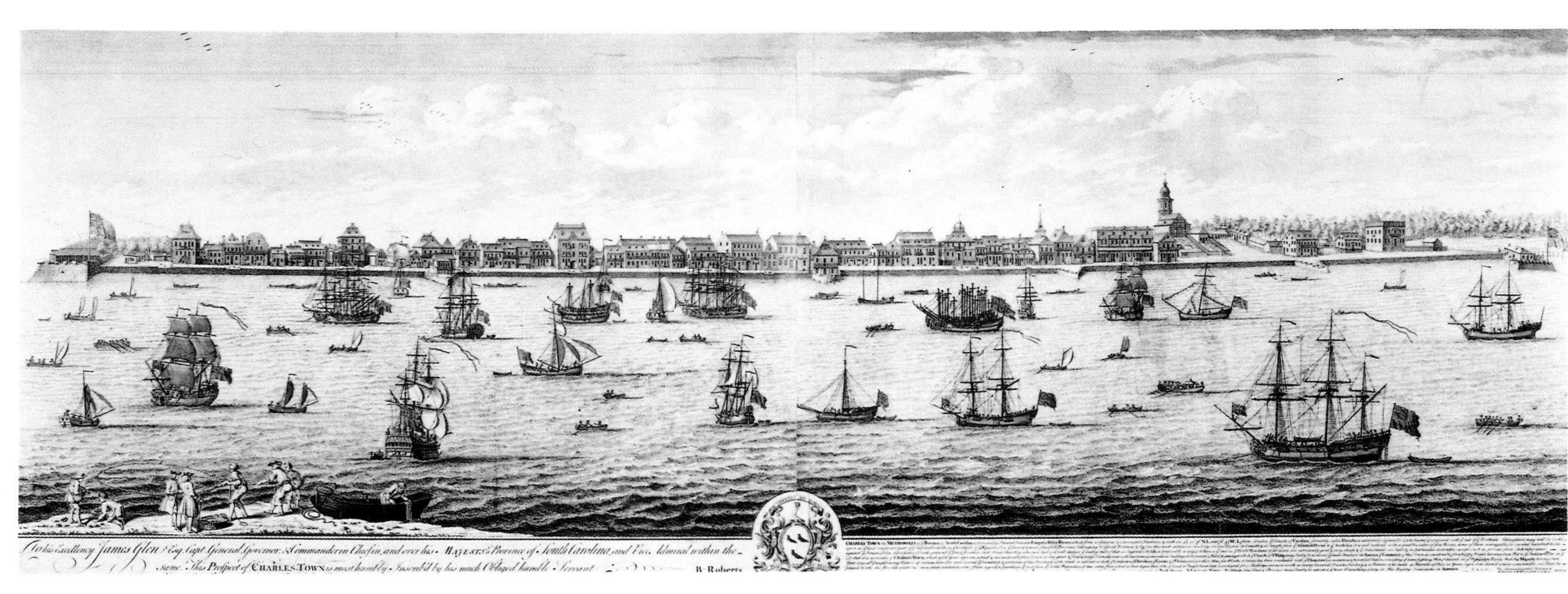
To his Excellency James Glen Esq. Capt. General Governor & Commander in Chief in, and over his MAJESTY'S Province of South Carolina, and Vice Admiral within the same. This Prospect of CHARLES TOWN is most humbly Inscrib'd by his much Obliged humble Servant
B. Roberts

6.

George Heap (d. 1752), delineator
Nicholas Scull (n.a.), publisher
Gerard Vandergucht (1695/6-1776), engraver

AN EAST PROSPECT OF THE CITY OF PHILADELPHIA; taken by GEORGE HEAP from the JERSEY SHORE, under the Direction of NICHOLAS SKULL Surveyor General of the PROVINCE of PENNSYLVANIA. To the Honourable Thomas Penn and Richard Penn, true and absolute Proprietors of the Province of PENNSYLVANIA: and Counties of NEWCASTLE, KENT and SUSSEX on DELAWARE, this Perspective View is humbly Dedicated by Nicholas Skull.

London, first state, September 1, 1754
Line etching with burin work
Laid paper, countermark of "IV" on each sheet

Overall size:
62.7 x 211.0 cm
Image (left section):
53.2 x 51.9 cm

59.2155

Thomas Penn (1702-1775) wanted no less than a great prospect of Philadelphia, which by 1750 was a wealthy and cosmopolitan city. At least three local artists tried to produce such a view, and all were unsuccessful.

Seizing the opportunity, George Heap went to draw the city from the New Jersey side of the Delaware River. In September of 1752, he and partner Nicholas Scull opened a subscription for the engraving of this view, which they proposed to be over seven inches (17.8 cm) in length when printed. Heap, on his way to London with the drawing before the end of the year, died before his ship left the Delaware River. His widow sold the drawing to Scull, who made arrangements to have it engraved. Printed from four copperplates, the Scull and Heap view measures eighty-two inches (208.3 cm). Initially, four hundred impressions were struck, each with Nicholas Scull's name misspelled "Skull." All but fifty of these came to America for the original subscribers. The plate was corrected to spell Scull properly, and an additional two hundred fifty impressions were pulled, most shipped for sale in the colonies at the price of three dollars each. The views were advertised from Boston to South Carolina.

References: Martin P. Snyder, *City of Independence: Views of Philadelphia Before 1800* (New York: Praeger Publishers, 1975), 42-44, no. 17; Nicholas B. Wainwright, "Scull and Heap's East Prospect of Philadelphia," *Pennsylvania Magazine of History and Biography* 73 (1949): 16-25.

Stokes and Haskell Before 1754—B-59

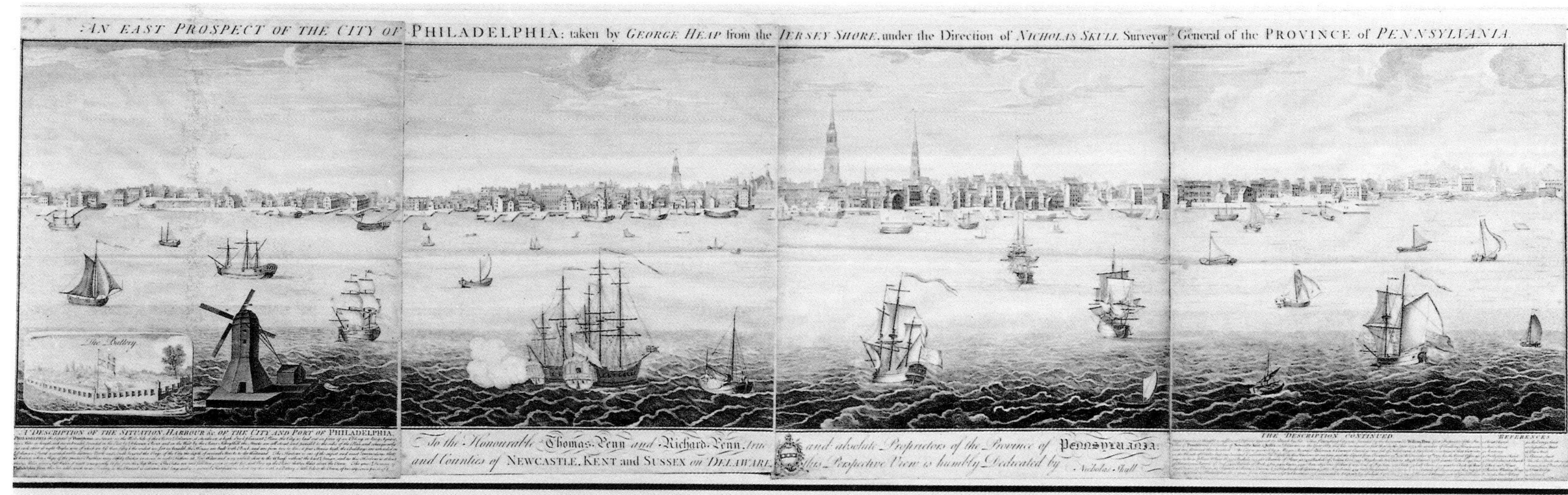
AN EAST PROSPECT OF THE CITY OF PHILADELPHIA: taken by GEORGE HEAP from the JERSEY SHORE, under the Direction of NICHOLAS SKULL Surveyor General of the PROVINCE of PENNSYLVANIA.
The Battery
A DESCRIPTION OF THE SITUATION HARBOUR &c. OF THE CITY AND PORT OF PHILADELPHIA.
To the Honourable Thomas Penn and Richard Penn, true and absolute Proprietors of the Province of PENNSYLVANIA:
and Counties of NEWCASTLE, KENT and SUSSEX on DELAWARE, this Perspective View is humbly Dedicated by Nicholas Skull
THE DESCRIPTION CONTINUED.
REFERENCES.

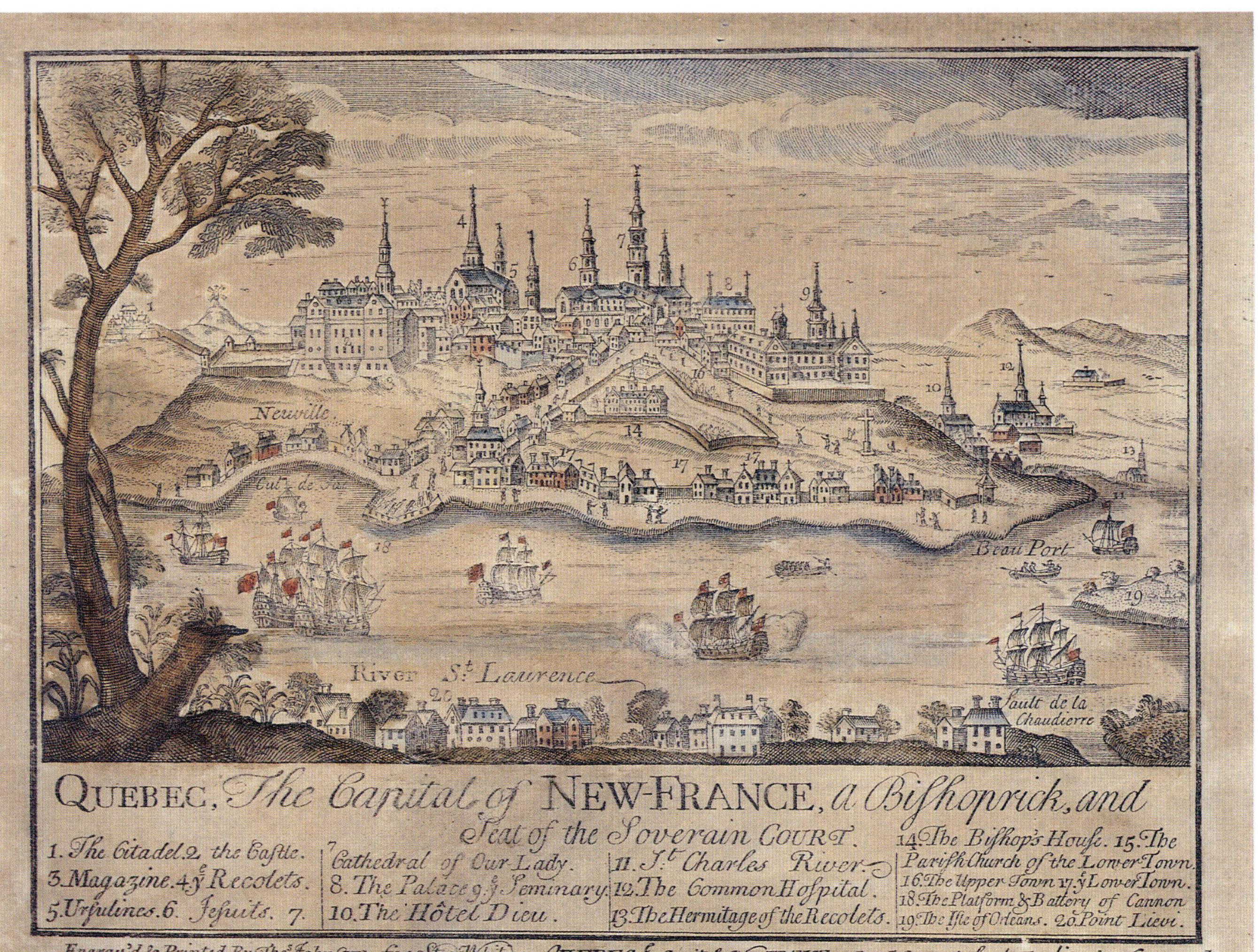
Neuville
Cul de Sac
Beau Port
River S.t Laurence
Sault de la Chaudierre
QUEBEC, The Capital of NEW-FRANCE, a Bishoprick, and Seat of the Soverain COURT.
1. The Citadel. 2. the Castle. 3. Magazine. 4. ye Recolets. 5. Ursulines. 6. Jesuits. 7. Cathedral of Our Lady. 8. The Palace 9. ye Seminary. 10. The Hôtel Dieu. 11. S.t Charles River. 12. The Common Hospital. 13. The Hermitage of the Recolets. 14. The Bishop's House. 15. The Parish Church of the Lower Town. 16. The Upper Town 17. ye Lower Town. 18. The Platform & Battery of Cannon 19. The Isle of Orleans. 20. Point Lievi.
Engrav'd & Printed By Tho.s Johnston for Step.n Whiting. QUEBEC ye Capital of New FRANCE, reduced formerly by the English in 1629 and deliverd up 1632. Unsuccessfully attempted twice, since 1690. & 1711. But surrenderd to his Brit: Majesty Sep: 17 1759, after a Battle near it on ye 13.th of Sep: wherein both ye Brave Gen: Wolfe & ye French Gen; lost their lives, The Enemy were about 12,000 strong ye Brit: army 4 or 5,000 Killed and wounded of ye former 12, or 1500 . of ye latter 5 or 600 Brig: Gen: Townshend Commanded the Brit: Troops when ye CITY surrendred.

7.

Thomas Johnston (ca. 1708-1767), engraver and printer
Stephen Whiting (n.a.), seller

QUEBEC. The Capital of NEW-FRANCE, a Bishoprick and Seat of the Soverain Court.

Boston, second state, dating after September 17, 1759, and before October 1, 1759
Line engraving and etching, watercolors
Laid paper, watermark of "W"

Overall size: 20.5 x 24.8 cm
Image (within border):
17.2 x 22.7 cm

60.13

Thomas Johnston, a native Bostonian, was a man of many skills and talents. He worked as a japanner, a painter, and a musical instrument maker, and he had his own shop at the age of twenty-four. Johnston was also an engraver of some talent, to whose credit are over thirty printed works, including trade cards and bills, maps and charts. Among his engravings is this view of the French city of Quebec as seen from the opposite shore of the St. Lawrence River.

Johnston first issued this view in August of 1759 and advertised it in the August 13 issue of the *Boston Gazette*. A month to the day later British forces attacked Quebec and engaged the French in a battle on the Plains of Abraham, just outside the city. It was a costly victory for the British, one that took the lives of Generals Marquis Louis Joseph de Montcalm de Saint-Veran (1712-1759), leader of the French forces, and James Wolfe (1727-1759), commander of the British troops. The outcome prompted Johnston to reissue the view, this time with a description of the results of the assault.

It was not unusual for American engravers, like their European contemporaries, to consult previously published views and plans as a basis for new designs that would bear appropriately updated information. Wendy Shadwell has pointed out that Johnston borrowed this view of Quebec from an earlier inset on a Paris publication of 1713. The fact that Johnston had previously suffered some embarrassment in being forced to admit he borrowed from other sources for a publication in 1753 apparently did not discourage him from this widespread practice.

References: Advertisement of Stephen Whiting in the *Boston News-Letter*, August 16, 1759, as quoted in Dow, *Arts & Crafts in New England,* 24; Sinclair H. Hitchings, "Thomas Johnston," in *Boston Prints and Printmakers 1670-1775* (Boston: Colonial Society of Massachusetts, 1973), 83-131; Shadwell, *American Printmaking*, 23-24, no. 25.

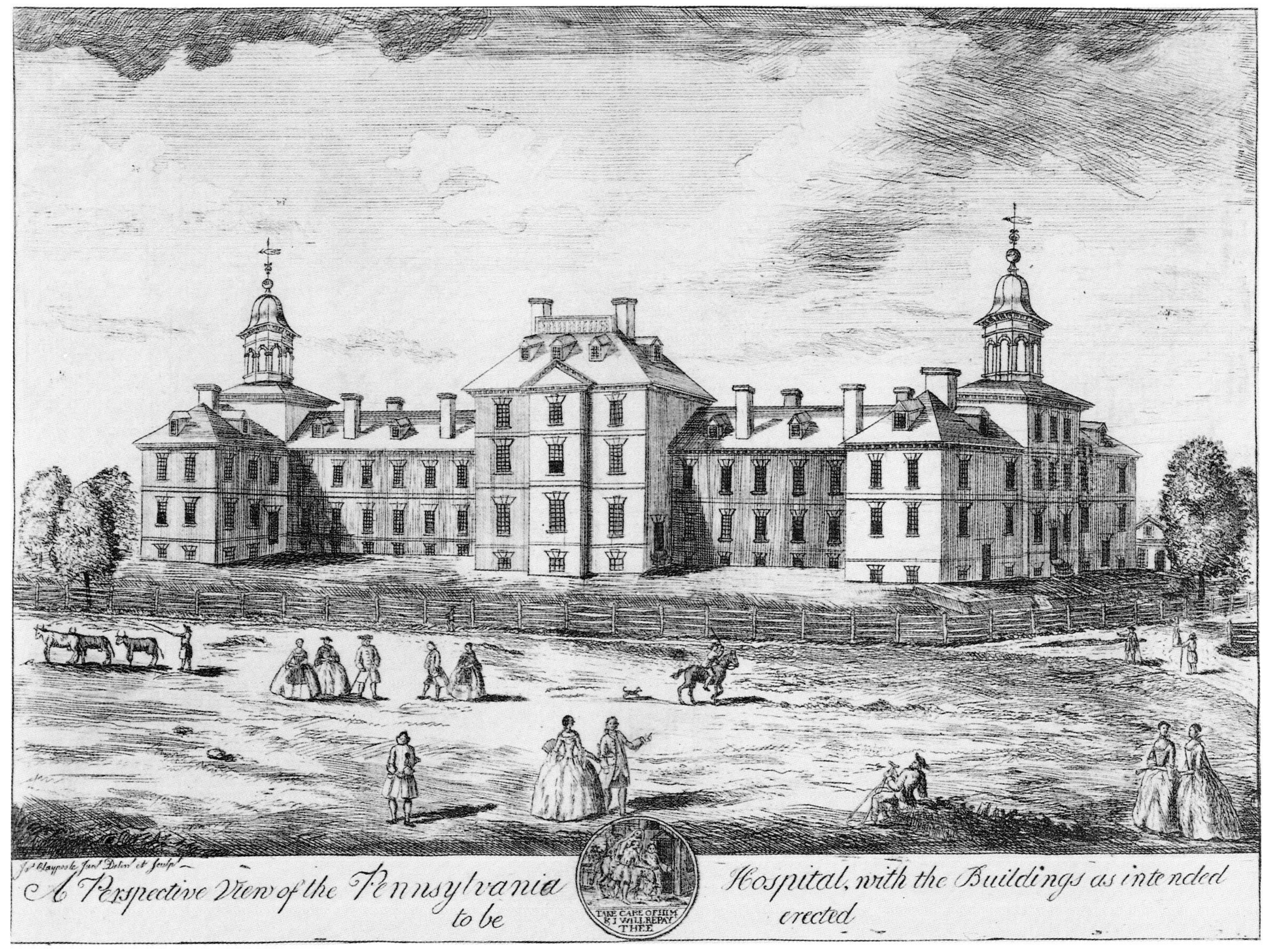
A Perspective View of the Pennsylvania Hospital, with the Buildings as intended to be erected
TAKE CARE OF HIM & I WILL REPAY THEE

8.

James Claypoole, Jr.
(w. 1761-d. 1796), artist, engraver, and publisher

A Perspective View of the Pennsylvania Hospital, with the Buildings as intended to be erected

Philadelphia, Pennsylvania, October 29, 1761
Line etching and engraving
Laid paper, watermark of Pro-patria and countermark of "G R" under crown

Overall size: 30.3 x 39.7 cm
Platemark: 27.0 x 35.9 cm
Image: 23.6 x 34.6 cm

59.1551

Perspective views of colonial cities were intended to support promises of burgeoning economic opportunities, yet Americans were justly proud of educational and humanitarian achievements within these cities. By early July of 1726, *A Prospect of the Colledges in Cambridge in New England* (recently determined to be the work of William Burgis) was advertised in the *Boston News-Letter*, and in 1749 Thomas Johnston engraved the *Prospect of Yale College* after John Greenwood.

Ground was broken in 1755 at the corner of Eighth and Pine Streets in Philadelphia for the Pennsylvania Hospital. This ambitious undertaking was worthy of broad attention. Funding for the structure was on a subscription basis. In 1761, the Board of Managers of the project agreed to commission an engraving of framing size that would depict the complex as it would appear when completed. Such pictures could be given as an acknowledgement to past subscribers and as an award for future contributions. Officially, the printseller Robert Kennedy was to organize the publication. He contacted artists to prepare the drawing and a leading Philadelphia engraver to execute the copperplate.

James Claypoole, Jr., in the spirit of enterprise and independence, undertook to produce a suitable image that he would execute in its entirety. On October 22, 1761, Kennedy announced that finished views of the hospital, "coloured, framed and glaized," would be ready in two weeks. The following week Claypoole had his view ready for the public and promptly announced that it could be purchased from him or from David Hall for the price of one shilling plain or two shillings "neatly coloured."

References: Richard B. Hodman, "William Burgis," in *Boston Prints and Printmakers: 1670-1755*, ed. Walter Muir Whitehall and Sinclair H. Hitchings (Boston: Colonial Society of Massachusetts, 1973), 65-67; Snyder, *City of Independence*, 53-57, nos. 23, 24.

Stauffer 396

9.

Carington Bowles (1724-1793), publisher

An East Perspective view of the CITY of PHILADELPHIA, in the PROVINCE of PENSYLVANIA, in NORTH AMERICA: taken from the JERSEY Shore. [Followed by fourteen numbered references.] The other Streets are not to be seen from the point of Sight. Engraved from the Original Drawing sent over from Philadelphia in the possession of Carington Bowles. Printed for and Sold by CARINGTON BOWLES, at his Map & Print Warehouse, No. 69 in St Pauls Church Yard, LONDON.

London, unrecorded state from first issue, "1 Jany. 1778" (four other states known)
Etching with burin work, watercolors
Laid paper, watermark of "I VILLEDARY"

Overall size: 34.0 x 48.6 cm
Platemark: 27.7 x 42.9 cm
Image: 24.3 x 41.4 cm

59.1385

By 1778, George Heap's drawing of Philadelphia (cat. no. 6) was in the possession of Carington Bowles, one of London's most prolific publishers of popular views. Bowles' shop served as a gathering place for the fashionable bourgeois and the upper classes who were in search of an afternoon's entertainment browsing through portraits, genre and satire, and the latest views. Philadelphia, which had been occupied by British forces since October of the preceding year, no doubt was then on the minds of many of Bowles' customers.

Bowles greatly reduced the scale of Heap's original design to approximately ten by sixteen inches (25.4 by 40.6 cm), a size that was suitable for use with the popular perspective glass. The diminished size was also far less expensive to glaze and frame, should the purchaser simply wish to exhibit the picture on the wall.

To accommodate the smaller format, Bowles eliminated part of the Philadelphia skyline south of Market Street. He retained the principal points of interest along the city's skyline. Although this impression lacks a plate number, many impressions of the same image are known, all having been taken from the plate after the number "38" was added. Undoubtedly this number signifies its place in a series of two hundred seventy-one views produced for the perspective glass, which Bowles carried in his inventory. Typical of views designed for the perspective glass, this one was brightly colored with opaque watercolors, but unlike most, this impression was once stretched around strainers, a strong indication that from the outset it was intended to be framed for the wall.

Reference: Snyder, *City of Independence*, 119.

Stokes and Haskell P. 1731-36—B-60; Snyder 100, 100A

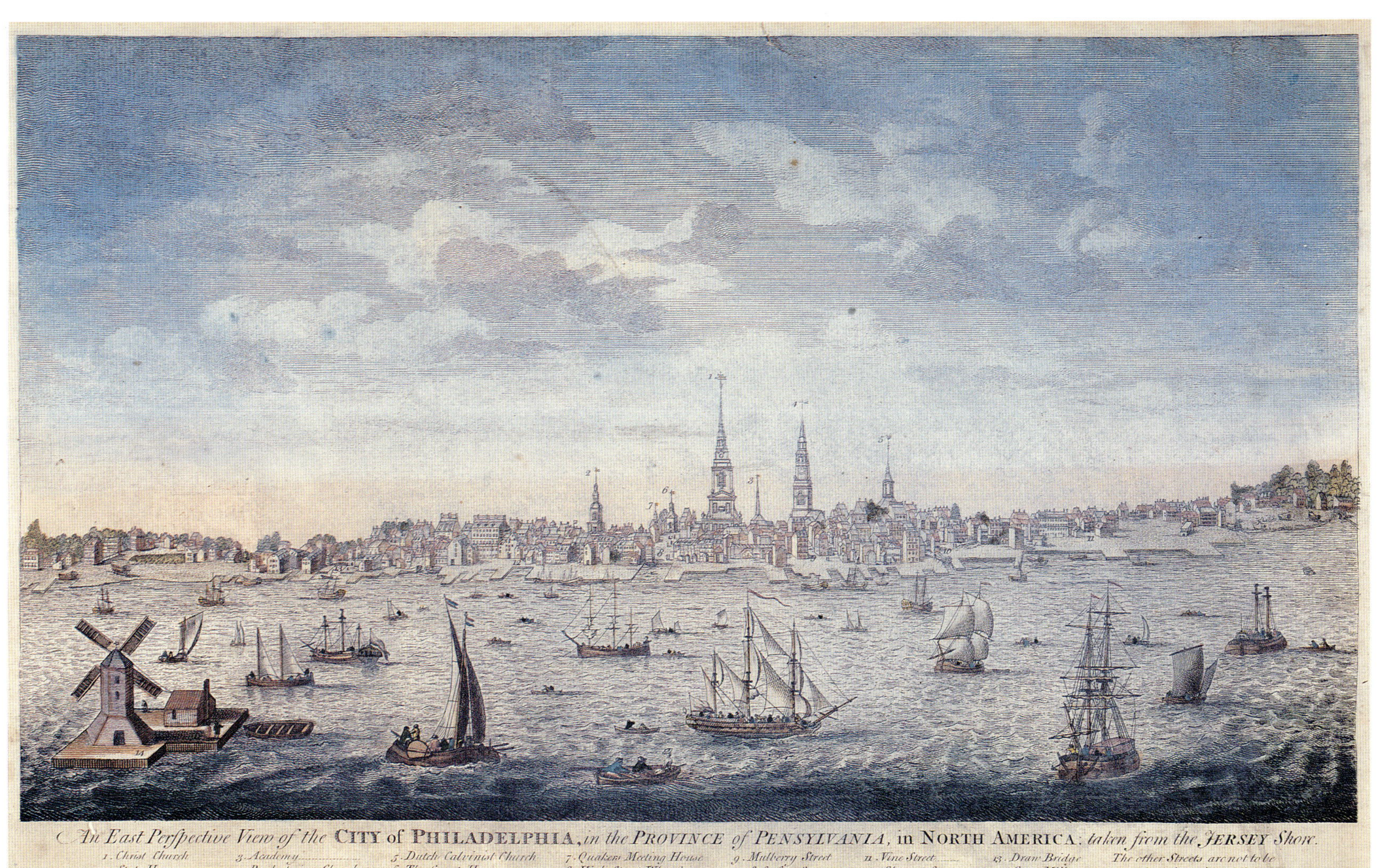
An East Perspective View of the CITY of PHILADELPHIA, in the PROVINCE of PENSYLVANIA, in NORTH AMERICA; taken from the JERSEY Shore.
1. Christ Church
2. State House
3. Academy
4. Presbyterian Church
5. Dutch Calvinist Church
6. The Court House
7. Quakers Meeting House
8. High Street Wharf
9. Mulberry Street
10. Saſsafras Street
11. Vine Street
12. Chesnut Street
13. Draw Bridge
14. Corn Mill
The other Streets are not to be seen from the point of Sight.
Engraved from the Original Drawing sent over from Philadelphia in the poſseſsion of Carington Bowles.
Printed for and Sold by CARINGTON BOWLES, at his Map & Print Warehouse, No. 69 in St. Pauls Church Yard LONDON. Publish'd as the Act directs, 1 Jany. 1778.

10.

Captain Thomas Howdell (n.a.), delineator
Pierre Canot (1710-1777), engraver
John Bowles (1701-1779), Thomas Jefferys (b. 1710, ac. 1732-d. 1771), Carington Bowles (1724-1793), Henry Parker (ac. 1758-1773), publishers

A South East View of the City of New York, in NORTH AMERICA.
Drawn on the SPOT by Capt. Thomas Howdell, of the Royal Artillery. [Followed by seven numbered references.]

London, third state, 1768
Published in *Scenographia Americana, or A Collection of Views in North America and the West Indies...* (London: Printed for John Bowles, 1768)
Line etching with burin work
Laid paper

Overall size: 45.8 x 61.0 cm
Platemark: 35.7 x 52.9 cm
Image: 31.7 x 49.8 cm

64.1232

The cityscape and landscape continued to gain popularity into the eighteenth century. As a result, the topographical artist became an increasingly important source of designs for the engraver. Many who learned the art of drawing the landscape, such as Thomas Howdell, did so as part of their training for the military, where an ability to make correct records of the terrain was critical in reconnaissance and useful in reporting military encounters.

In 1768, twenty-eight views of North America were published under the title of *Scenographia Americana* and sold for slightly under five pounds. The collection comprised several sets that had been issued from 1761. One of a set of two views to be first offered by Thomas Jefferys, this view of New York actually delineates little of the city beyond a few church spires and the large, new building at King's College, which had been granted a Royal Charter in 1754 and was named Columbia University on May 1, 1784, by act of the legislature of New York. Seemingly more important to the artist are the two young men who find the serenity of the place conducive to thoughtful conversation.

References: Isaac Newton Phelps Stokes, *Iconography of Manhattan Island 1498-1909,* 3 vols. (New York: Robert H. Dodd, 1915), 1:281ff; Ronald Russell, *Guide to British Topographical Prints* (London: Newton Abbott, England, and North Pomfret, Vt.: David & Charles, 1979), 9-12, 31-35; Irving S. Olds, *Bits and Pieces of American History* (New York: Privately printed, 1951), 6-9.

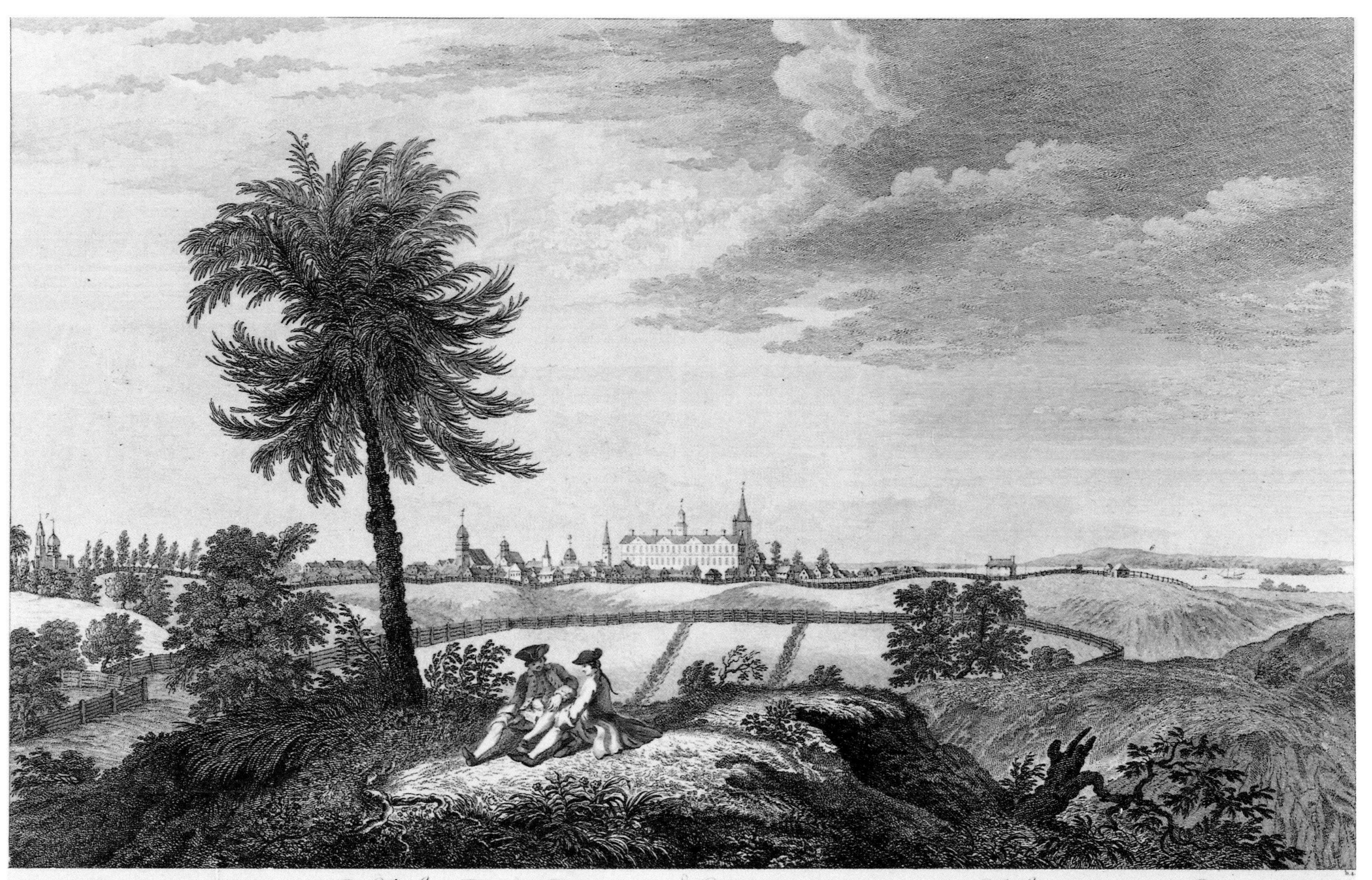
A South East View of the City of New York, in NORTH AMERICA.
Vue du Sud Est de la Ville de New York, dans L'AMERIQUE SEPTENTRIONALE.
Drawn on the SPOT by Capt. Thomas Howdell, of the Royal Artillery. Engraved by P. Canot.
1. New Colledge. 2 Old English Church. 3 City Hall. 4 French Church.
5 North River. 6 Staten Island. 7 The Prison.

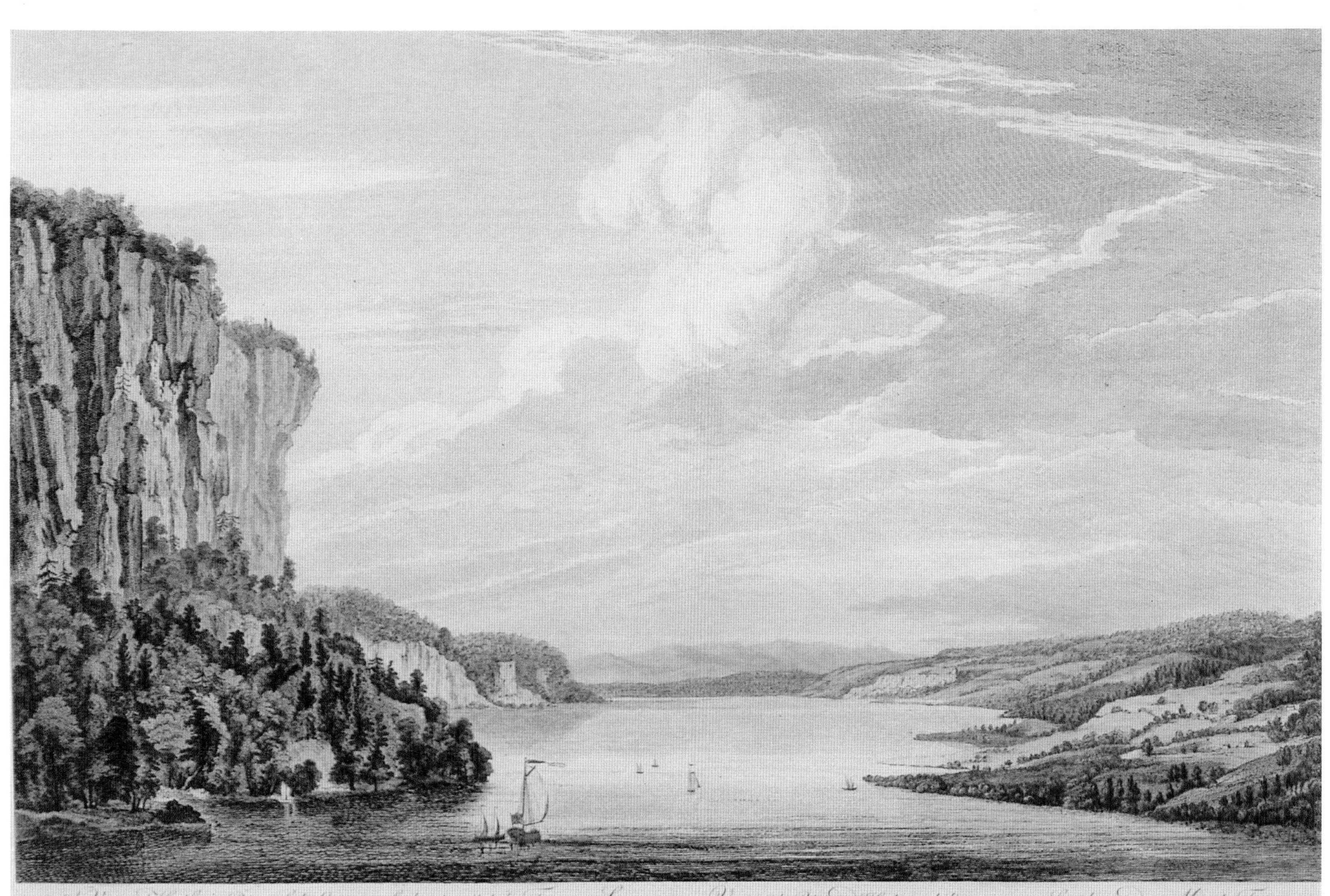
A View in Hudson's River of the Entrance of what is called the Topan Sea.
Vue sur la Rivière d'Hudson, de l'entrée counue sous le nom de Mer de Topan.
Sketch'd on the SPOT by his Excellency Governor Pownal, Painted by Paul Sandby, Engraved by Peter Benazech.

11.

Thomas Pownall (1722-1805), artist
Paul Sandby (1730-1809), delineator
Peter Benazech (n.a.), engraver
John Bowles (1701-1779), Robert Sayer (b. 1725, ac. 1751-d. 1794), Thomas Jefferys (b. 1710, ac. 1732-d. 1771), Carington Bowles (1724-1793), Henry Parker (ac. 1758-1773), publishers

A View in Hudson's River of the Entrance of what is called the Topan Sea.
Sketched on the SPOT by his Excellency Governor Pownal...

London, 1768
Published in *Scenographia Americana*
Line etching with burin work, watercolors
Laid paper

Overall size: 43.2 x 57.1 cm
Platemark: 35.7 x 52.9 cm
Image: 31.7 x 49.8 cm

74.31

Although members of the Royal Academy held that landscape ranked just behind history as a suitable subject for the artist's pencil, their reference was to the idealized landscape. For eighteenth-century print buyers, the art of landscape could be either the more pedestrian topographical studies, which concentrated on delineation of a place, or the emotionally charged and imaginary places found in the classical and romantic tradition of Claude Lorraine, Salvatore Rosa, or Poussin.

Thomas Pownall's moody and evocative sketch of the palisades at the entrance to the Topan Sea, as interpreted by Paul Sandby for the engraver, is full of light and shadows and serves as an early precursor of the American school of painting that took its name from the river depicted here. Pownall was a militarist who made sketches and kept careful notes, which he prepared for publication after the Revolutionary War. He demanded detail. Sandby, as chief drawing master at the Royal Military Academy, could understand the need for precision, but he was also an artist who viewed the landscape as being complex and worthy of expression as a higher art form.

This work was designed as part of a set of *Six Remarkable Views,* first published in 1761 and reissued with other sets of views in *Scenographia Americana* in 1768.

References: Thomas Pownall, *A Topographical Description of the Dominions of the United States of America*, ed. Lois Mulkearn (London, 1776; Pittsburgh: University of Pittsburgh Press, 1949), 39; Dale Roylance, "Aquatint Engraving in England," in Gloria-Gilda Deák, *William James Bennett: Master of the Aquatint View* (New York: New York Public Library, 1988), 3-4.

12.

James Smither (d. 1797), engraver
Thomas Mann (n.a.), printer
John Reed (n.a.), publisher

To the Honourable House of Representatives of the Freeman of Pennsylvania this
Map of the City and Liberties of Philadelphia
With the Catalogue of Purchasers is Humbly Dedicated by their most Obedient Servant John Reed

Philadelphia, Pennsylvania, 1774
Line engraving, printed in red from three copperplates on linen textile

Overall size: 233.9 x 155.1 cm

61.238

The Liberties outside the city of Philadelphia consisted of lots that had been offered by William Penn (1644-1718) as bonuses to early purchasers of city property. Problems noticed at the outset between actual surveys and Penn's records remained unreconciled. In the third quarter of the eighteenth century, a number of descendants were determined to set matters straight. John Reed, being one of them, undertook to get to the bottom of the matter and in 1774, with financial support from other heirs, published his results.

Reed's book was accompanied by a map of the city and the Liberties, a lengthy list of the first purchasers and their occupations, and an enlarged plan of the center city. It was a complex issue and to present it graphically required a large format. Reed included an elaborate cartouche at top center, along with views of the Pennsylvania Hospital, the State House and the House of Employment, and the Alms House, all of which he borrowed from previously published Philadelphia views.

In announcing completion of the map, Reed gave notice in the *Pennsylvania Gazette* on July 13, 1774, that anyone wishing to have the map "framed, painted, gilded and varnished" could have it done by either Mr. Brooks or Mr. James Gilliangham. Such treatment was usual for maps printed on paper. This impression on linen, although now framed, was equally suitable for mounting on rollers or for folding into a case to be used as a field map.

References: Snyder, *City of Independence*, 89-93; Oliver Hough, "Captain Thomas Holme, Surveyor-General of Pennsylvania and Provincial Councillor," *Pennsylvania Magazine of History and Biography* 38, no. 2 (1913): 246; Receipt of May 30, 1774, Box 8, Case 4, John Reed Papers, Gratz Collection, Historical Society of Pennsylvania; *The Arader Grading System for Maps, Books and Prints*, ed. Donald H. Cresswell and W. Graham Arader III, Catalogue of W. Graham Arader III, vol. 28 (Philadelphia: Arader, 1981), item 54.

Stauffer 2986

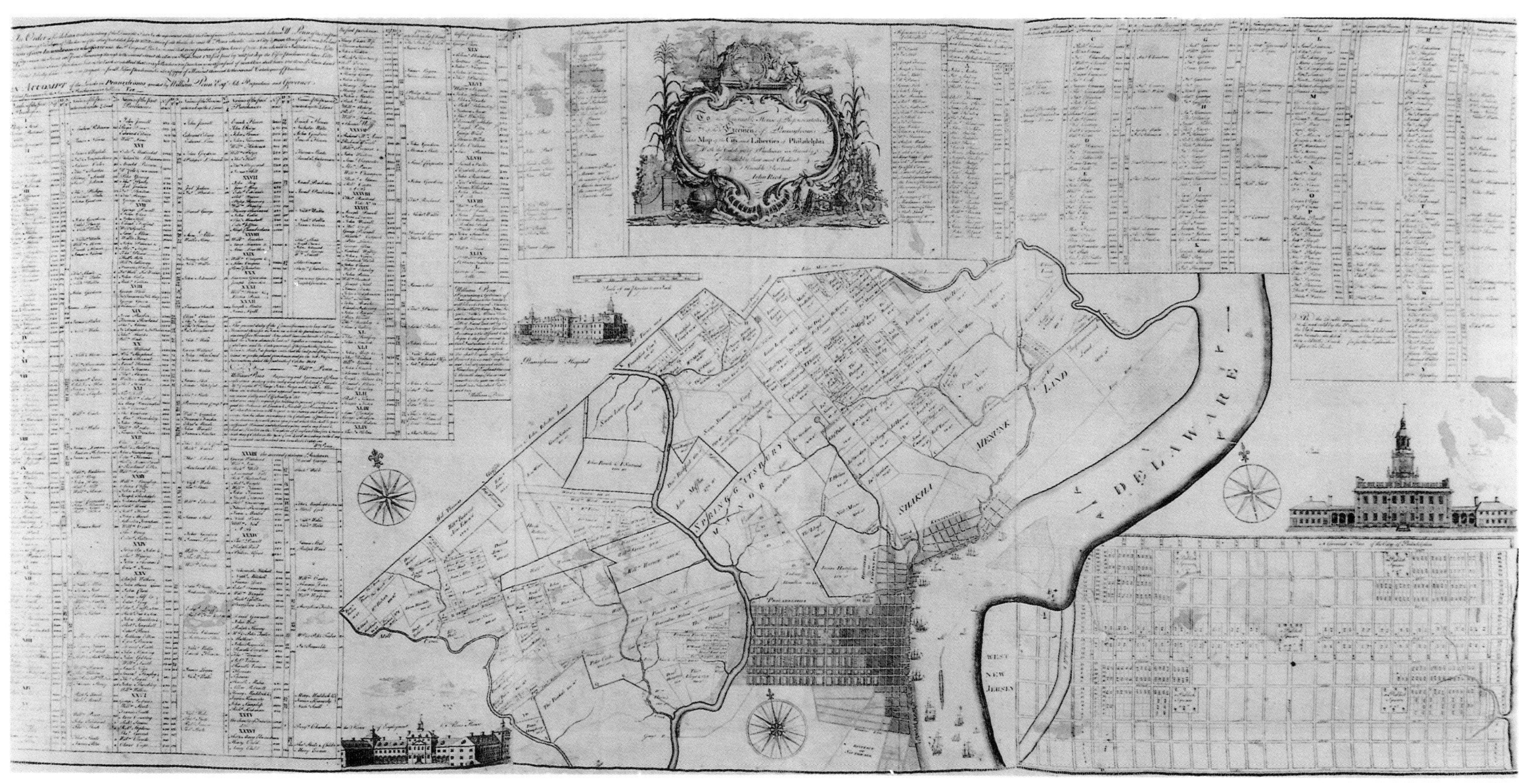
DELAWARE
WEST NEW JERSEY

13.

Charles Willson Peale (1741-1827), artist, engraver, and publisher

The ACCIDENT in LOMBARD-STREET PHILADA. 1787

Philadelphia, Pennsylvania, 1787
Line etching
Laid paper

Overall size: 20.9 x 30.1 cm
Image: 18.5 x 28.4 cm

62.88
Funds gift of the Caroline Clendenin Ryan Foundation, Inc.

Of his many activities, Charles Willson Peale's work as a topographical artist remains the least explored. He is known to have gone on sketching trips in the company of some of his patrons. A number of his portraits incorporate detailed vignettes as background, and engravings after his sketches of local scenes were published in several issues of *Columbian Magazine*.

In the fall of 1787, Peale turned his attentions to a more common genre that had proven profitable to London printmakers: the street scene. Earlier in the century William Hogarth had used the streets as environments for his comments on *Election Day*, *Gin Lane*, and *Beer Street*. And more recently, the Bowleses and the Darlys, eighteenth-century London families of publishers, had used the streets of London as background for their chronicles and ridicule of the Macaroni, or the English dandies. The street scene, transferred to Philadelphia, held the potential of being both familiar and humorous.

Peale placed an advertisement in the *Pennsylvania Packet* for November 5, 1787, in which he offered a "New Print," being "A Perspective View of Lombard-street." He further promised his subscribers that this view was the first in a series "to be taken of the principal streets in Philadelphia." Although Peale did not call attention to his process in the advertisement, those who came to purchase one of the prints found that in his haste to get the image on the market Peale had used etching, a line process. It was *not* a technique that he had mastered. Peale used the etcher's needle or stylus much as he would have used a pencil. With short, overlapping strokes focused on small details, he ignored the variety and vitality of line that characterized line etching as practiced by topographical engravers, and he gave a minimum of consideration to bringing the whole image into a point of focus through a judicious use of chiaroscuro.

For whatever reason, this first plate of the series did not attract the number of customers Peale felt necessary to continue the project. Instead, he found an audience for his views of the architecture and neighborhoods of Philadelphia among the readers of the newly established *Columbian Magazine* (Philadelphia, 1787-95).

References: Advertisement of Charles Willson Peale in the *Pennsylvania Packet*, November 5, 1787, as quoted in Alfred Coxe Prime, *The Arts and Crafts in Philadelphia, Maryland, and South Carolina, 1786-1800*, series 2 (Topsfield, Mass.: Walpole Society, 1932), 22; Edgar Preston Richardson, "Charles Willson Peale's Engravings in the Year of National Crisis, 1787," in *Winterthur Portfolio One*, ed. Edgar P. Richardson, John D. Morse, and Milo M. Naeve (Winterthur, Del.: Henry Francis du Pont Winterthur Museum, Inc., 1964),166, 178ff.; Charles Coleman Sellers, *Portraits and Miniatures by Charles Willson Peale* 42, pt. 1 of Transactions of the American Philosophical Society (Philadelphia: American Philosophical Society, 1952), 238-39; Snyder, *City of Independence,* 136-46.

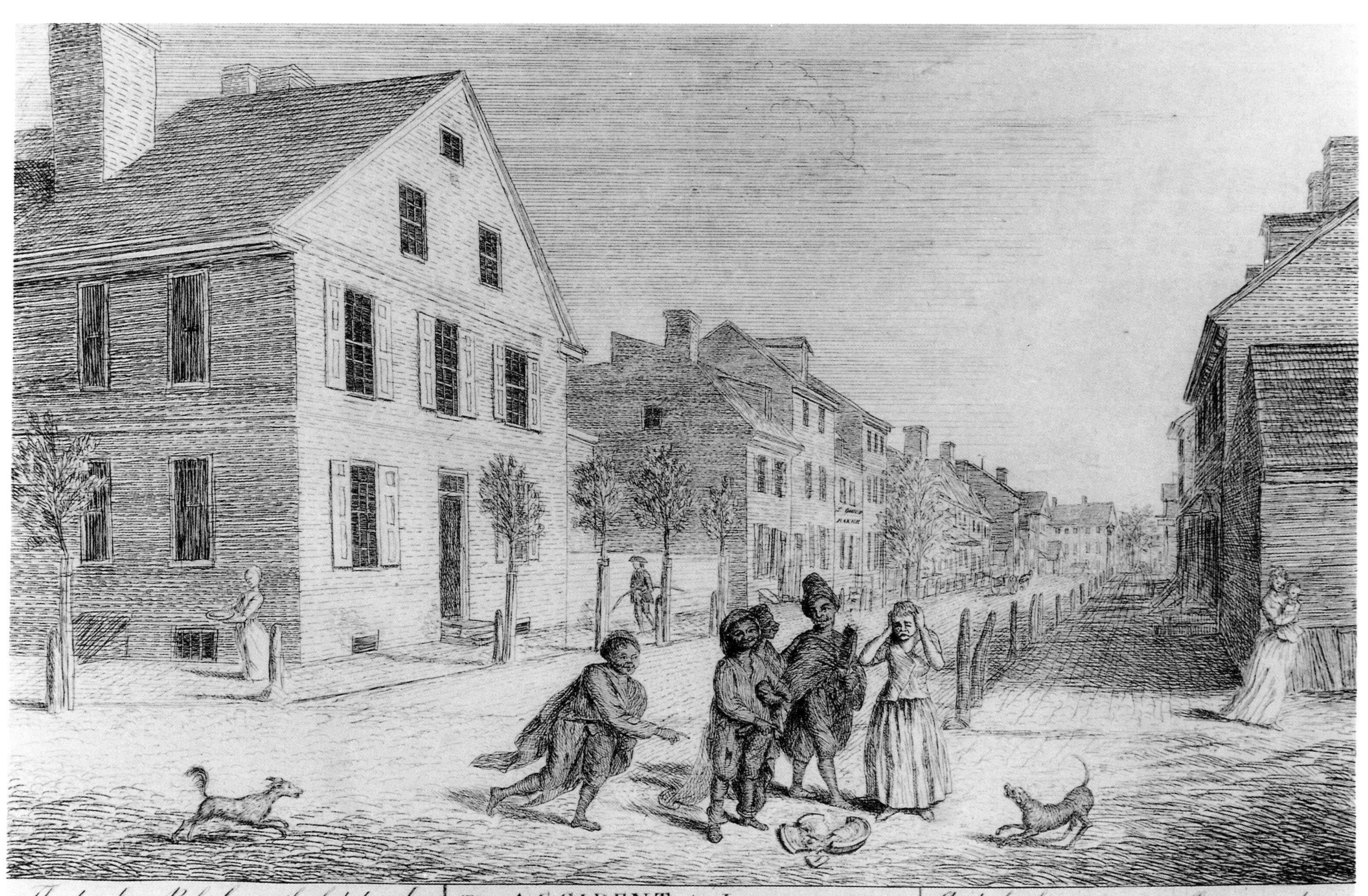
The pye from Bake-house she had brought
But let it fall for want of thought
The ACCIDENT in LOMBARD-STREET
PHILADA. 1787
designed & engraved by C.W. Peale
And laughing Sweeps collect around
The pye that's scatter'd on the ground
No. 1

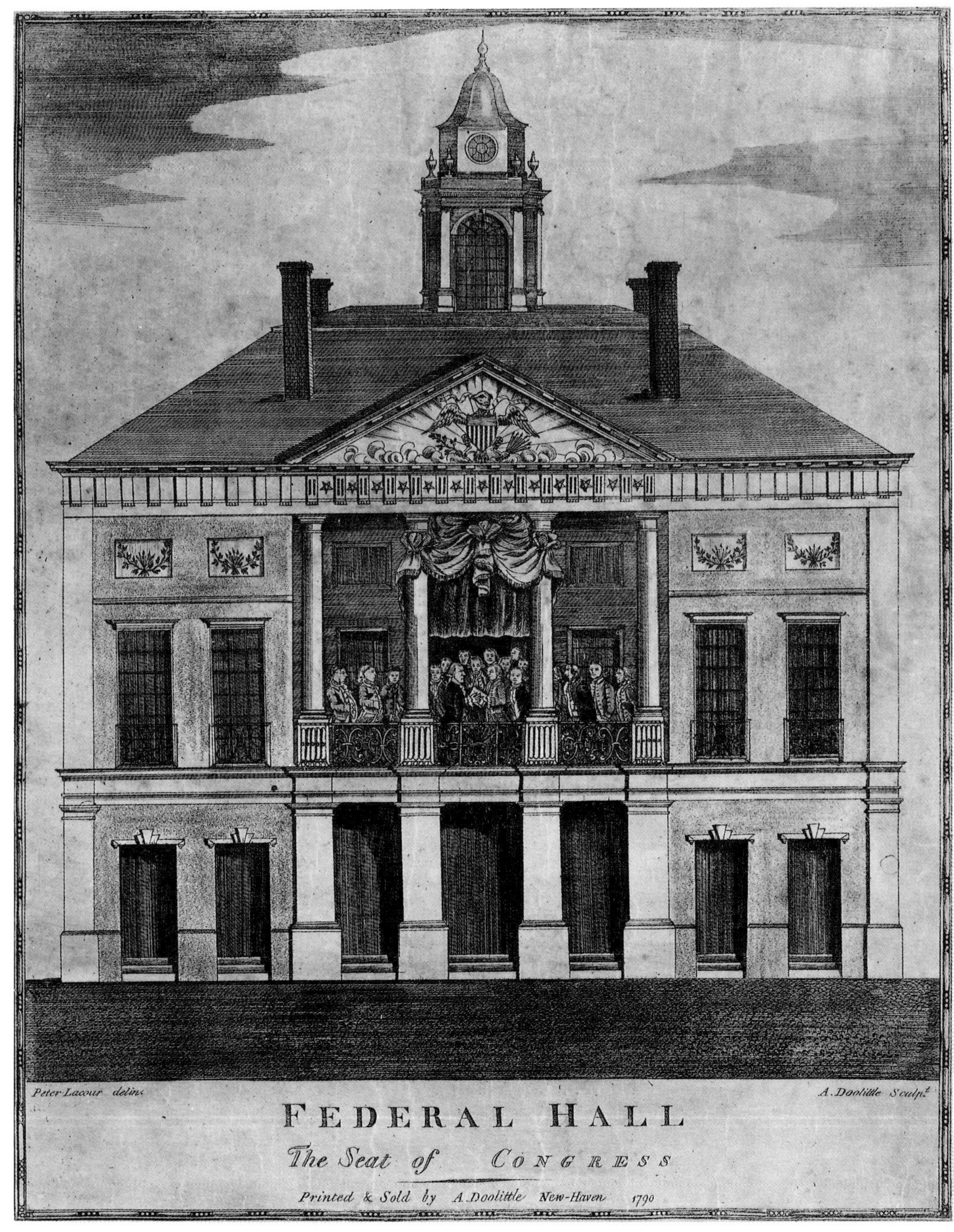
Peter Lacour delin.
A. Doolittle Sculpt.
FEDERAL HALL
The Seat of CONGRESS
Printed & Sold by A. Doolittle New-Haven 1790

14.

Amos Doolittle (1754-1832), engraver and publisher
Pierre or Peter Lacour (w. in New York 1785-1799), artist

FEDERAL HALL
The Seat of CONGRESS

New Haven, Connecticut, 1790
Line and stipple etching with some burin work, watercolors
Laid paper

Overall size: 46.4 x 36.6 cm
Platemark: (indistinct)
Image: 42.0 x 32.2 cm

57.816

In preparation for the inauguration of George Washington and with the hope that the seat of national government could be attracted from Philadelphia, the city of New York undertook a major renovation of its old City Hall. Pierre Charles L'Enfant (1754-1825) was hired as architect for the project.

On April 30, 1789, Washington was sworn to the presidency on the balcony of City Hall (renamed Federal Hall after renovations) below a pediment emblazoned with the seal of the United States and a frieze with thirteen stars. Somewhere on the street below Pierre Lacour, a drawing teacher, was in the crowd. He made the sketch that Amos Doolittle later etched on copperplate. Doolittle gave a suggestion of form and shadow in this view with the judicious use of stipple, a dotted method of developing tone within the etching procedure. Limited splashes of watercolor may have been the work of Doolittle or an early owner of the print.

Reference: I. N. Phelps Stokes and Daniel C. Haskell, *American Historical Prints: Early Views of American Cities, Etc.* (New York: New York Public Library, 1932), 35-36, 1789—B-124.

Stauffer 533

15.

Gilbert Fox (1776-ca. 1806), engraver
John Joseph Holland (ca. 1776-1820), artist

View OF THE CITY OF Philadelphia.

Philadelphia, Pennsylvania, probably 1796
Line etching, watercolors
Wove paper, watermark of "1794 J WHATMAN"

Overall size: 46.4 x 61.3 cm
Platemark: (trimmed) x 57.8 cm
Image: 38.2 x 52.8 cm

59.606

By the 1790s a measurable interest in landscape painting had emerged in America, an interest that in the next decades not only would encourage native artists but, more importantly for the immediate state of the arts, would also attract both established and fresh talents from England. Some, such as the English artists William Groombridge (1748-1811, ac. in America from 1795), William Winstanly (ac. in America 1793-1803), George Beck (1748/9-1812, ac. in America from 1795), and Francis Guy (1760-1820), came to paint the landscape in oil. Others journeyed to prepare detailed drawings in ink and watercolors to be engraved abroad, and still others ventured to engrave these views for local publishers.

John Joseph Holland, a theatrical scenery painter and topographical artist, arrived from London in 1796, preceded by Gilbert Fox a year or so earlier. It is believed that within a year of his arrival in Philadelphia, Holland made the drawing from which this romantic view of the city was engraved. Framed between two great trees, the city shimmers in the distance. In dark contrast, the foreground is peopled with proportionately large figures. Given the effects of theatrical lighting and Holland's principal occupation, there is the possibility that this bucolic design was initially conceived as a very real and accurate theatrical backdrop.

References: Snyder, *City of Independence*, 194-96; Jacob Hall Pleasants, *Four Late Eighteenth Century Anglo-American Landscape Painters* (Worcester, Mass.: American Antiquarian Society, 1943); Stiles Tuttle Colwill, *Francis Guy 1760-1820* (Baltimore: Museum and Library of Maryland History, Maryland Historical Society, 1981).

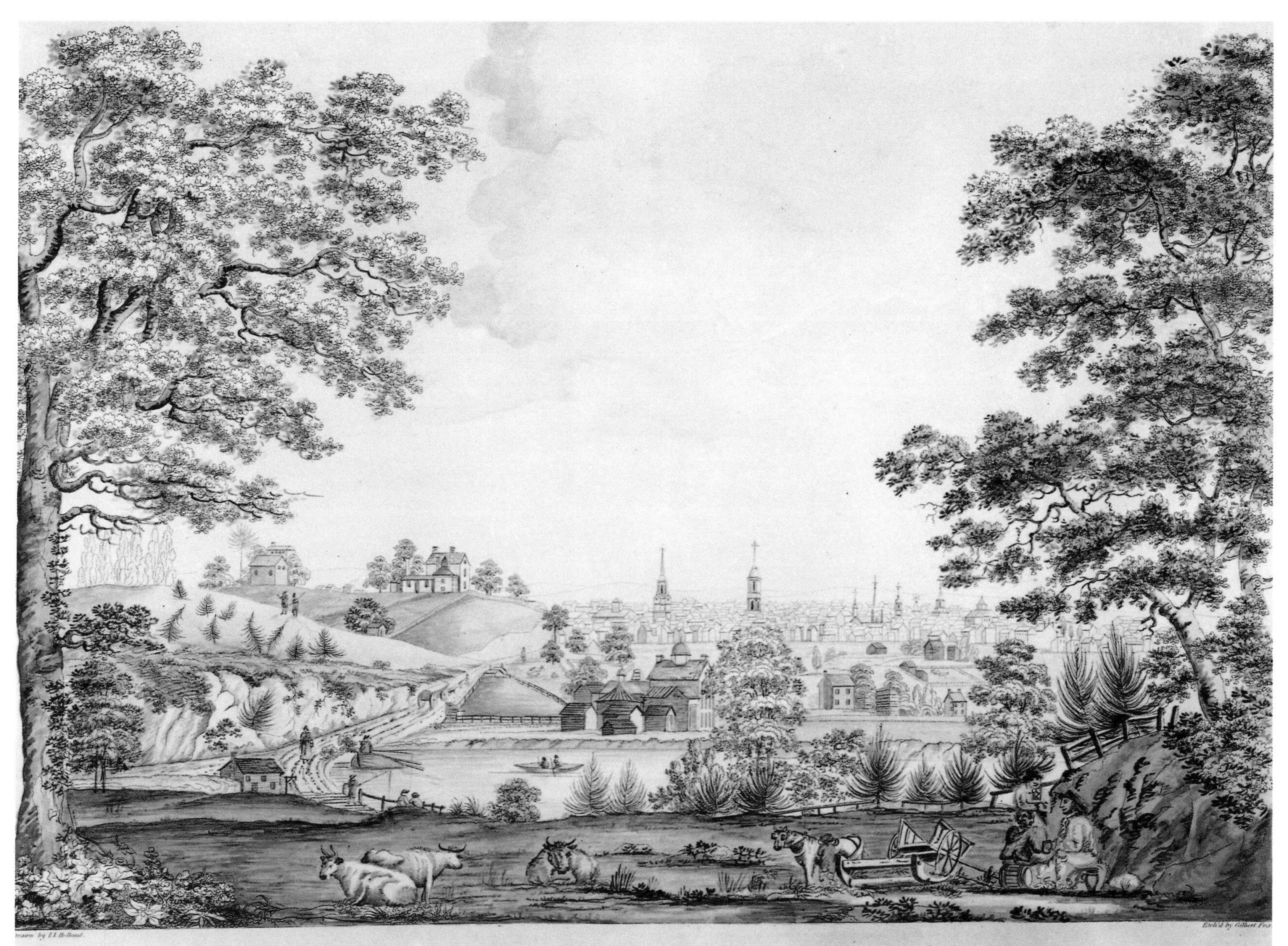

View OF THE City OF Philadelphia.

PORTRAITS

16.

Bernard Lens, Sr. (1659-1725), artist
Bernard Lens, Jr. (1680-1740), engraver

The Four Indian Kings. Tee Yee Neen Ho Ga Row. Emperour of the Six Nations. Sa Ga Yeath Qua Pieth Tow. King of the Maquas. Ho Nee Yeath Taw No Riow. King of Ganajoh-Hore. E Tow Oh Koam. King of the River Nation.

London, 1710
Mezzotint with minimal burin work
Laid paper

Overall size: 34.4 x 25.1 cm
Platemark: 34.0 x 25.1 cm
Image: 32.7 x 25.0 cm

69.218

With the frontier nearby and skirmishes or threats of hostile engagement reported frequently, native Americans were not subjects colonists were likely to choose as pictures to adorn the walls of their seventeenth-century houses. To a limited extent, attitudes changed at the beginning of the eighteenth century, when British authorities decided it was in their best interest to join in support of the Iroquois people, a confederation of the Mohawk, Oneida, Onondaga, Cayuga, and Seneca nations and later the Tuscarora, who had been resisting invasion from the north by Frenchmen and their Indian confederates. With a promise of material support from England, the Iroquois and a militia under the commands of Peter Schuyler and Francis Nicholson began an advance into Canada. Supplies did not reach the advancing forces, and the Iroquois were forced to retreat. Thus giving the appearance of defeat, the Indians were put in a humiliating position.

To relieve these new tensions between the British and the Iroquois, a trip to London was arranged for several of the Indian princes. They were to be received at court, feted, and otherwise impressed with the might of Britain. On April 19, 1710, the Iroquois representatives Tee Yee Neen Ho Ga Row, Sa Ga Yeath Qua Pieth Tow, Ho Nee Yeath Taw No Row, and Etow Oh Koam were presented to Queen Anne. For two months thereafter, the four Indian nobles were taken from one reception to another, plied with gifts, and painted by celebrated English portrait painters.

Among them was Bernard Lens, Jr., who executed their portraits in miniature. Capitalizing on the mania that was sweeping London, his father, Bernard Lens, Sr., designed a single sheet composition that replicated the miniature portraits and wreathed them in an elaborate set of borders surmounted with crowns of five feathers. Each of the subjects was shown in the court attire that had been tailored for him upon arrival. One, Sa Ga Yean Qua Rah Tow, kept his blouse opened from the neck to reveal an intricately tattooed torso.

References: John G. Garratt, "The Four Indian Kings," in *History Today* (London) 18, no. 2 (February 1968): 93-101; John Chaloner Smith, *British Mezzotinto Portraits: Being a Descriptive Catalogue of These Engravings From the Introduction of the Art to the Early Part of the Present Century*, 4 vols. (London: Henry Sotheran & Co., 1884), 1:288, 4:1692-93; Bradford F. Swan, "Prints of the American Indians, 1670-1775," in *Boston Prints and Printmakers, 1670-1775*, ed. Walter Muir Whitehill and Sinclair H. Hitchings (Boston: Colonial Society of Massachusetts, 1973), 245-59.

J. C. Smith, "Engraver Not Ascertained," Class II, no. 54

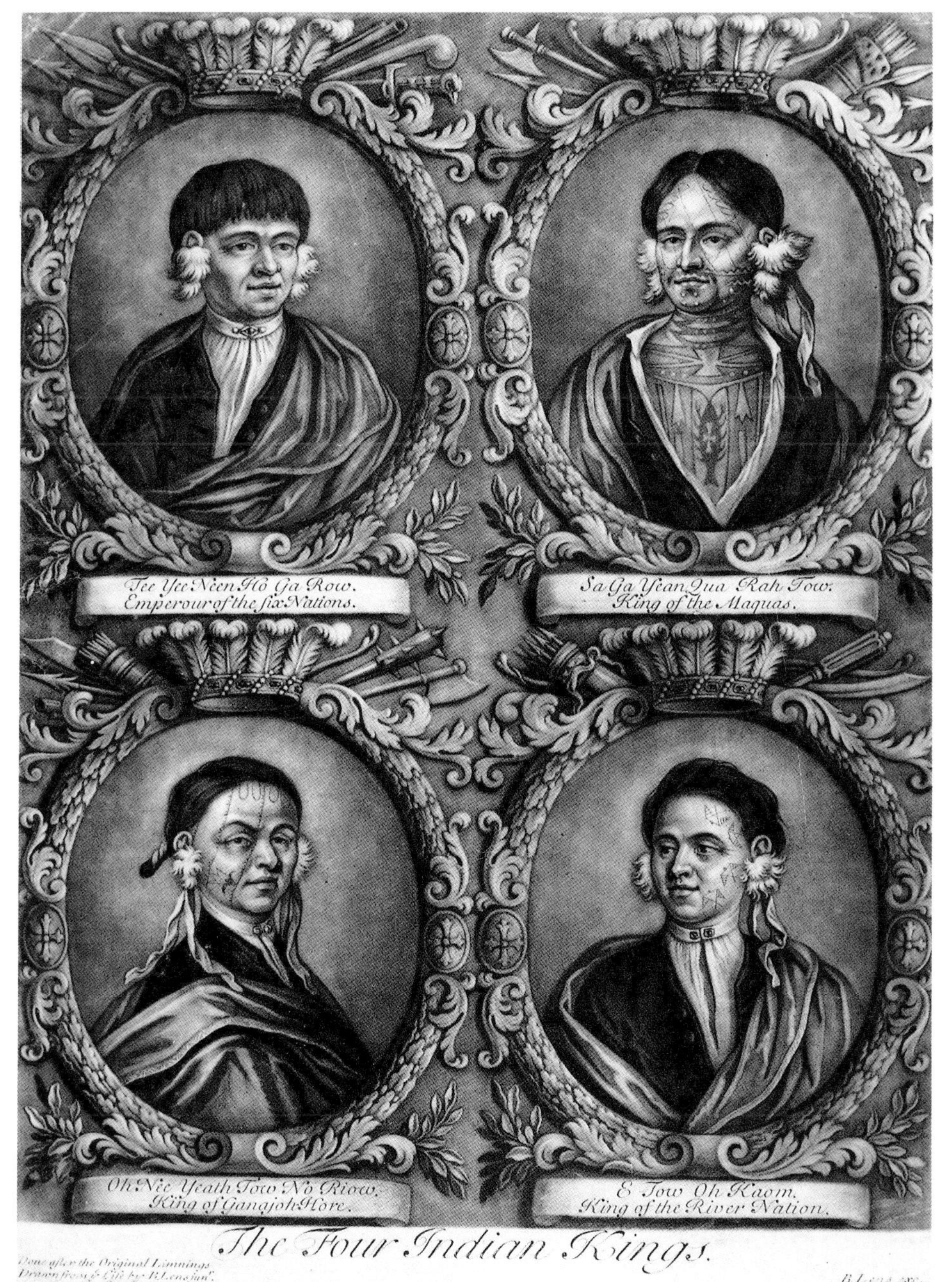
Tee Yee Neen Ho Ga Row.
Emperour of the six Nations.
Sa Ga Yean Qua Rah Tow.
King of the Maquas.
Oh Nee Yeath Tow No Riow.
King of Ganajoh Hore.
E Tow Oh Koam.
King of the River Nation.
The Four Indian Kings.
Done after the Original Limnings
Drawn from ye Life by B.Lens jun.
B.Lens exc.

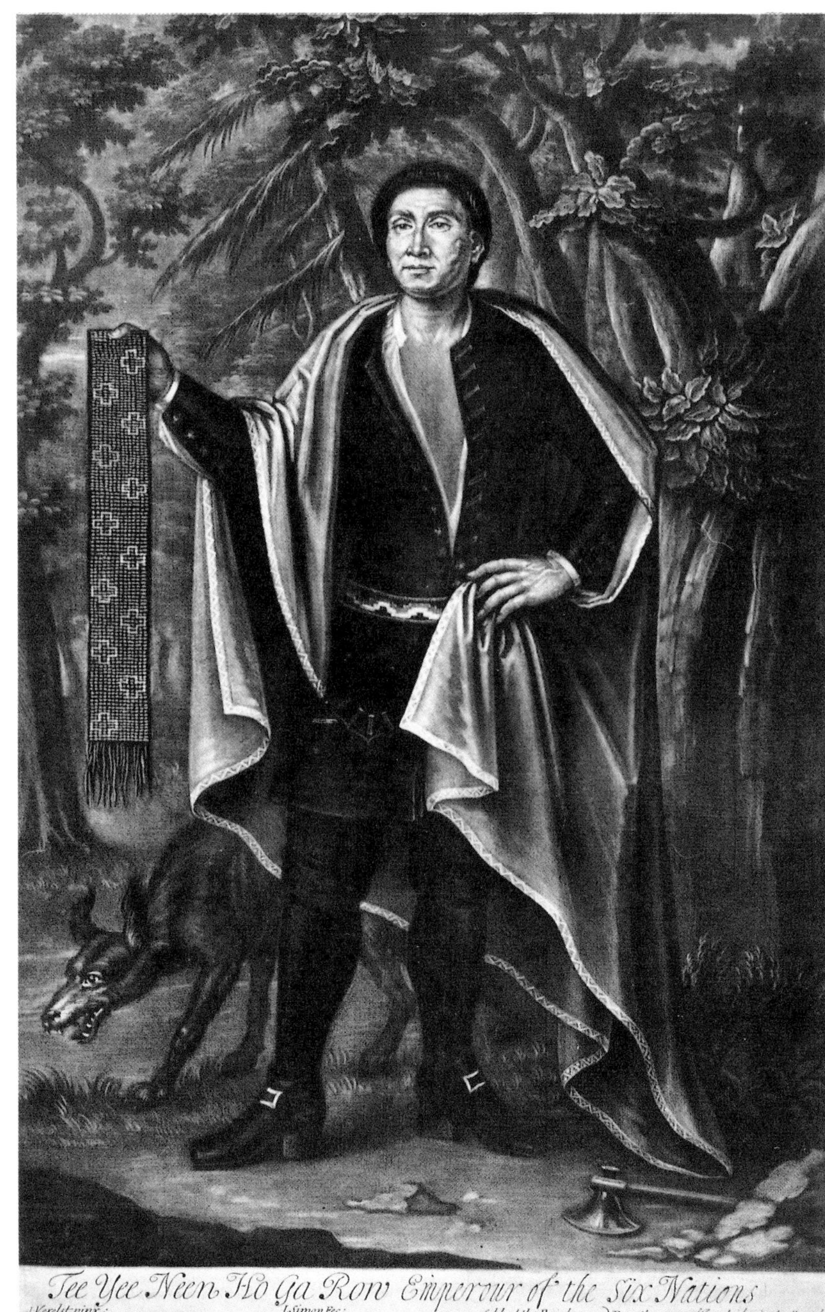
Tee Yee Neen Ho Ga Row Emperour of the Six Nations
I Verelst pinx:
I Simon Fec:
Sold at the Rainbow and Dove the corner of Ivey bridge in the Strand

17.

John Verelst (1648-1734, ac. in London 1691-1719), artist
John Simon (1675-ca. 1755), engraver

Tee Yee Neen Ho Ga Row Emperour of the Six Nations

London, first state, 1710
Mezzotint
Laid paper

Overall size: 42.3 x 26.7 cm
Platemark: 41.6 x 26.7 cm
Image: 39.8 x 25.8 cm

56.82.1
Funds gift of Charles K. Davis

Tee Yee Neen Ho Ga Row was given the title Emperor of the Six Nations by the English. Verelst painted him in the classical pose of authority, wearing his black court suit swathed in a brightly edged cloak, and displaying the wampum belt he had brought as his gift to another monarch, Queen Anne. A peculiar juxtaposition is evident as this regal figure in European dress and classical demeanor stands against a wilderness, with his clan's totem, a snarling wolf, at his heel.

References: Swan, "Prints of the American Indians," 245-59; Garratt, "The Four Indian Kings," in *History Today,* 93-101; John A. Garratt and Bruce Robertson, *The Four Indian Kings* (Ottawa: Public Archives of Canada, 1985); Hugh Honour, *The European Vision of America* (Cleveland: Cleveland Museum of Art, 1975), 198-99, cat. no. 170; Freda F. Waldon, "Queen Anne and 'The Four Kings of Canada,'" *Canadian Historical Review* 16, no. 3 (September 1935), 274.

J. C. Smith, Simon 84

18.

John Verelst (1648-1734, ac. in London 1691-1719), artist
John Simon (1675-ca. 1755), engraver

Sa Ga Yeath Qua Pieth Tow, King of the Maquas

London, first state, 1710
Mezzotint
Laid paper, watermark of Strasburg lily

Overall size: 41.5 x 26.0 cm
Platemark: 41.1 x 25.4 cm
Image: 39.3 x 25.4 cm

70.5

John Verelst painted individual full-length portraits of the Iroquois leaders for Queen Anne's palace at Kensington. Before the end of 1710, the *Tatler* carried four notices to Londoners that mezzotint prints of each were ready for subscribers.

Simon was a leading engraver in mezzotint. His translation of Verelst's portrait of Sa Ga Yeath Qua Pieth Tow (who was also a member of the wolf clan), like those of Etow Oh Koam and Ho Nee Yeath Taw No Row, reproduce a wide variety of textures, from the sheer blouse to the great cloak that is recorded as having been made of red edged in gilt.

References: Tatler, no. 165 (May 11-13, 1710); *Tatler*, no. 171 (November 14, 1710): 253, 256, 257; Richmond P. Bond, *Queen Anne's American Kings* (reprint, Oxford: Clarendon Press, 1952); Shadwell, *American Printmaking*, 18-19, cat. nos. 8-9; Garratt and Robertson, *The Four Indian Kings*.

J. C. Smith, Simon 84

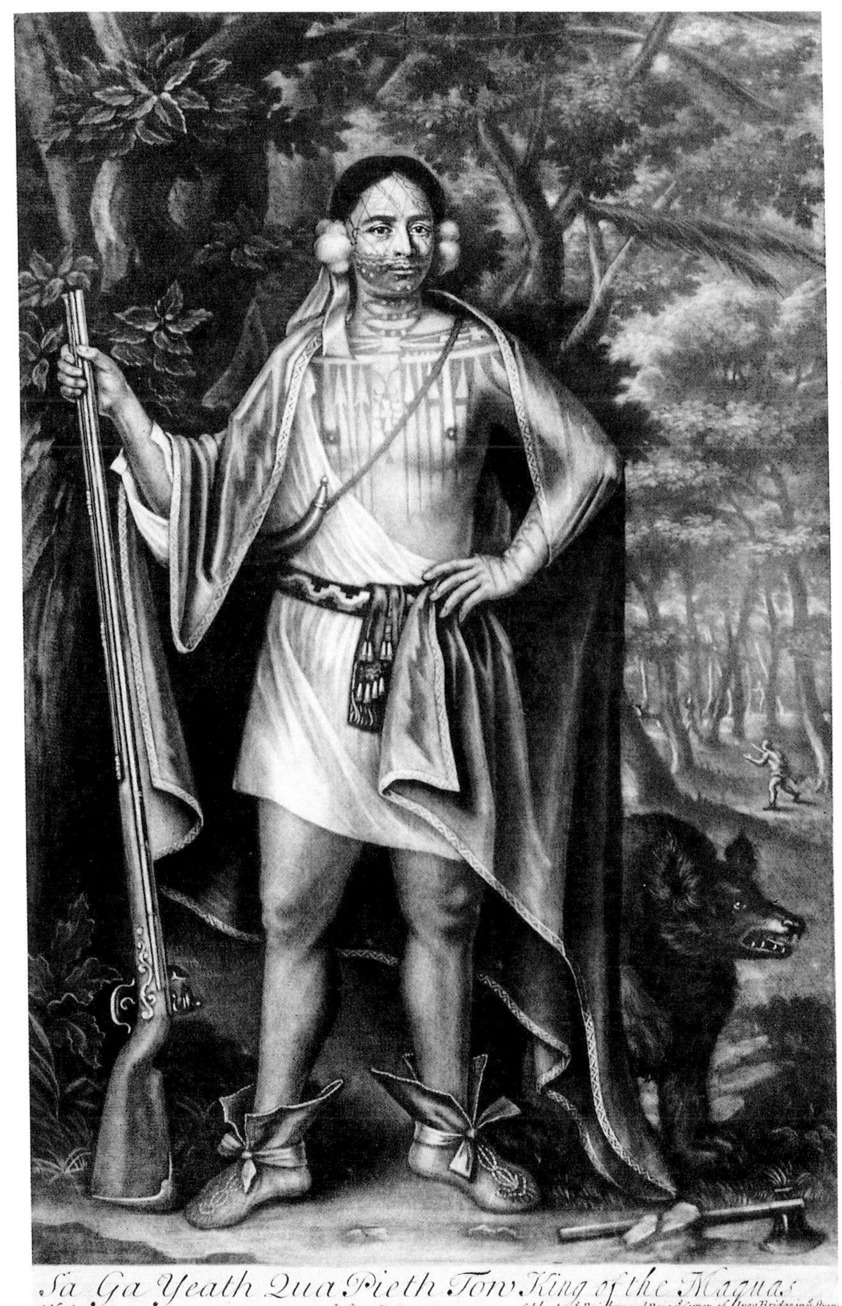
Sa Ga Yeath Qua Pieth Tow King of the Maguas
I. Verelst pinx.
I. Simon Fecit

19.

John Verelst (1648-1734, ac. in London 1691-1719), artist
John Simon (1675-ca. 1755), engraver

Etow Oh Koam King of the River Nation I. Verelst pinx: Simon Fecit Sold at ye Rain Bow & Dove ye Corner of Ivey Bridge in the Strand

London, first state, 1710
Mezzotint
Laid paper, watermark of fleur-de-lis (partial)

Overall size: 42.6 x 26.5 cm
Platemark: 41.5 x 25.8 cm
Image: 39.8 x 25.8 cm

56.82.2
Funds gift of Charles K. Davis

Etow Oh Koam of the Mohawk Nation stands beside a turtle, a symbol of his clan.

The Four Indian Kings were back in Boston on July 15, 1710. As a goodwill gesture, the following year Col. Sir Francis Nicholson, former governor of Virginia, brought sets of unframed prints to each of the nations and a framed set for the Onondaga Castle (west of present-day Albany), where the council of the Iroquois confederacy met. Other sets, both framed and unframed, were delivered to governments in Massachusetts, New Hampshire, Rhode Island, Connecticut, New York, New Jersey, and Pennsylvania.

J. C. Smith, Simon 84

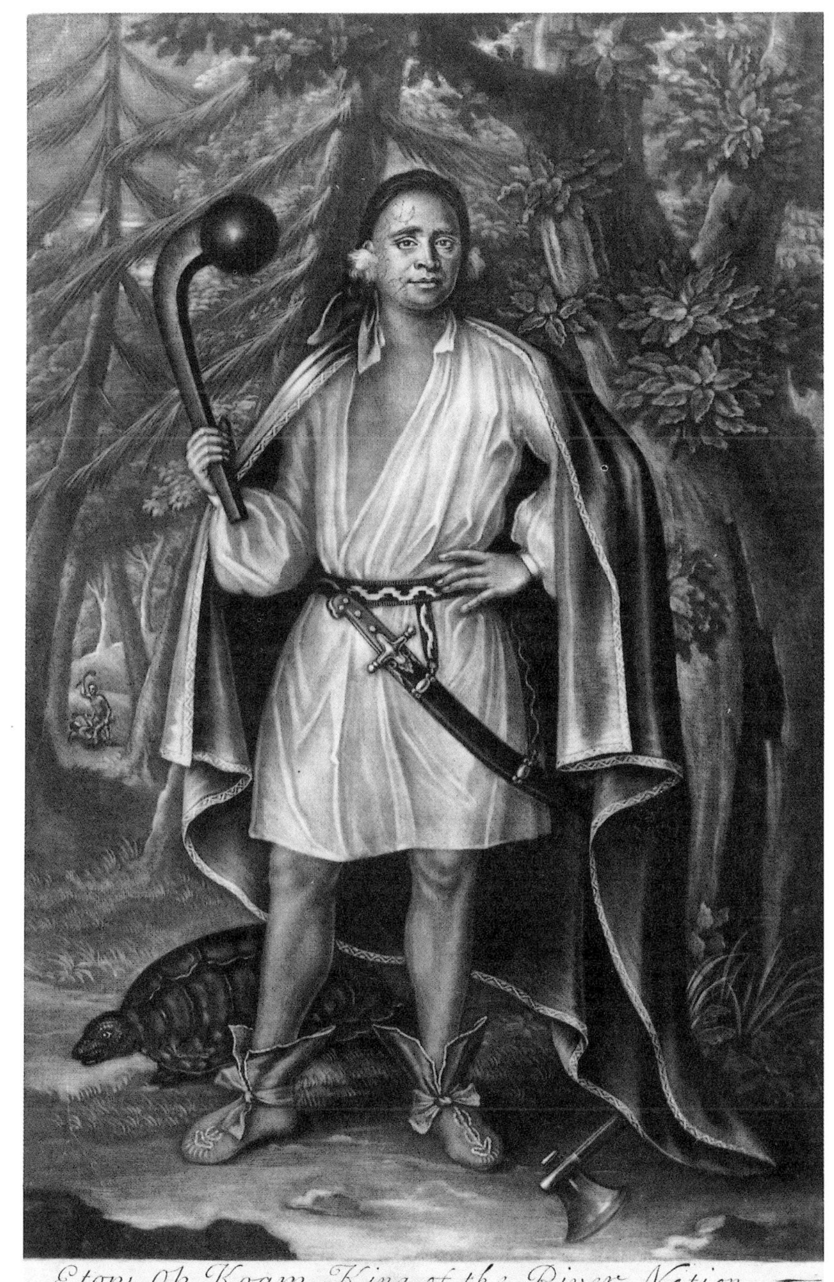
Etow Oh Koam King of the River Nation
I Verelst pinx:
Simon Fecit
Sold at ye Rain Bow & Dove ye Corner of Ivey Bridge in the Strand

20.

John Verelst (1648-1734, ac. in London 1691-1719), artist
John Simon (1675-ca. 1755), engraver

Ho Nee Yeath Taw No Row, King of the Generethgarieb
I. Verelst pinx. I. Simon fecit
Sold at ye Rainbow and Dove ye Corner of Ivey Bridge in ye S[trand]

London, first state, 1710
Mezzotint
Laid paper, watermark of Strasburg lily

Overall size: 41.5 x 26.0 cm
Platemark: 41.2 x 25.6 cm
Image: 39.5 x 25.5 cm

70.4

John Verelst's four paintings of the Indian leaders were acquired a number of years ago by the Archives of Canada and more recently have been on view in the National Gallery of Canada. Simon's copperplates of the Iroquois sachems are known in this state as well as in a second state, which bears the publication line "Printed & Sold by John King at ye Globe in ye Poultry London," and a third, which bears the line "Printed for Jno. Bowles & Son" (partners 1754-ca. 1764). These additions are testimony to the long-term popularity of the images and the collective respect for the Six Nations' friendly support of the British in North America.

J. C. Smith, Simon 84

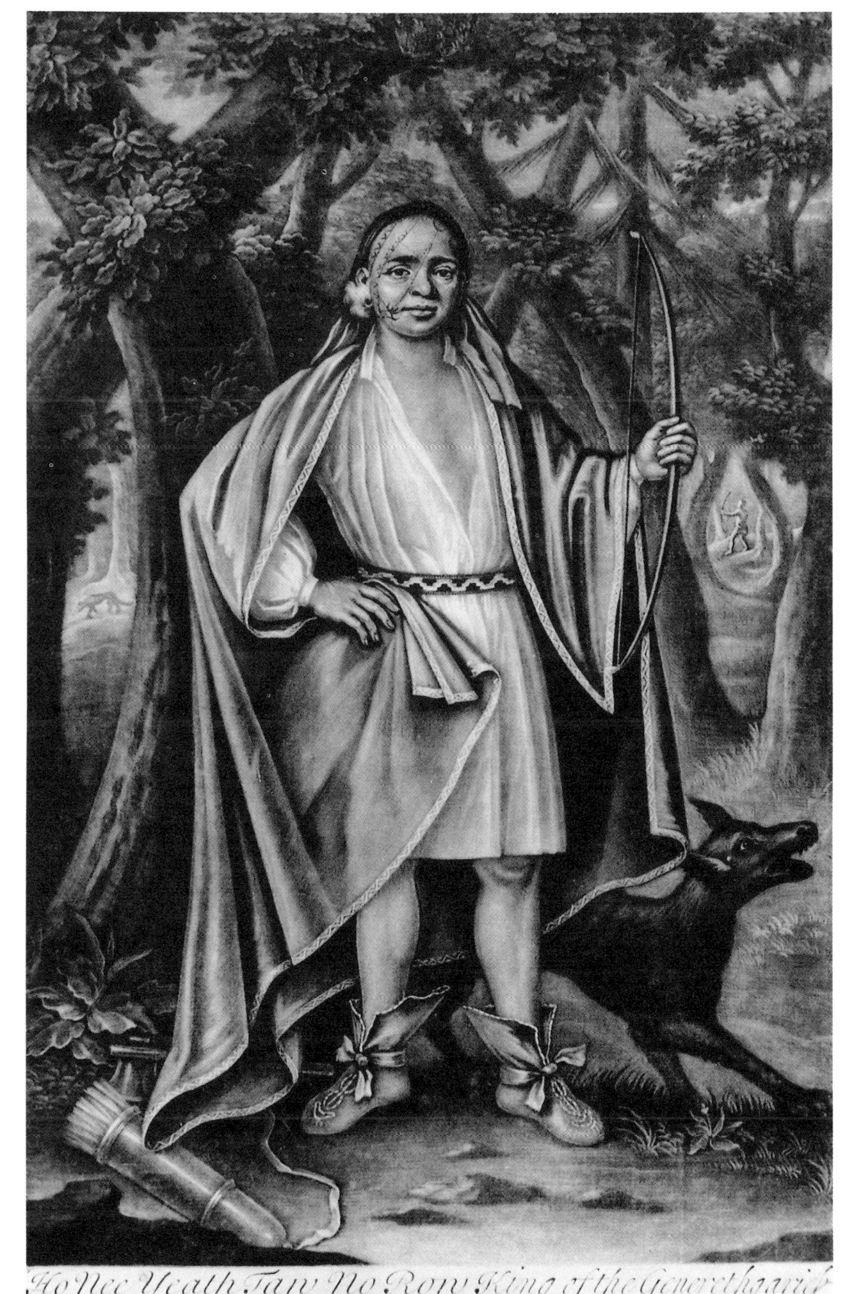
Ho Nee Yeath Taw No Row King of the Generethgarich
I. Verelst pinx
I. Simon fecit

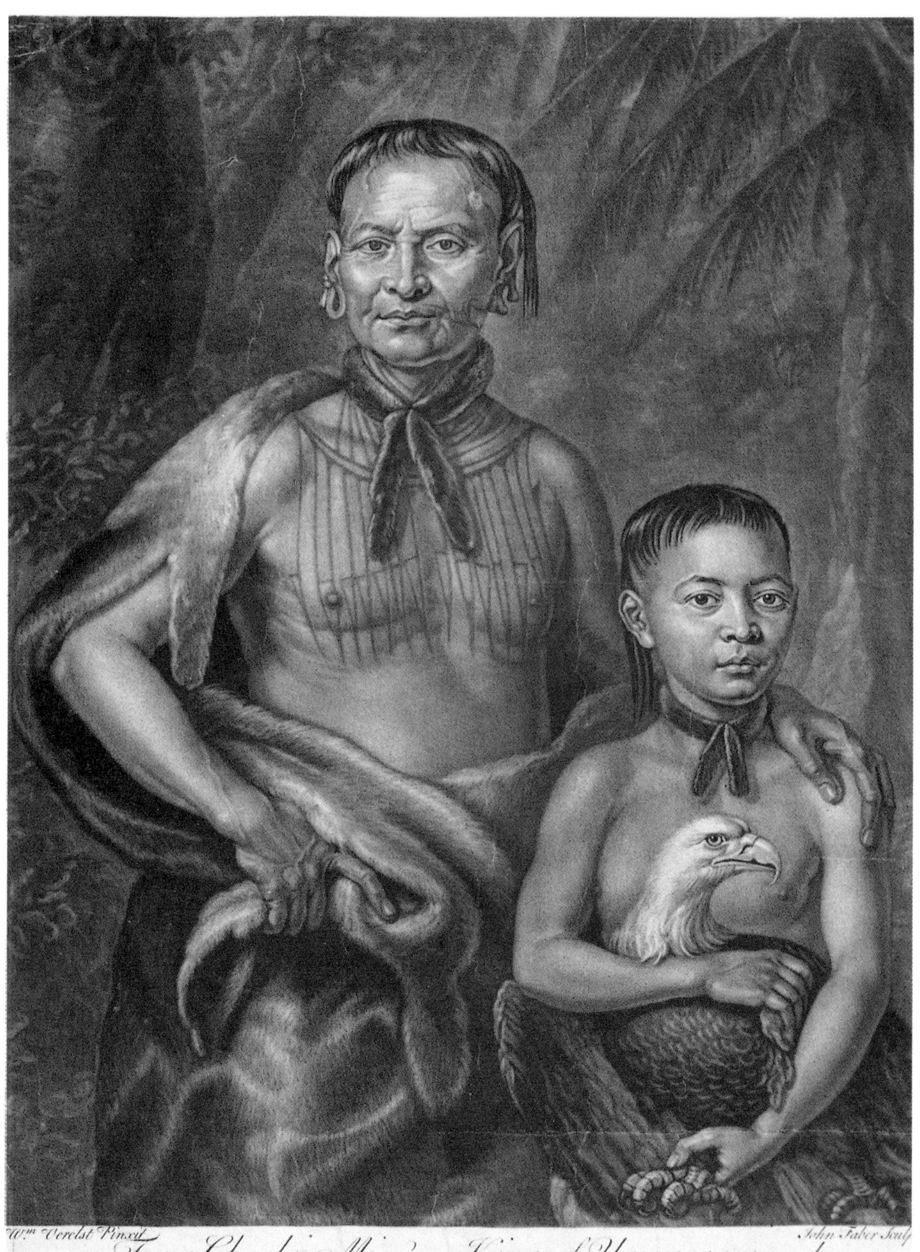
W.m Verelst Pinxit
John Faber Sculp
Tomo Chachi Mico or King of Yamacraw, and
Tooanahowi his Nephew, Son to the Mico of the Etchitas.

21.

William Verelst (ac. in London 1733-d. ca. 1756), artist
John Faber, Jr. (1695-1756), engraver

Tomo Chachi Mico or King of Yamacraw, and Tooanahowi his Nephew, Son to the Mico to the Etchitas.

London, probably 1734
Mezzotint
Laid paper

Overall size: 35.0 x 24.7 cm
Image: 32.3 x 24.7 cm

66.291

Twenty-four years after the London visit of the four representatives of the Iroquois people, James Oglethorpe and Peter Gordon took Tomochichi [or Tomochachi], his wife Senauki, and his nephew Tooanahowi to be presented to the Trustees of Georgia. They sailed from Savannah on May 7, 1734, on board a man-of-war, the *Aldborough*, and arrived in London on June 20, 1734. Their meeting with the Trustees was recreated on canvas (now in the Winterthur Museum collection) by William Verelst.

Sometime before Tomochichi embarked on the return voyage to Georgia in October of 1734, Verelst prepared a half-length portrait of the chief and his nephew, which John Faber, Jr., engraved in mezzotint. Again, the advantage of this technique in the reproduction of textures is evident in the softness of the feathers of the eagle that Tooanahowi holds. And most surely Londoners noticed the sumptuous furs worn by Tomochichi, a commodity that trappers were trading at the port of Savannah for shipment to markets abroad.

Reference: Temple and Coleman, *Georgia Journeys*, 64.

J. C. Smith, Faber, Junr., 349

22.

Hans Huyssing (Huysing, Hysing) (ac. 1700-1735), artist
Peter Pelham (ca. 1697-1751), engraver

Jacobus Gibbs, Architectus

London, 1720-26
Mezzotint with minimal burin work
Laid paper

Overall size: 35.6 x 25.6 cm
Image: 31.7 x 25.2 cm

77.52

Today, viewers are more likely to recognize Peter Pelham for his mezzotint portraits of New England ministers. Before leaving England for New England in 1727, however, Pelham had to his credit over twenty engraved portraits of the British nobility and upper classes. The earliest of these date from 1720. In London, Pelham had the best of mezzotint engravers as a constant source of competition and inspiration. He learned his craft in the shop of John Simon, and he had as models some of the best of English portraiture.

Hans Huyssing had come from Sweden to England to become an assistant in the studio of the painter Michael Dahl. Huyssing quickly adopted the style of his master and at Dahl's death took over his studio. He enjoyed the support of Dahl's patrons, including George II and the royal family.

James Gibbs (1682-1754) studied architecture in Rome under Carlo Steffano Fontana (1634-1714), a master of the late Baroque and architect of several important chapels from 1661 to 1705. Gibbs' publication of 1728, *A Book of Architecture*, was intended to reduce the mysteries of architecture to terms workmen could understand; it became a standard reference. His popularity made him a logical subject for an engraved portrait, one for which the publisher could expect sales throughout Britain and the American colonies.

Gibbs was well established as an architect when Pelham scraped this mezzotint after Huyssing's painting. St. Mary-le-Strand, his first important commission, was one of fifty churches built in tribute to Queen Anne beginning in 1711. Appropriately, Gibbs is posed holding a partially unrolled plan of the church's ground floor as he leans with classical nonchalance on the base of a column.

Reference: Rudolph Wittkower, *Art and Architecture in Italy 1650-1750* (reprint, Baltimore: Penguin Books, 1958), 244-46.

J. C. Smith, Pelham 21

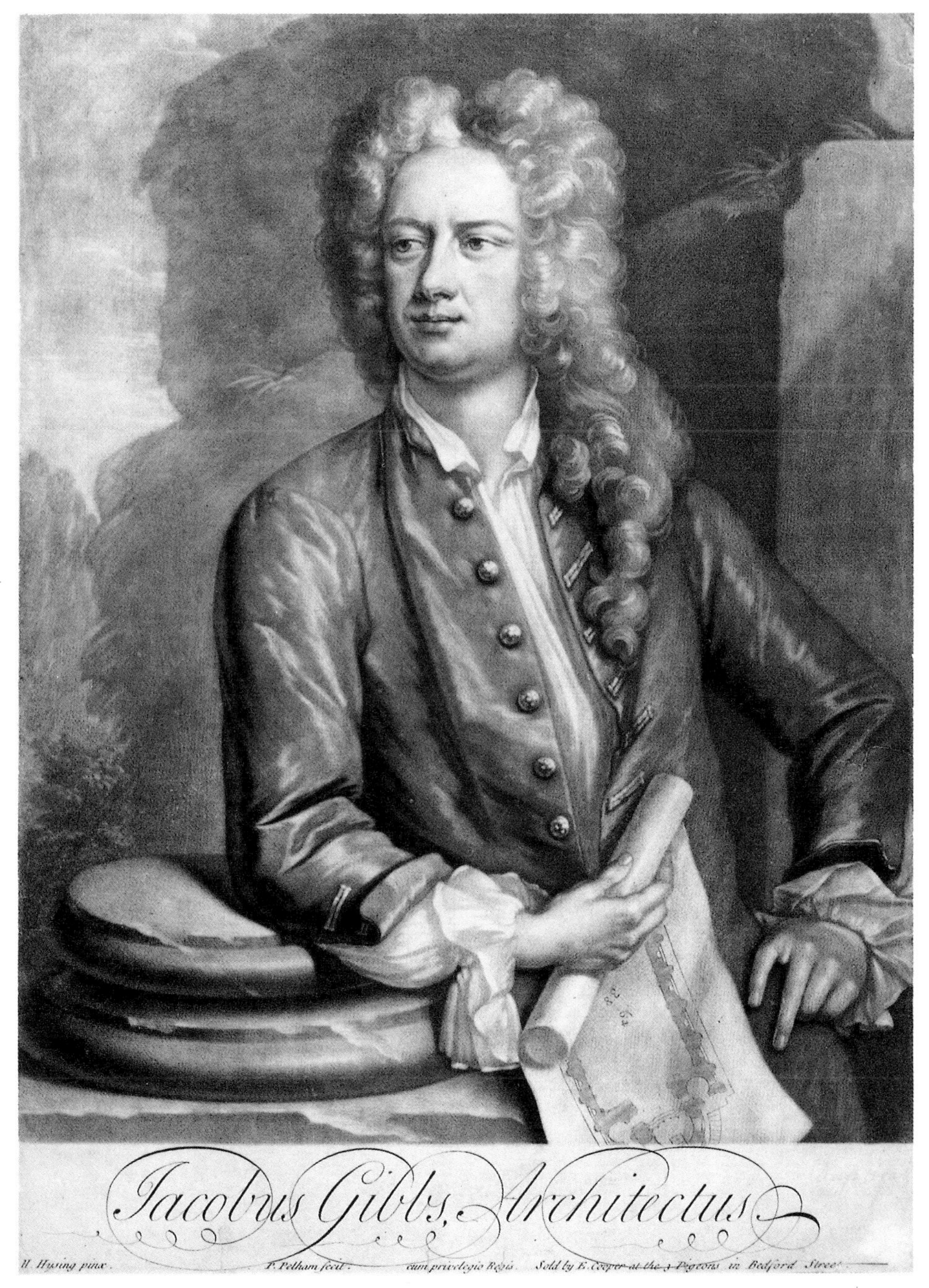
Jacobus Gibbs, Architectus
H. Hysing pinx.
P. Pelham fecit.
cum privelegio Regis.
Sold by E. Cooper at the 3 Pigeons in Bedford Street

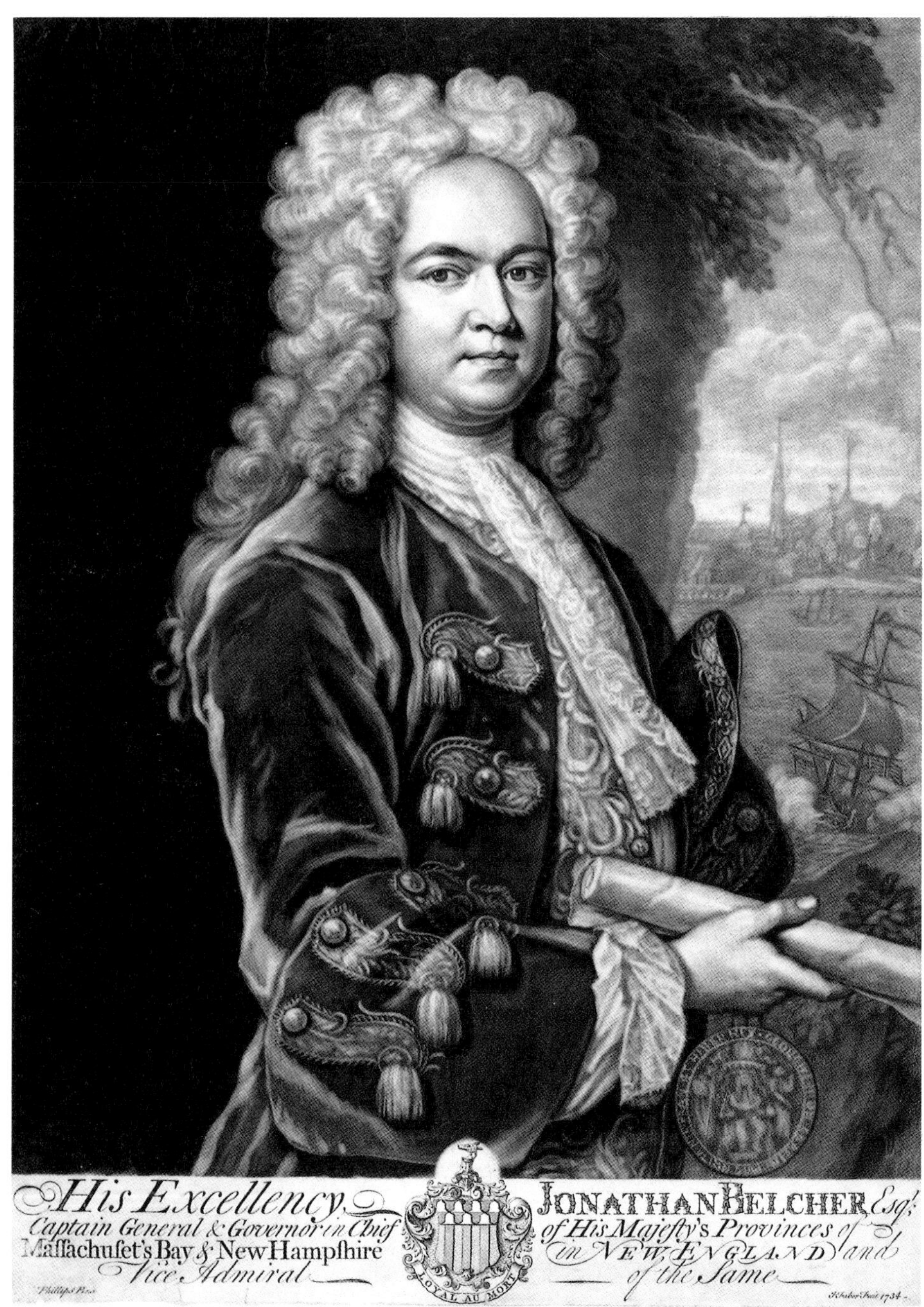
His Excellency JONATHAN BELCHER Esq:
Captain General & Governor in Chief of His Majesty's Provinces of
Massachuset's Bay & New Hampshire in NEW ENGLAND and
Vice Admiral of the Same
LOYAL AU MORT
J. Faber Fecit 1734

23.

Richard Phillips (1681-1741), artist
John Faber, Jr. (1695-1756), engraver

His Excellency, JONATHAN BELCHER Esqr; Captain General & Governor in Chief of His Majesty's Provinces of Massachusetts Bay & New Hampshire in NEW ENGLAND and Vice Admiral of the Same.

London, 1734
Mezzotint
Laid paper, watermark of lily above a shield with four bars

Overall size: 35.8 x 26.2 cm
Platemark: 34.9 x 26.2 cm
Image: 31.5 x 24.8 cm

52.20

Jonathan Belcher (1682-1757) became governor of Massachusetts in 1730. Three years later, William Price, following a practice to which printmakers who hoped to secure famous names as underwriters to their projects had long resorted, dedicated to Belcher his revised edition of an engraved plan of the *Great Town of Boston* by John Bonner (1646-1725/6). Presumably, such a consideration would have been viewed by a recipient as a true compliment, and it usually brought not only the official patron's endorsement but also his or her purchase of copies of the publication for distribution to family and close friends.

In the early eighteenth century, however, a certain decorum was attached to the matter of having one's portrait scraped in mezzotint. To have a publisher or an engraver undertake the project independently was flattering testimony to an individual's position, popularity, influence, or handsomeness of features.

If, on the other hand, one was ambitious and impatient to attract the public's attention for political or business reasons, the more impetuous person might seek an engraver and commission a mezzotint portrait. In the most polite circles, this was *not* the first choice.

In 1734, and to Belcher's dismay, his son ordered John Faber to prepare a mezzotint from a portrait of the Massachusetts governor that had probably been painted on a trip to London in 1729-30. Behind Belcher can be seen a partial view of the town of Boston, which the artist borrowed from William Burgis' *South East View*, engraved in London in 1723-25.

Reference: Richard H. Saunders and Ellen G. Miles, *American Colonial Portraits: 1700-1776* (Washington City: Smithsonian Institution Press for The National Portrait Gallery, 1987), 151-52.

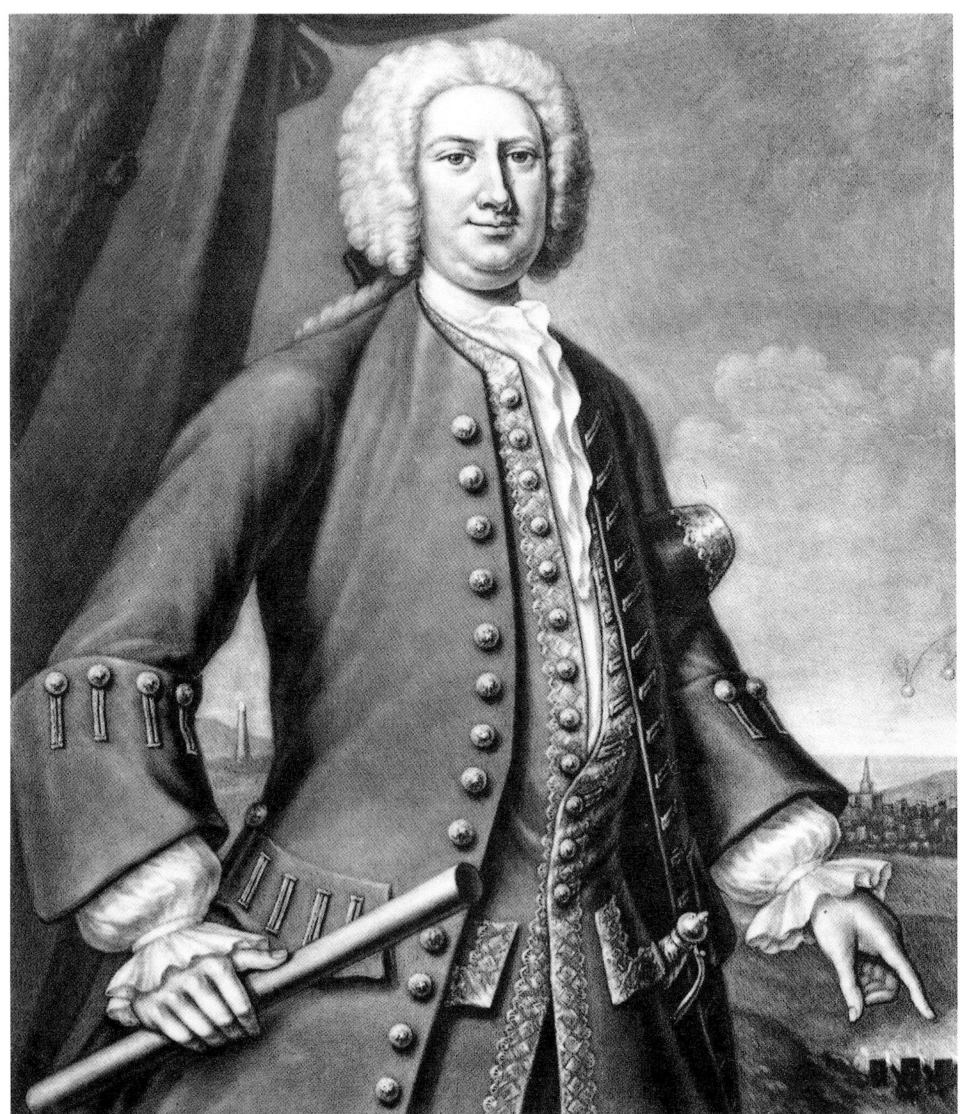
Sir William Pepperrell Bar.t Colonel of one of his Majesty's Regiments
of Foot, who was Lieutenant General and Commander in Chief of the American
Forces Employ'd in the Expedition against the Island of Cape Breton which was
happily Reduced to the Obedience of his Britanick Majesty June the 17. 1745
J: Smibert Pinx:
Sold by J. Buck in Queen street Boston
P. Pelham fecit et ex: 1747.

24.

Peter Pelham (ca. 1697-1751), engraver
John Smibert (1688-1751), artist
Sold by J. Buck in Queens Street

Sir William Pepperrell Bart.

Boston, 1747
Mezzotint
Laid paper, watermark of Strasburg lily and bend

Overall size: 44.6 x 30.1 cm
Platemark: 35.2 x 25.0 cm
Image: 29.9 x 24.8 cm

67.232

Mezzotint portraits were among the first prints to be advertised for sale in the American colonies. William Price offered "fine Metzotinto" pictures at his shop on King Street near the east end of the town hall in Boston as early as May 20, 1728. In December of 1749, James Buck was promoting "a choice Sortment of Maps, Prints, Metzotintos, &c. in Frames and Glass, or without," and by April of 1758, Stephen Whiting was presenting for sale "a great variety of very beautiful Metzotinto and other Pictures." Indeed, newspaper advertisements of recently imported mezzotint portraits appeared with noteworthy frequency under the names of booksellers, upholsterers, housepainters, and wallpaper hangers, in addition to those of print-sellers, until the last decade of the eighteenth century.

The honor of being the first to engrave portraits, indeed the first to execute any engraving in mezzotint in the colonies, belongs to Peter Pelham. Upon arriving in Boston at the age of thirty, Pelham set about looking for portrait subjects of such high regard that he was certain to find many admirers and buyers for his work. He began with a portrait of the venerable Réverend Cotton Mather (1663-1728), pastor of North or Second Church, executed in the last year of the cleric's life and published posthumously. This was followed by engraved portraits of fourteen other prominent men, including ten members of the clergy. Initially, Pelham worked from his own paintings, but with the arrival of John Smibert in Boston in 1729, Pelham found an artist upon whose portraits he could rely, thus freeing him to concentrate on the subtleties of engraving.

In the summer of 1745, William Pepperrell, a merchant from Kittery, Maine, joined with Governor William Shirley of Massachusetts to lead an expedition of forces successfully against the French at Louisbourg. Smibert was engaged by a group of citizens to paint Governor Shirley's portrait in December of that year; the artist executed a portrait of Pepperrell in 1746. In 1747, Pelham scraped both portraits in mezzotint. Pelham clearly intended that the mezzotints serve as a set. Each was completed in three-quarter length, but unlike many companion portraits, both subjects face to the right instead of in opposition. The portrait of Shirley was advertised for sale in July of 1747; the portrait of Pepperrell was dedicated to "his Britanick Majesty" on June 17, 1747. Three years later Benjamin Franklin wrote from Philadelphia to his brother James in Boston, "Pray send me the Heads of Shirley and Pepperrell with the price."

Reference: Andrew Oliver, "Peter Pelham (ca. 1697-1751): Sometime Printmaker of Boston," in *Boston Prints and Printmakers, 1670-1775*, ed. Walter Muir Whitehill and Sinclair H. Hitchings (Boston: Colonial Society of Massachusetts, 1973), 155-58, 171-72.

25.

Nathaniel Hurd (1730-1777), designer, engraver, and publisher

BRITONS-BEHOLD The Best of KINGS. Beloved by the Bravest of People. Justly admired by all, By his Enemies Dreaded— May he live long and happy. No Evil and Corrupt Ministers Dare to Approach his Sacred presence, Let none but such as Imitate his Virtues, have any Power, then shall Britannia be Blest for Ever. The man resolv'd & steady to his trust Inflexible to ill, & obstinately just. **GEORGIUS. III REX THE RIGHT HONOURABLE WILLIAM PITT. -Major General JAMES WOLFE. The British HERO.**

Boston, Massachusetts, 1762
Line engraving, watercolors
Laid paper

Overall size: 11.2 x 14.6 cm
Platemark: 9.9 x 13.1 cm
Image: 9.6 x 12.6 cm

58.2374

Portrait engravings, or "heads," came in a wide variety of sizes in the eighteenth century, from a frontispiece in an octavo edition to an impressive nineteen-by-twenty-three-inch (48.3 by 58.4 cm) copy of John Zoffany's painting (1769-70) of George III and Queen Charlotte with their royal offspring, engraved by Richard Earlom in 1770. Most, however, were published in the popular fourteen-by-ten-inch (35.5 by 25.4 cm) format, called "posture size."

Among the smallest portraits executed in the colonies were those of George III, William Pitt, and General James Wolfe. Engraved and published by Nathaniel Hurd, the three likenesses could be framed as presented within a border, or each of the faces could be cut out and placed inside the cover of a watch. Hurd advertised to that effect in the *Boston Evening-Post* for December 20, 1762.

It is interesting to observe in this example that Hurd cut the copperplate to conform to the design. The shallow arch above the portrait of George III may have been readily executed by a silversmith accustomed to sawing complex outlines, but it is a feature that contemporary London publishers would have been likely to dismiss on the basis of added cost.

As a silversmith, Hurd was capable of handling a burin to engrave cyphers, emblems, heraldic devices, and other intricate designs on both curved and flat surfaces. And like other colonial silversmiths, he cut dies, seals, and engraved copperplates for currency as authorized for official use. To further capitalize on his abilities with a burin, he prepared trade cards, book plates, and similar items for customers on a commission basis. As the colonial interest in framing prints developed, Hurd and others ventured to engrave subjects of local interest.

References: Martha Gandy Fales, "Heraldic and Emblematic Engravers of Colonial Boston," in *Boston Prints and Printmakers, 1670-1775*, ed. Walter Muir Whitehill and Sinclair H. Hitchings (Boston: Colonial Society of Massachusetts, 1973), 185-220; See *Sayer and Bennetts Catalogue of Prints for 1775*, 79-80, for listing of sixty-three designs for watch cases, including portraits of George III, Pitt, and Wolfe.

Fielding 739

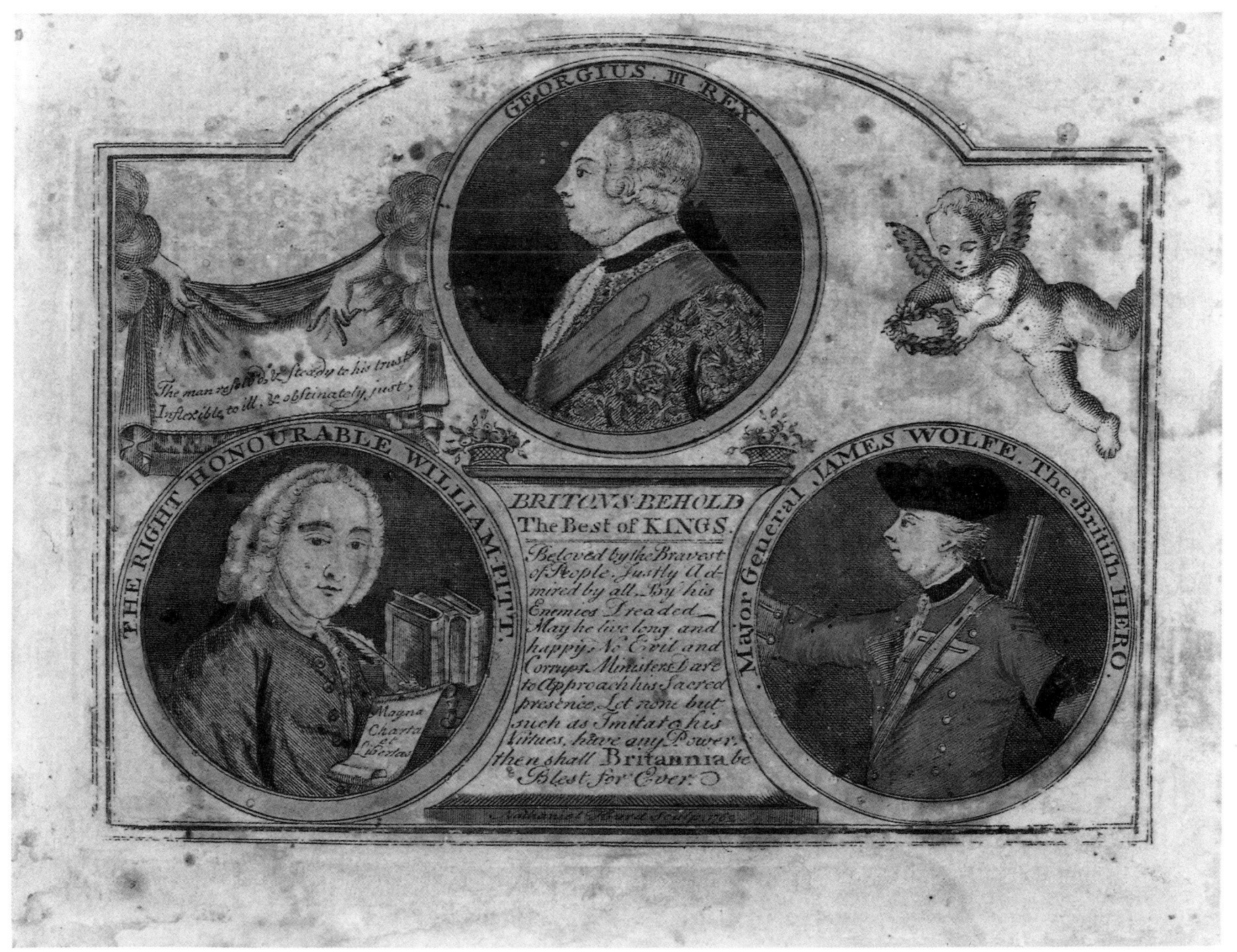
GEORGIUS III REX.
The man resolv'd, & steady to his trust,
Inflexible to ill, & obstinately just,
THE RIGHT HONOURABLE WILLIAM PITT.
Magna Charta et Libertas
BRITONS BEHOLD
The Best of KINGS.
Beloved by the Bravest of People, Justly Admired by all, By his Enemies Dreaded—
May he live long and happy; No Evil and Corrupt Ministers Dare to Approach his Sacred presence, Let none but such as Imitate his Virtues, have any Power.
then shall Britannia be Blest for Ever.
Major General JAMES WOLFE, The British HERO.

26.

Joshua Reynolds (1723-1792), artist
Richard Purcell (1736-1765/6), engraver after MacArdell's mezzotint
James MacArdell (1729-1765), delineator and engraver
Robert Sayer (b. 1725, ac. 1751-d. 1794), publisher

Caroline. Dutchess of Marlborough.
Lady Caroline Russell

London, 1762-66
(or after MacArdell's engraving of ca. 1760)
Mezzotint
Laid paper

Overall size: 43.0 x 29.2 cm
Platemark: 35.5 x 24.4 cm
Image: 31.6 x 24.3 cm

65.2954

In Philadelphia during the 1760s, Robert Kennedy was offering prints of "ladies of quality and celebrated Beauties" at his shop on Second Street, and he was prepared to frame them according to the latest London taste.

Lady Caroline Russell was the daughter of John Russell, fourth duke of Bedford, and not yet married when Joshua Reynolds painted her seated and holding a King Charles spaniel, a popular pet among eighteenth-century English nobility. James MacArdell copied Reynold's painting in mezzotint about 1760. In 1762, the Lady Caroline became the duchess of Marlborough, wife of the third duke. Between then and 1766, Richard Purcell, working for the print publisher and seller Robert Sayer, prepared the plate from which this impression was struck. Purcell may have worked directly from Reynold's painting, or even reworked an old MacArdell plate at the command of his employer. It is equally possible that Purcell made a copy directly from MacArdell's mezzotint. The two prints are very similar, although this image measures nearly a half centimeter larger in both dimensions than known impressions by MacArdell.

John Singleton Copley (1738-1815) wrote to his half-brother Henry Pelham (1749-1806) of his interest in MacArdell's work, and it is documented that he owned several MacArdell engravings, although this one is not mentioned specifically. For his design of a portrait painted about 1767 and traditionally identified as Mrs. Jerathmael Bowers, Copley could have borrowed from either MacArdell or Purcell's mezzotint of the duchess of Marlborough, down to the smallest details of costume and pet spaniel. That may never be known for certain. Perhaps Copley chose the prototype for his sitter, or if she were sufficiently familiar with the reigning English beauties, she may have selected her own model.

References: Jules David Prown, *John Singleton Copley in America, 1738-1774* (Cambridge, Mass.: Harvard University Press for the National Gallery of Art, Washington, D.C., 1960), 210, no. 219; Waldron Phoenix Belknap, Jr., *American Colonial Painting: Materials for A History* (Cambridge, Mass.: Belknap Press of Harvard University Press, 1959), 274; "William Price," *Boston Gazette*, May 20/27, 1728, "James Buck," *Boston Evening-Post*, December 11, 1749, and "Stephen Whiting," *Boston News-Letter*, April 7, 1758, as quoted in Dow, *Arts & Crafts in New England*, 18, 21, 23; "Robert & Thomas Kennedy," *Pennsylvania Chronicle*, December 12, 1768, as quoted in Prime, *Arts and Crafts in Philadelphia, 1721-1785,* 33; Saunders and Miles, *American Colonial Portraits*, 237, no. 75 and 247, no. 79.

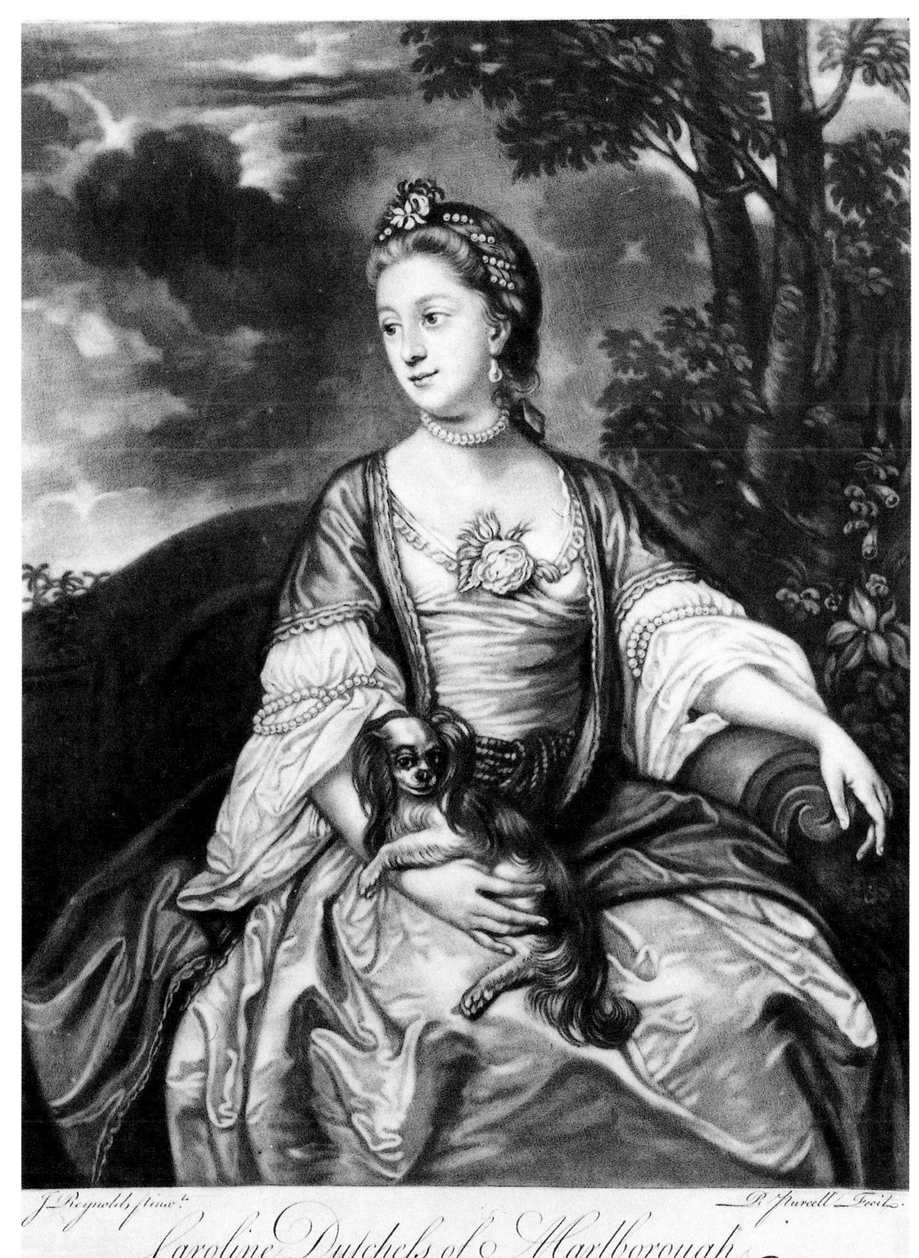
J. Reynolds pinxt.
R. Purcell Fecit.
Caroline, Dutchess of Marlborough.
Printed for Rob. Sayer near Serjeants Inn Fleet Street.

27.

Charles Willson Peale (1741-1827), artist, engraver, and publisher

Worthy of Liberty, Mr. Pitt scorns to invade the Liberties of other People.

London, 1768
Mezzotint with minimal burin work
Laid paper, watermark of the mill of T. Dupuy, Auvergne, 1742

Overall size: 59.0 x 38.0 cm
Image: 55.2 x 37.6 cm

59.1488
Ex coll. Whitelaw Reid

From the beginning of the eighteenth century, collaboration between the artist and the engraver grew to be profitable for both. Many English painters found their fame spread far more quickly through the sale of prints after their paintings than could otherwise have been realized. Charles Willson Peale, who determined at a somewhat mature age that he was destined to become a painter, was in London in the spring of 1767, at the height of this synergistic relationship between artist and engraver. He was quick to grasp that a finely scraped mezzotint plate was the best kind of advertising for an artist, as well as an excellent way of making a respectable profit. Six years earlier John Boydell began an enterprise that brought him the handsome sum of £2,000 from the sale of prints of a landscape engraved by William Woollett after Richard Wilson's *The Destruction of the Children of Niobe*. By the time Peale arrived in England, Woollett and other leading engravers were adroitly picking and choosing whose and which work they would reproduce. Artists who might have otherwise declared that engraving was not an art form of the highest order soon found themselves in the position of attempting to gain the engraver's favor.

Peale, ever attuned to a financially rewarding endeavor, set about learning the art of scraping a mezzotint, a skill he surely anticipated putting to good use when he returned to Philadelphia. It is not clear who prepared the ground for Peale's engraving of William Pitt in 1768-69. The ground is densely and evenly executed and may have been the work of a London technician, not the first attempt of an American painter. The actual scraping Peale claimed for himself in a broadside that announced "A DESCRIPTION OF THE PICTURE AND MEZZOTINTO OF MR. PITT DONE BY CHARLES WILLSON PEALE, OF MARYLAND."

Peale used as the model for this mezzotint his own portrait of William Pitt, commissioned by Edmund Jennings for a group of Westmoreland County (Virginia) planters. The design was a complex, iconographic essay, which Peale found necessary to explain in some detail to the public. According to the broadside, Pitt, in the dress of a Roman senator, holds in his left hand a copy of the Magna Charta—the British Bill of Rights—as he gestures to a figure of Liberty, which tramples a petition from the Colonial Congress of 1765. Ironies and contrasts repeated in other visual counterpoints have been explored in detail in several significant publications.

Early impressions of the engraving were struck in London. Peale vigorously promoted his work after his return to America in 1769. Once home he chose to send one of his prints of Pitt and the explanatory broadside to Copley. Praise from so respected a figure in American painting could only help Peale's sale of the engravings. Copley was complimentary, but for Peale this foray into combining patriotism with intellectual and artistic outreach never fulfilled his expectations.

He complained that he barely made enough to cover the cost of materials, an assertion that his biographer and descendant, Charles Coleman Sellers, disputed.

At first glance the watermark would indicate that the paper on which this impression was struck was made twenty-four years before the print. In fact, a British tariff passed in 1741 decreed that beginning in January of the following year, all papers were to be marked 1742. French papermakers heeded the letter of the law and continued to use the same year as their watermarks until the end of the century.

References: Sellers, *Portraits and Miniatures by Charles Willson Peale,* 172-73, nos. 693-95; Frank H. Sommers III, "Thomas Hollis and the Arts of Dissent," in *Prints in and of America to 1850*, ed. John D. Morse (Charlottesville: University Press of Virginia for the Henry Francis du Pont Winterthur Museum, 1970), 142-55; Charles Henry Hart, "Charles Willson Peale's Allegory of William Pitt, Earl of Chatham, and the Pitt Statues in Cork, Ireland and Charleston, South Carolina," in *Proceedings of the Massachusetts Historical Society* 48 (1915): 291-303. I am indebted to John Krill for bringing the particulars of the 1742 watermarks to my attention and for checking all the Auvergne watermarks in this collection.

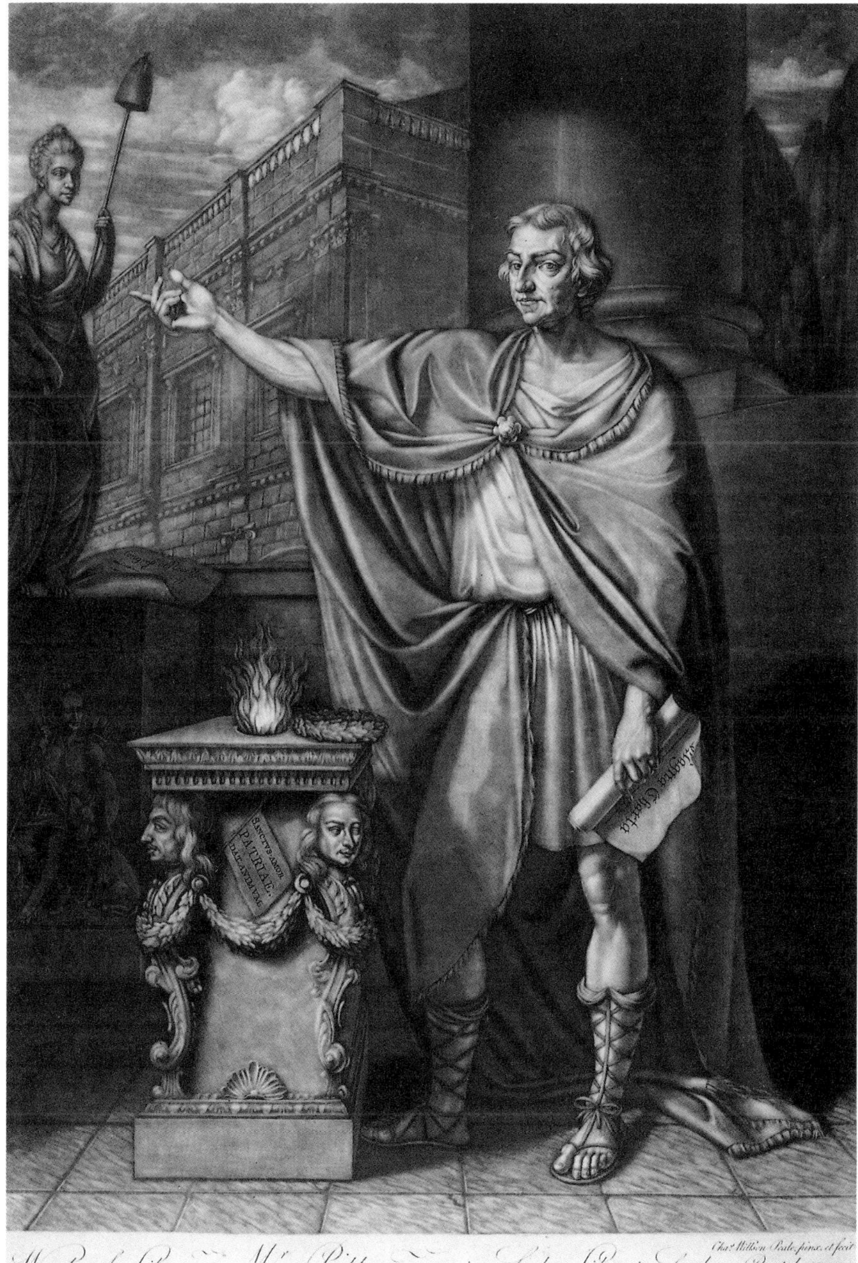

28.

Attributed to William Hoare (1706-1792), artist
Richard Houston (1722-1775), engraver
John Bowles & Son (firm ac. 1754-ca. 1764), publishers

The Right Honourable William Pitt, Esqr. One of His Majesty's Principal Secretary's of State.
And One of His Majesty's most Honble. Privy Council. Sold by Jno Bowles & Son at the Black Horse in Cornhill.

London, variant of second state, 1770-78
Mezzotint
Laid paper

Overall size: 39.05 x 27.94 cm
Image: 32.6 x 25.0 cm

65.2999

Engraved portraits of William Pitt the Elder, Lord Chatham (1708-1778), in more conventional attire appeared regularly in printsellers' catalogues and colonial advertisements during the second half of the eighteenth century. This engraving by Houston could be purchased in black and white, colored with watercolors, or transferred to glass and painted with oils or watercolors from the reverse. In at least one eighteenth-century print of the interior of a tavern, Houston's engraving of Pitt, or a pirated version thereof, is shown in an appropriate molded frame hung above the entrance door (see cat. no. 64, *Settling the Affairs of the Nation*).

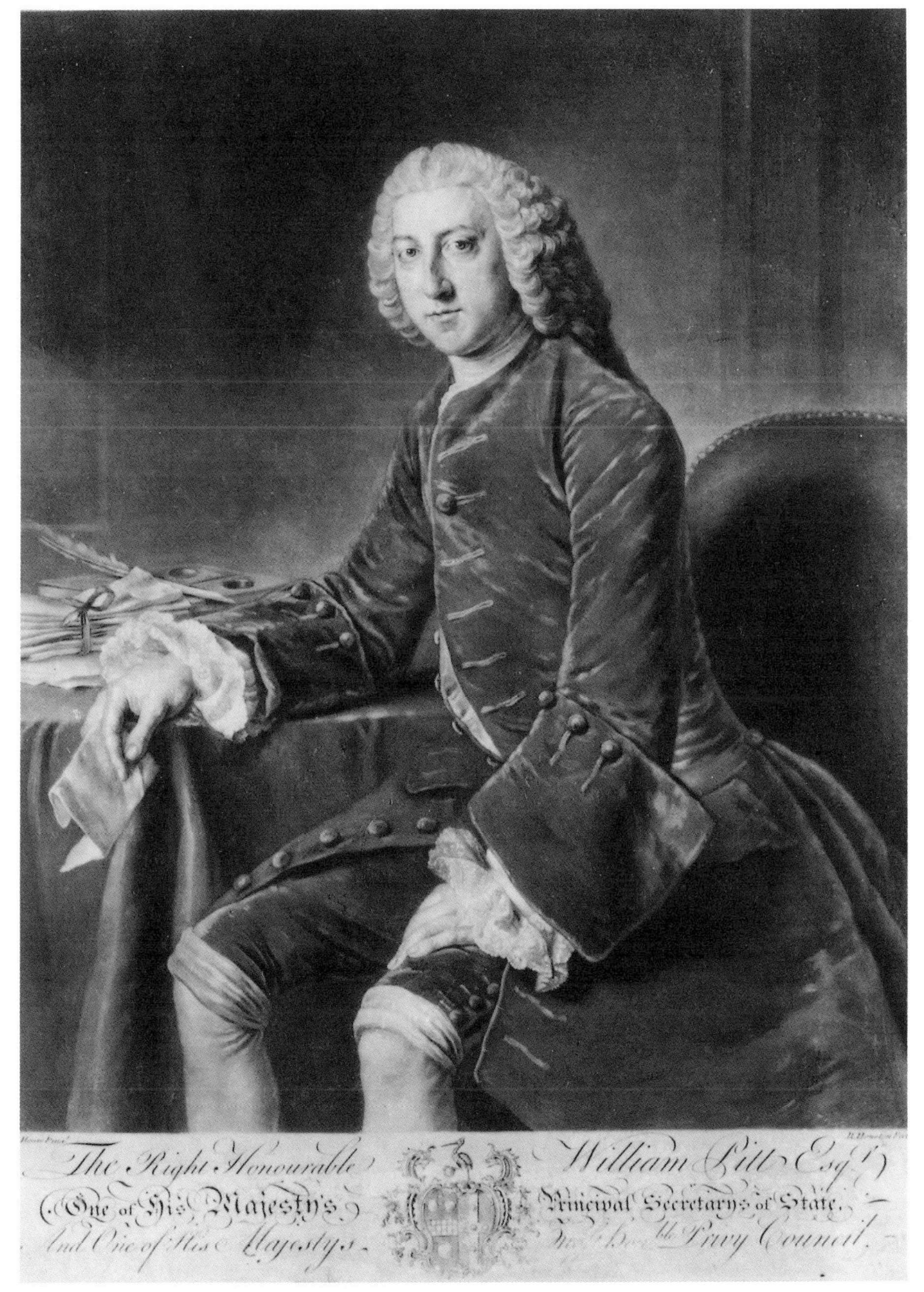
The Right Honourable William Pitt Esq.r
One of His Majesty's Principal Secretarys of State,
And One of His Majestys Privy Council.

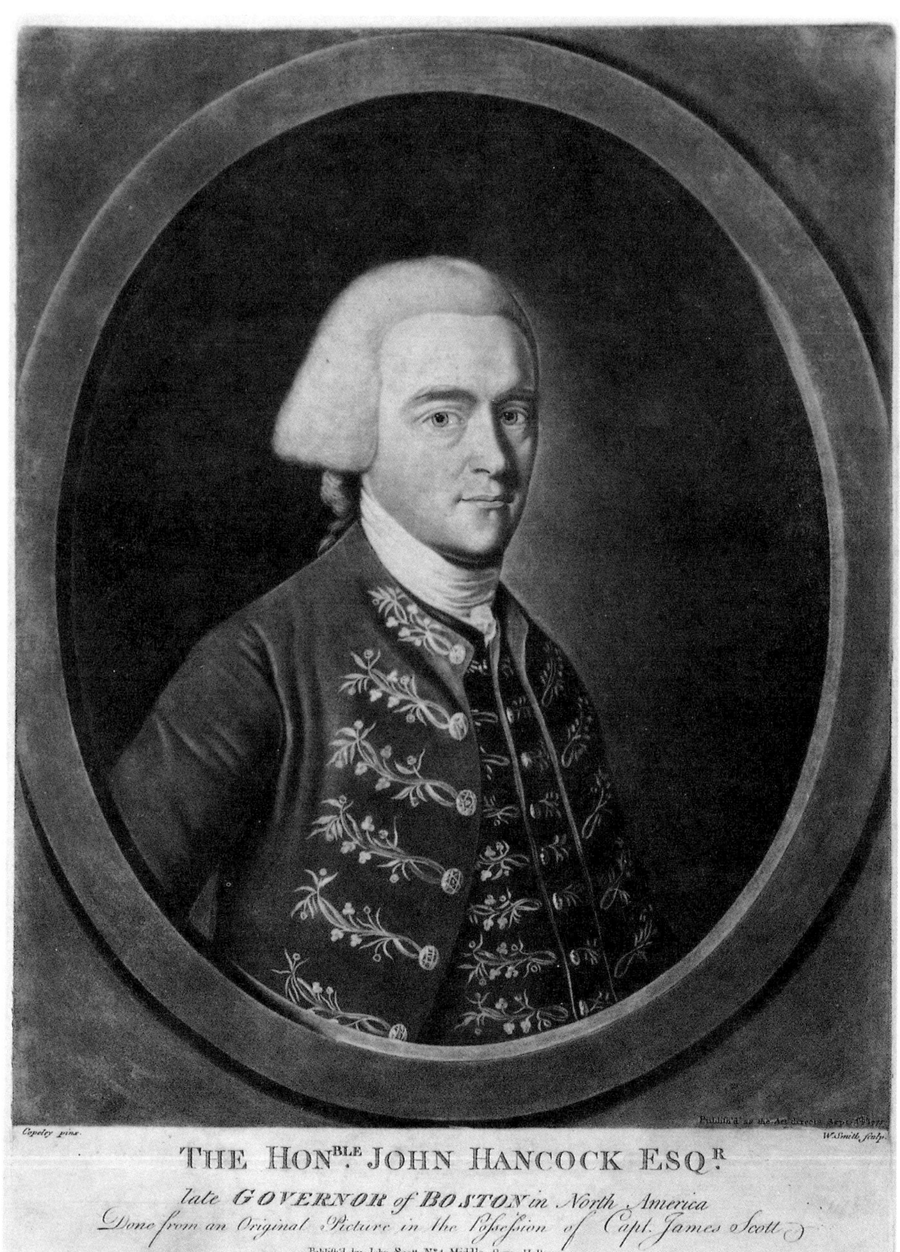
Copley pinx.
W. Smith sculp.
THE HON.BLE JOHN HANCOCK ESQ.R
late GOVERNOR of BOSTON in North America
Done from an Original Picture in the Possession of Capt. James Scott
Publish'd by John Scott No. 4, Middle Row, Holborn.

29.

John Singleton Copley (1738-1815), artist
William Smith (1707-1764), engraver
John Scott (1774-1828), publisher

THE HONBLE. JOHN HANCOCK ESQR. late GOVERNOR of BOSTON in North America
Done from an Original Picture in the Possession of Capt. James Scott

London, 1775
Mezzotint
Laid paper

Overall size: 36.9 x 27.0 cm
Platemark: 35.5 x 25.0 cm
Image: 31.6 x 25.0 cm

59.80

Self-assured, handsome and engaging, wealthy, and an aggressive businessman, John Hancock (1736/7-1793) was a natural leader. When a contest arose over a shipload of wine consigned to him, so many Bostonians came to his defense that the British reported Boston was a town in the hands of rabble. His style and his profound commitment to independence, well beyond his personal interests, were never more clear than in the flourishing signature he affixed to the Declaration of Independence.

Several years earlier, in 1772-76, John Singleton Copley had painted a waist-length portrait of Hancock looking through a porthole frame. At least one copy of this painting was made, since two are listed as being in private collections in Jules Prown's study of Copley's American paintings. In 1775, one version in the collection of Captain James Scott was engraved in mezzotint by William Smith in London for publication by John Scott, who certainly sensed a waiting market among both Americans and British who appreciated such commitment to liberty.

Framed and glazed impressions of Smith's mezzotint portrait of Hancock were in Philadelphia by November 1 of 1775 and in New York City by the first of the following year. Plain and unframed, the print was for sale at four shillings. For a shilling more it could be acquired suitably hand-colored, and for twice the amount it could be purchased framed and glazed.

References: Prown, *Copley in America*, 217, nos. 300, 301; Advertisement of Nicholas Brooks, *Pennsylvania Gazette* (Philadelphia), November 1, 1775, as quoted in Prime, *Arts and Crafts in Philadelphia, 1721-1785*, 16-17; Advertisement of Richard Sause, as published in *New York Gazette and Weekly Merchandizer* (January 15, 1776).

J. C. Smith, William Smith 2

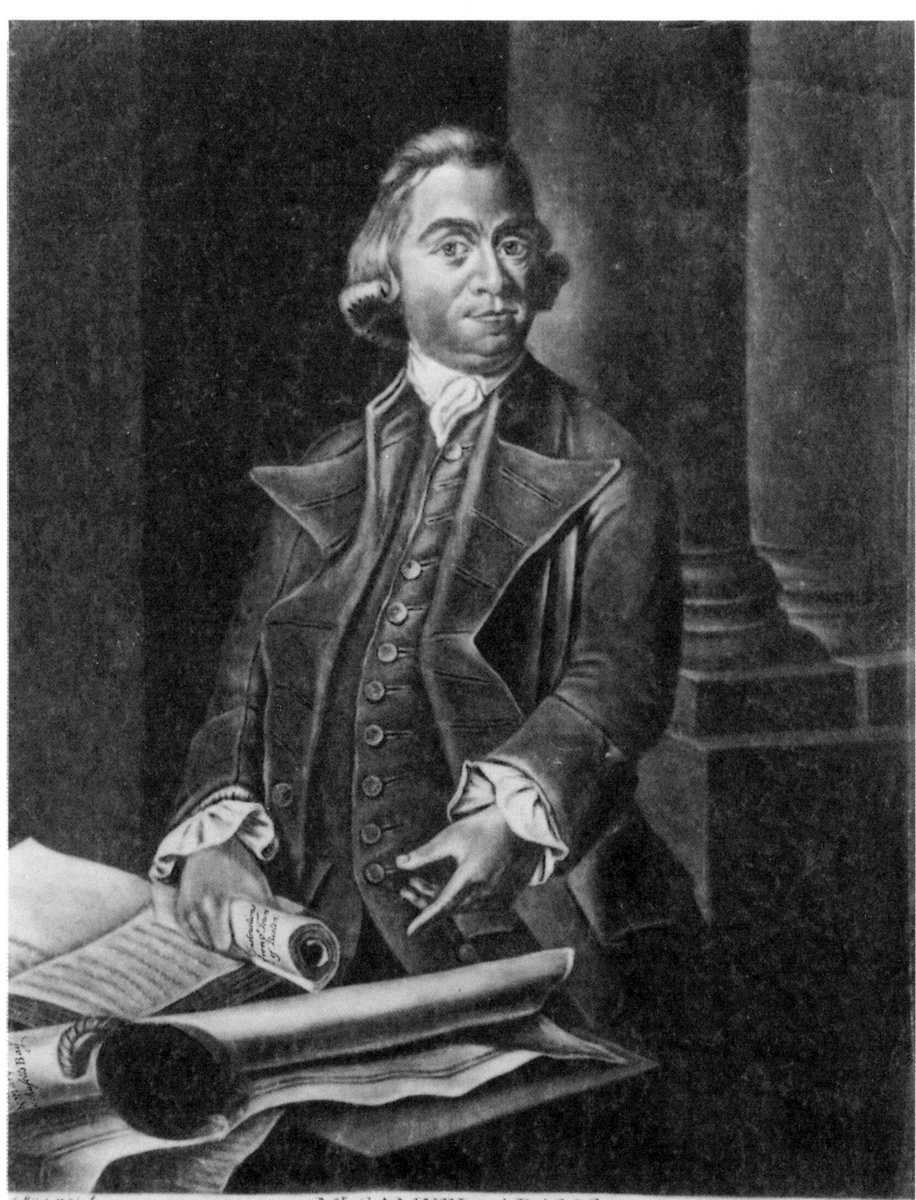
Mr. SAMUEL ADAMS.
When haughty NORTH impress'd wth proud Disdain
Spurn'd at the Virtue, which rejects his Chain:
Heard with a Tyrant Scorn our Rights implor'd
And when we sued for Justice, sent the Sword:
Lo: ADAMS rose, in Warfare nobly try'd,
His Country's Saviour, Father, Shield & Guide.
Urg'd by her Wrongs, he wag'd ye glorious Strife
Nor paus'd to waste a Coward Thought on Life.

30.

Samuel Okey (ac. in England 1765-1770; ac. in America 1773-1780), engraver
J. Mitchell (n.a.), delineator
John Singleton Copley (1738-1815), artist
Samuel Okey and Charles Reak (n.a.), publishers

Mr. SAMUEL ADAMS.

Newport, Rhode Island,
April 1775
Mezzotint with some burin work
Laid paper

Overall size: 34.8 x 24.7 cm
Image: 31.1 x 24.7 cm

56.11.4

Samuel Okey, like Peter Pelham, was trained and practiced as an engraver in mezzotint in London before emigrating to the colonies. In 1773, Okey and Charles Reak were in partnership in Newport, Rhode Island. For the present, the artist J. Mitchell would seem saved from obscurity only by this engraving made after a copy of Copley's original portrait of Samuel Adams (1722-1803).

Deeply influenced by the religious fervor of evangelist George Whitefield while a Harvard College student, Adams became an eloquent and emotional defender of Americans' rights to refuse taxes levied without due colonial representation. He was an influential member of such radical groups as the "Caucus Club," and he instinctively moved to energize others in acts of rebellion. Copley's portrait of Adams, painted between 1770 and 1772, captured the sitter's determination in both the intensity of his gaze and the force of his gesture toward the documents on the table. Okey's translation of the design into mezzotint accentuated both features.

References: Saunders and Miles, *American Colonial Portraits*, 316-17; David McNeely Stauffer, *American Engravers Upon Copper and Steel*, 2 vols. (New York: Grolier Club, 1907), 1:194, 2:391-92.

Stauffer 2370

31.

John Singleton Copley (1738-1815), artist
Valentine Green (1739-1813), engraver
John Stockdale (1749?-1814), publisher

HENRY LAURENS ESQR. PRESIDENT OF THE AMERICAN CONGRESS, 1778

London, open letter proof, October 1, 1782
Mezzotint with minimal etching
Laid paper, watermark of "IHS" in circle below a cross and above a heart, and countermark of "T DUPUY FIN AUVERGNE 1742"

Overall size: 65.8 x 43.0 cm
Platemark: 64.0 x 40.5 cm
Image: 58.8 x 40.5 cm

59.116
Ex coll. Henry Graves, Jr.

On his way to the Netherlands to arrange for a loan of ten million dollars in support of the American colonial cause, Henry Laurens (1724-1792) was captured when British seamen seized the ship. He was sent to fourteen months in the Tower of London. Upon his release in December of 1781, negotiated as a trade after the Americans had captured General Charles Cornwallis at Yorktown, Laurens sat for John Singleton Copley, who had left Boston for London in 1774. The artist painted Laurens amid the surroundings of a gentleman of great rank: chair and stool finished in gilt, turkey carpet as a tablecover, a raised platform set between column and pilaster. On the table are spread documents dating from 1778, when Laurens was president of the American Congress. The artist signed the portrait, which is now in the National Gallery of Art, Washington D.C., on the last step of the riser just below the footstool.

Copley, a member of the Royal Academy and a painter of high acclaim among British nobility, finished the portrait in 1782, the year Laurens joined Benjamin Franklin, John Adams, and John Jay to negotiate the preliminary treaty of peace with the British. John Stockdale published this mezzotint of the recently finished portrait in October of that year. He employed Valentine Green to scrape the plate. As "Mezzotint Engraver to his Majesty," Green was one of the best engravers working in London and was certainly equal to the task of capturing the nuances of Copley's painting.

J. C. Smith, Green 80

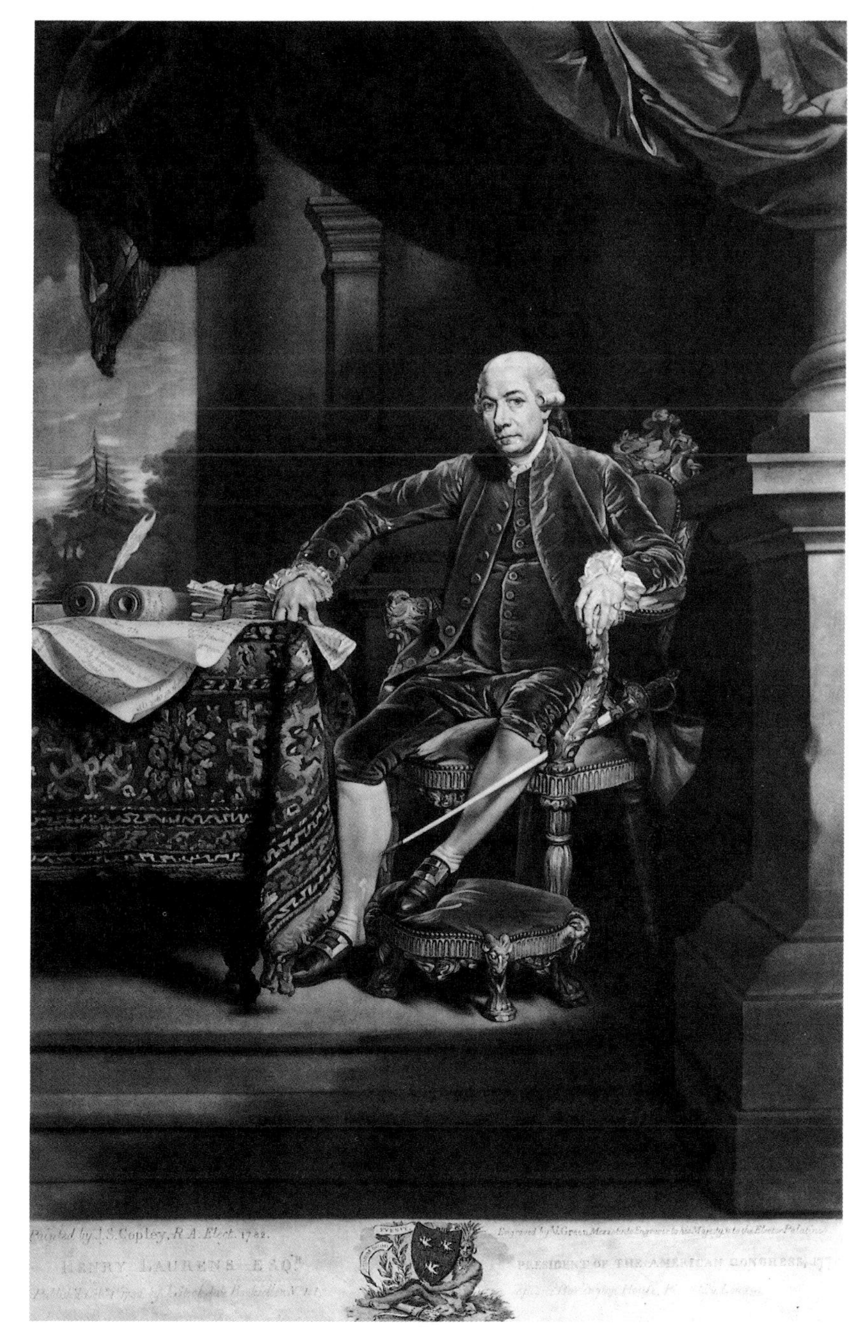
Painted by J.S. Copley, R.A. Elect. 1782.
HENRY LAURENS ESQ.R
PRESIDENT OF THE AMERICAN CONGRESS

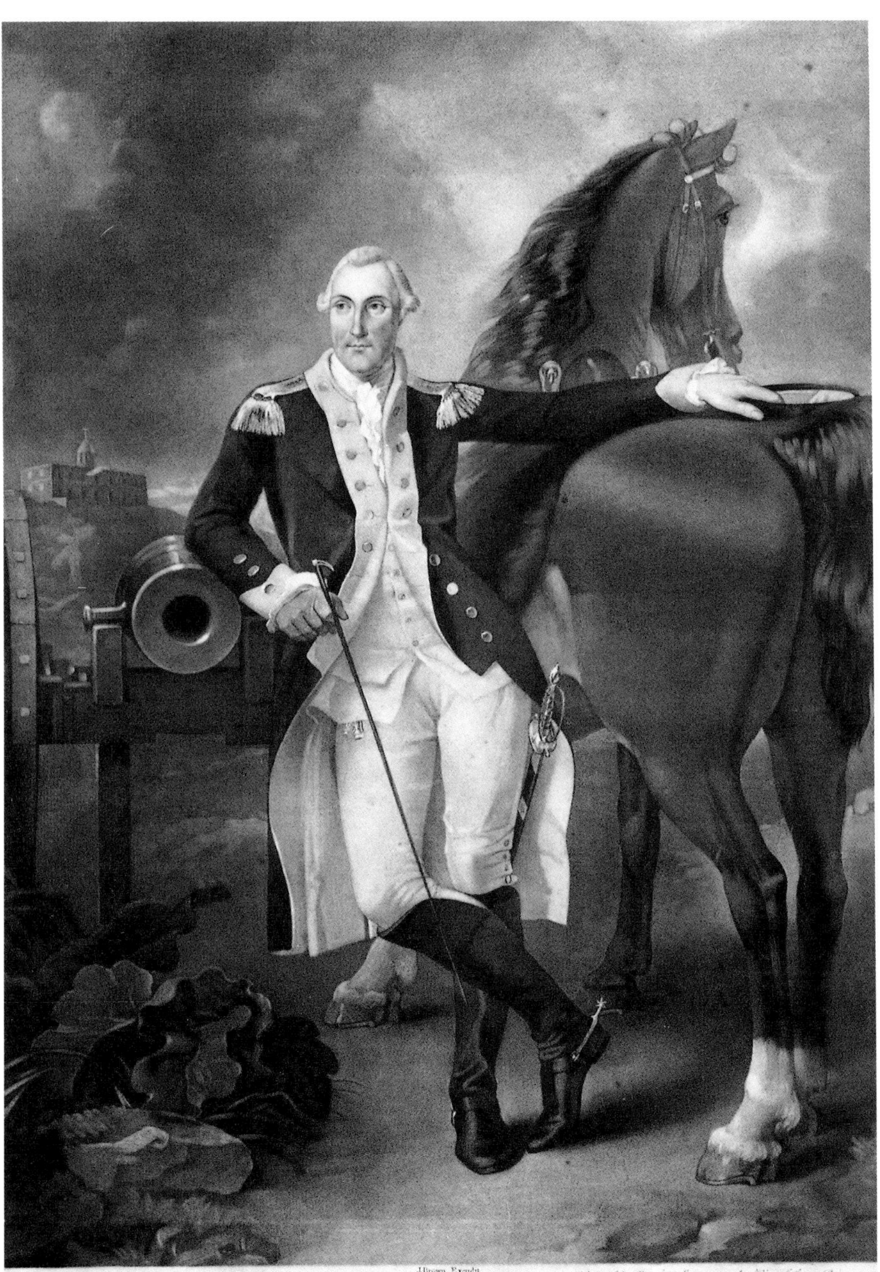
J.Brown Excudit
GENERAL WASHINGTON.

32.

Charles Willson Peale (1741-1827), artist
Thomas Stothard (1755-1834), delineator
Valentine Green (1739-1813), engraver
Joseph Brown (n.a.), publisher

GENERAL WASHINGTON.
George Washington

London, second state, April 22, 1785
Mezzotint with minimal burin work
Laid paper, watermark of "IHS" in circle below a cross and above a heart, and countermark of "FIN DUPUY AUVERGNE 1742"

Overall size: 56.0 x 40.4 cm
Platemark: 52.8 x 35.4 cm
Image: 50.2 x 35.4 cm

54.501

No artist painted George Washington (1732-1799) from life more than Charles Willson Peale. The general and statesman sat for him on seven occasions: in 1772, 1776, 1777, 1779, 1783, 1785, and finally in 1795. Despite a lively demand for copies in oil after the original studies, there was a limit to the artist's endurance. Peale decided to scrape a mezzotint after his full-length portrait of Washington posed against the Princeton battlefield. He put a notice in the *Pennsylvania Packet* for August 26, 1780.

> A new impression in Metzotinto; From the original Picture, belonging to the State of Pennsylvania; Posture size, i.e. 14 inches by 10 inches, exclusive of the margin; Price Two Dollars, or the value thereof in current money, or Six Pounds per Dozen to Shop Keepers, or any persons going abroad....

To adhere to the popular "posture size" for framing prints, Peale executed the engraved portrait as a three-quarter length version.

At the urging of American artist Benjamin West, Peale sent a full-size copy of the 1779 portrait to London. The painting was bought by the publisher Joseph Browne, who hired Thomas Stothard to prepare a working tonal study that was reduced to actual scale. This allowed the engraver to work directly from image to copperplate. Stothard exercised some artistic prerogative and in the process rearranged the composition to eliminate an aide to Washington, several trophies of the British defeat, and one horse. Although the muzzle of the cannon now threateningly faces the viewer, the composition that Stothard prepared and Valentine Green scraped, without the superfluous references to their nation's defeat, was less likely to offend any war-weary English printbuyers.

References: Sellers, *Portraits and Miniatures by Charles Willson Peale*, 216-33; Prime, *Arts and Crafts in Philadelphia, 1721-1785*, 6 and facing 8; Shadwell, *American Printmaking*, nos. 66, 70.

33.

Charles Willson Peale (1741-1827), artist, engraver, and publisher

HIS EXCEL: G: WASHINGTON ESQ: L.L.D.
LATE COMMANDER IN CHIEF OF THE ARMIES OF THE U. S. OF AMERICA & PRESIDENT OF THE CONVENTION OF 1787.

Philadelphia, second state, September 26, 1787
Mezzotint with minimal burin work
Laid paper

Overall size:
18.4 x 15.3 cm
Platemark: (trimmed) x 14.7 cm
Image: 13.2 x 10.4 cm
In original frame:
23.5 x 20.7 cm oval

63.58

Hart 3b; Stauffer 2429

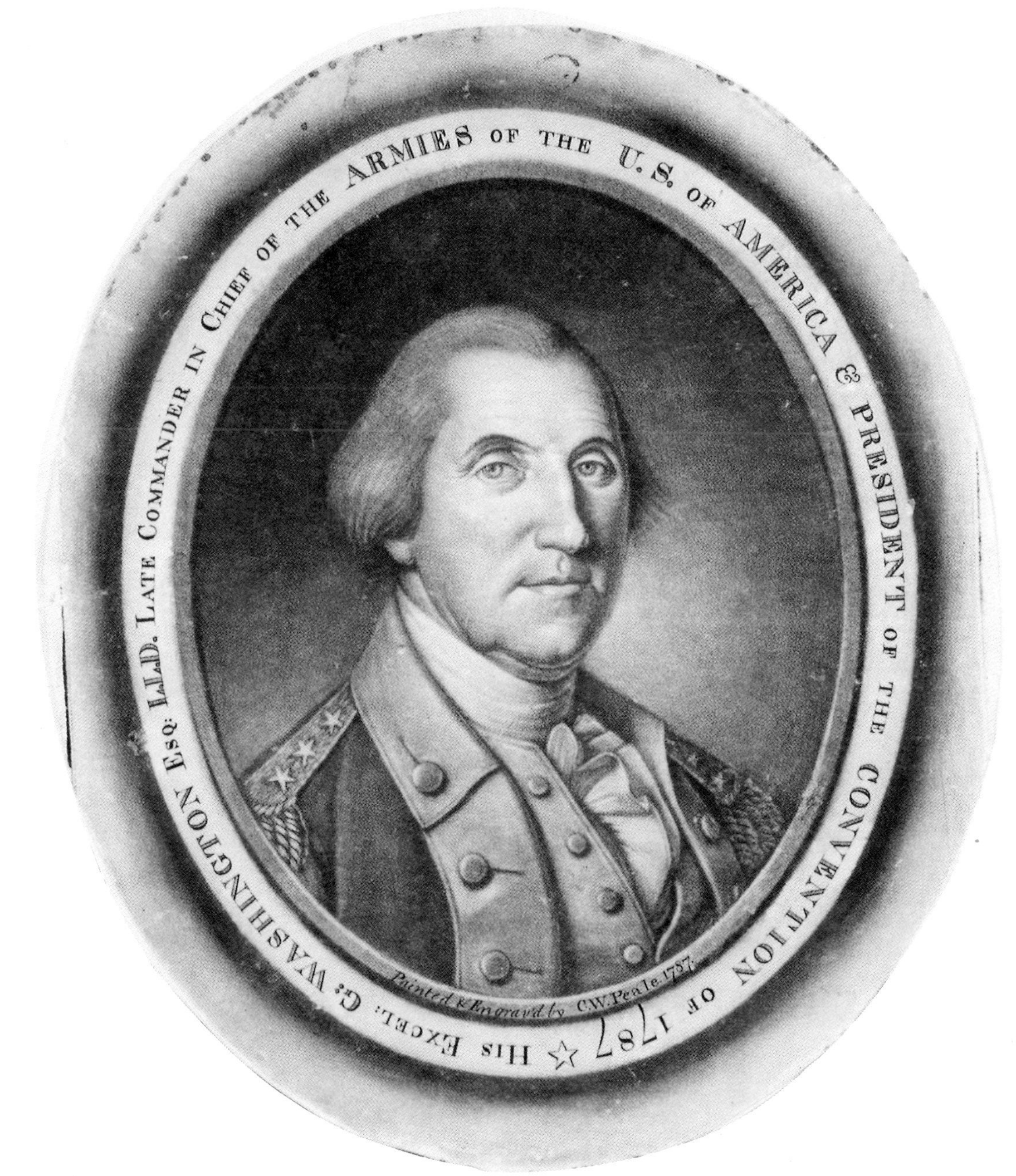
His Excel: G: WASHINGTON Esq: LL.D. Late Commander in Chief of the ARMIES of the U.S. of AMERICA & PRESIDENT of the CONVENTION of 1787 ☆
Painted & Engrav'd by C.W. Peale. 1787.

34.

Charles Willson Peale
(1741-1827), artist,
engraver, and publisher

HIS EXCELLENCY B. FRANKLIN L.L.D. F.R.S.
PRESIDENT OF PENNSYLVANIA, & LATE MINISTER OF THE UNITED STATES OF AMERICA AT THE COURT OF FRANCE.

Philadelphia, February, 1787
Mezzotint with minimal burin work
Laid paper

Overall size:
18.3 x 15.7 cm
Platemark: 16.3 x 14.4 cm
Image: 13.0 x 10.3 cm
In original frame:
23.5 x 20.7 cm oval

63.59

Early in 1787, Charles Willson Peale proposed publication of a series of mezzotints taken from the collection of oil portraits of illustrious personages on view in his museum. On March 30 of that year, Peale initiated the series with a portrait of Benjamin Franklin; this was followed by one of Lafayette on sale by April 20. A portrait of the Reverend Joseph Pilmore, a charismatic evangelist and rector of Trinity, St. Thomas, and All Saints churches was published next. Fourth in the series, a portrait of George Washington as commander of the armies and president of the convention of 1787, was on sale by September 26. It proved to be the last.

At the beginning of this enterprise, Peale wrote to Dr. David Ramsay of both his enthusiasm for the project and his expectation that it would cause him some difficulty since he would have the task of preparing and "roughing" the copperplates and otherwise doing the whole business himself, including the printing. This would seem to confirm the suggestion that Peale had help from professionals in London in both laying the mezzotint ground and printing his earlier portrait of William Pitt (cat. no. 27).

Peale took great pains with the project, selecting for his subjects three distinguished and respected champions of American liberty and a preacher of wide popularity. Double frames of the best materials, designed as ovals according to the latest and most elegant taste, were provided with each impression for fifteen shillings at the outset. In September each framed portrait was priced at two dollars, but by October the cost of the print had been reduced to two-thirds of a dollar. The cost of the frame remained at one dollar. Whether due to the continuous competition from imported and attractively framed prints or just a fickle market, Peale was unable to gain sufficient public approbation to continue the series.

References: Sellers, *Portraits and Miniatures by Charles Willson Peale*, 81-82, 119, 172, 236-39; Richardson, "Peale's Engravings in the Year of National Crisis, 1787," 166-81; Wendy J. Shadwell, "The Portrait Engravings of Charles Willson Peale," in *Eighteenth Century Prints in Colonial America: To Educate and Decorate*, ed. Joan D. Dolmetsch (Williamsburg: Colonial Williamsburg Foundation, 1979), 123-44.

Stauffer 2423

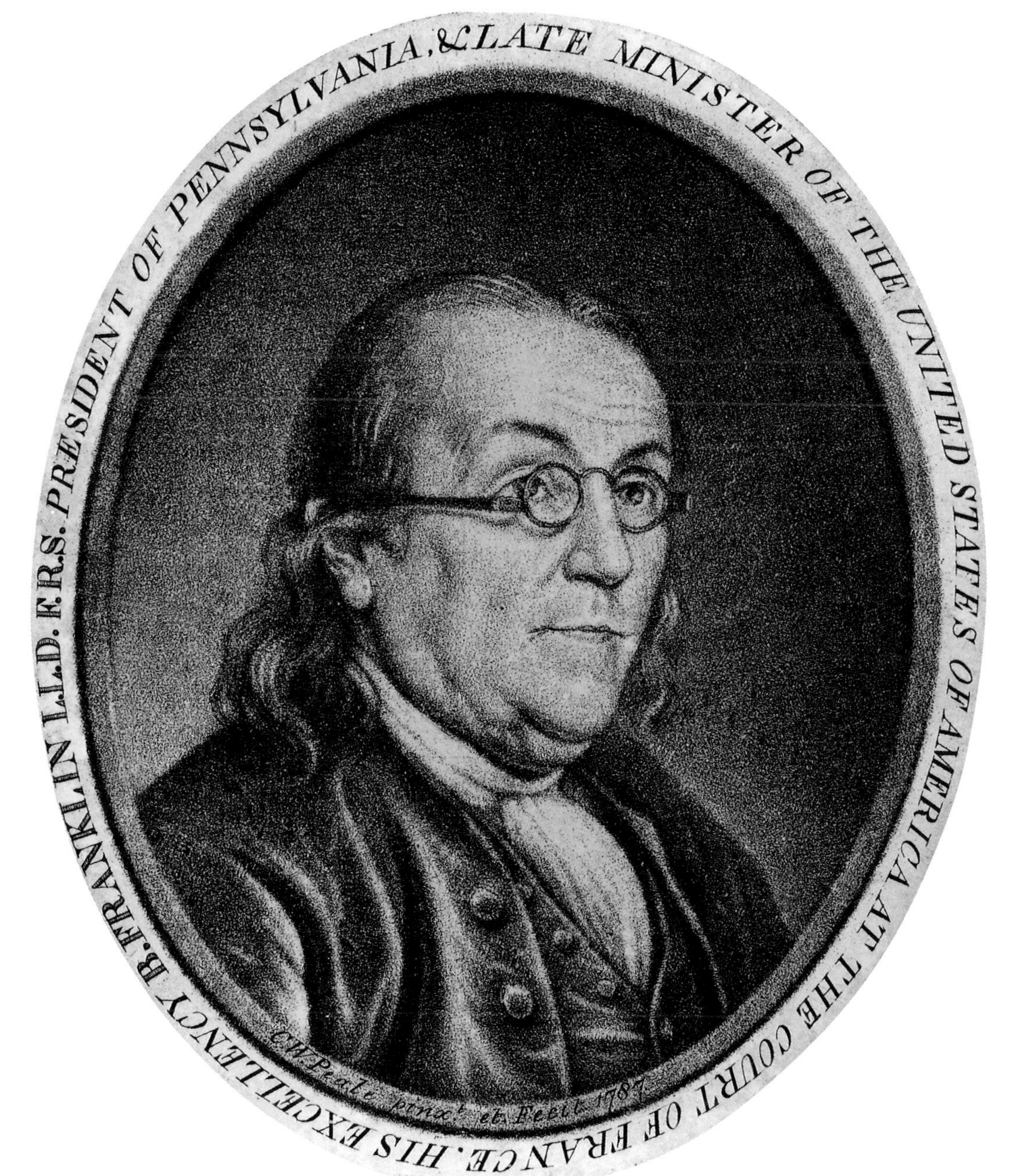
HIS EXCELLENCY B.FRANKLIN L.L.D. F.R.S. PRÆSIDENT OF PENNSYLVANIA, & LATE MINISTER OF THE UNITED STATES OF AMERICA AT THE COURT OF FRANCE.
C.W.Peale pinxt. et Fecit 1787

35.

Amos Doolittle (1754-1832), engraver and publisher

A DISPLAY of the UNITED STATES of AMERICA
GEORGE WASHINGTON President of the UNITED STATES of AMERICA. The Protector of his COUNTRY, and the Supporter of the rights of MANKIND. BORN 11th FEB 1732.

New Haven, Connecticut, October 1, 1791
Line engraving and etching, stipple, watercolors
Laid paper, two sheets joined before printing

Overall size: 60.0 x 49.5 cm
Platemark: 53.1 x 43.3 cm
Image: 51.9 x 43.3 cm

61.1742

Amos Doolittle learned engraving as an apprentice in the shop of a jeweler and silversmith. Over a long career he engraved bookplates and heraldic devices, a set of the Prodigal Son, and four plates from which were printed the most prized of eighteenth-century American engravings: scenes of the battles at Lexington and Concord (see cat. no. 49).

In 1789, Doolittle published an ambitious, complicated broadside celebrating the first president of the United States. It included a chain of state seals surrounding a three-quarter portrait of Washington, which had been copied from a 1787 engraving by James Trenchard (b. in England 1747, ac. in America 1777-ca. 1794, d. in England). In 1790, Doolittle reworked the portrait, erasing the three-quarter view with a scraper and burnisher, and re-engraving the central portion with a profile of Washington in the uniform of commander of the armies that was based on an earlier portrait by Joseph Wright. Doolittle's training as an engraver did not include the technical shortcuts used to minimize such changes, and the effects are still visible in this impression from the fourth state of the plate. With the exception of updated statistics relative to population growth, there is little change between the second, third, and fourth states of the plate. The remaining fifth and sixth states of this broadside included states newly added to the union.

In spite of its large size and the added expense involved for those who wished to have impressions framed, this *Display* was sufficiently popular that Doolittle designed and executed another in a similar format in 1799, this time to honor John Adams upon his assuming the presidency. By then Doolittle was sufficiently certain of its success to include in the credit line a note that this broadside was available at wholesale rates, an accommodation to distant shopkeepers and traveling salesmen. A third *Display* representing the presidency of Thomas Jefferson was designed and printed in 1803.

Reference: The Reverend William A. Beardsley, "An Old New Haven Engraver and His Work: Amos Doolittle," in *Papers of the New Haven Historical Society* 8 (1914): 132-50.

Hart 840b; Stauffer 521

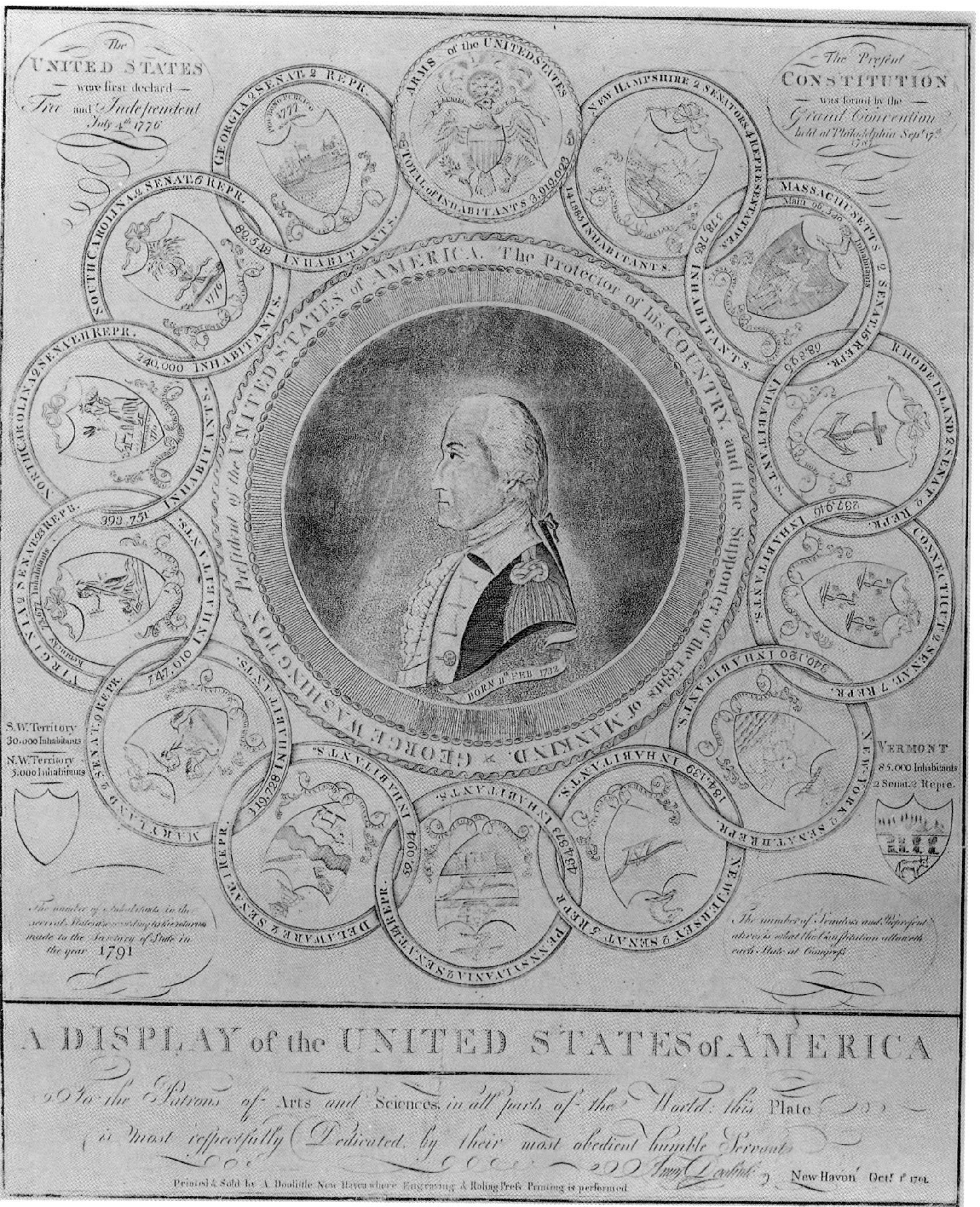
The UNITED STATES were first declard Free and Independent July 4th 1776
The Present CONSTITUTION was formd by the Grand Convention held at Philadelphia Sept 17th
ARMS of the UNITED STATES
TOTAL of INHABITANTS 3,919,023
GEORGIA 2 SENAT. 2 REPR.
82,548 INHABITANTS.
NEW HAMPSHIRE 2 SENATORS 4 REPRESENTATIVES.
141,885 INHABITANTS.
President of the UNITED STATES of AMERICA. The Protector of his COUNTRY, and the Supporter of the rights of MANKIND.
GEORGE WASHINGTON
BORN 11th FEB 1732
S.W. Territory 30,000 Inhabitants
N.W. Territory 5,000 Inhabitants
VERMONT 85,000 Inhabitants 2 Senat. 2 Repre.
The number of Inhabitants in the several States is according to the returns made to the Secretary of State in the year 1791
The number of Senators and Representatives is what the Constitution alloweth each State at Congress
A DISPLAY of the UNITED STATES of AMERICA
To the Patrons of Arts and Sciences, in all parts of the World, this Plate is most respectfully Dedicated, by their most obedient humble Servant
New Haven
Printed & Sold by A. Doolittle New Haven where Engraving & Roling Press Printing is performed

36.

Edward Savage (1761-1817), engraver and publisher
Charles Willson Peale (1741-1827), artist

DAVID RITTENHOUSE. L.L.D. F.R.S.
President of the American Philosophical Society.

Philadelphia, Pennsylvania, December 10, 1796
Mezzotint with minimal burin work
Wove paper

Overall size: 53.0 x 41.9 cm
Platemark: 50.7 x 35.2 cm
Image: 45.2 x 34.8 cm

60.366
Ex coll. Albert Rosenthal

Edward Savage went to London in 1790 to study under Benjamin West, to make important contacts, and to master the art of engraving on copperplate. As Peale had earlier done, he undertook to learn the mysteries of mezzotint. During his stay in London, Savage completed two large essays using this technique. One was a portrait of Washington after his own painting; the other was a companion piece that he had copied from David Martin's (1737-1798) so-called thumb portrait of Benjamin Franklin in 1793. Savage returned to Boston, married, and moved with his wife to Philadelphia in 1795.

David Rittenhouse (1732-1796) was an instrument and clockmaker by occupation and an astronomer and mathematician by avocation. In 1791, the American Philosophical Society recognized his genius and elected him president. Charles Willson Peale, also a member of the Society, was engaged to paint Rittenhouse's portrait. Working from a replica, Savage scraped this mezzotint, which he first offered in December of 1796 as a posthumous tribute to Rittenhouse, one that could be purchased for nine dollars in an "elegant and burnished" frame.

With skilled mezzotint engravers working in the United States, American printsellers and print collectors were no longer completely dependent upon the portrait subjects chosen by foreign entrepreneurs, nor did they have to suffer the inevitable delays that occurred when designs or paintings made in America had to be sent to a European atelier. It was once again possible to have a prominent citizen honored in a print as readily as it had been during Peter Pelham's years in Boston (1727-51).

References: William Barton, *Memoirs of the Life of David Rittenhouse* (Philadelphia: Printed by W. Brown for Edward Parker, 1813); Sellers, *Portraits and Miniatures by Charles Willson Peale*, 181-83, no. 741; Advertisement of Edward Savage, published in *Gazette of the United States* (Philadelphia), December 29, 1796, as quoted in Prime, *Arts and Crafts in Philadelphia, 1786-1800*, 72.

Stauffer 2748

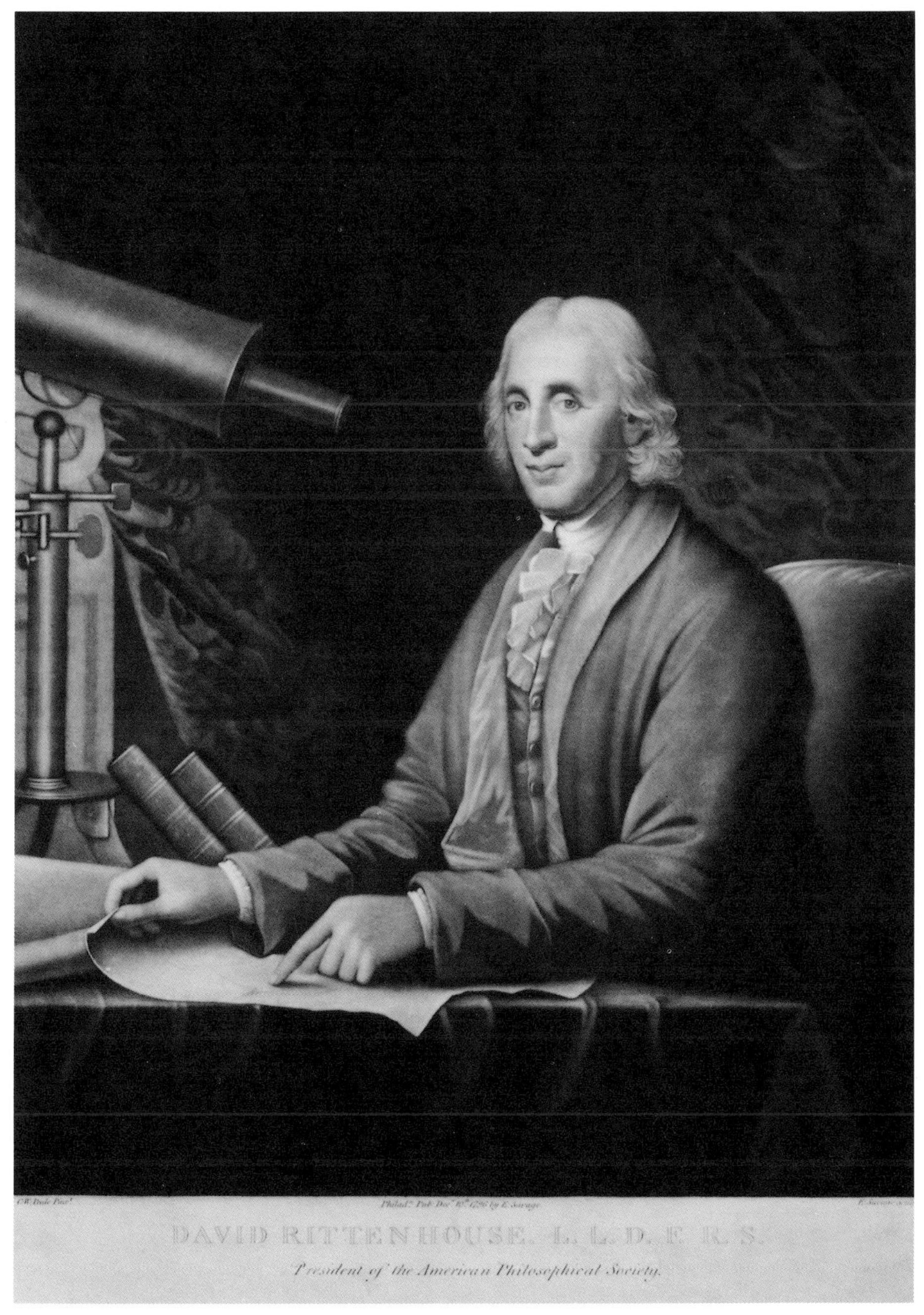
DAVID RITTENHOUSE. L. L. D. F. R. S.
President of the American Philosophical Society.

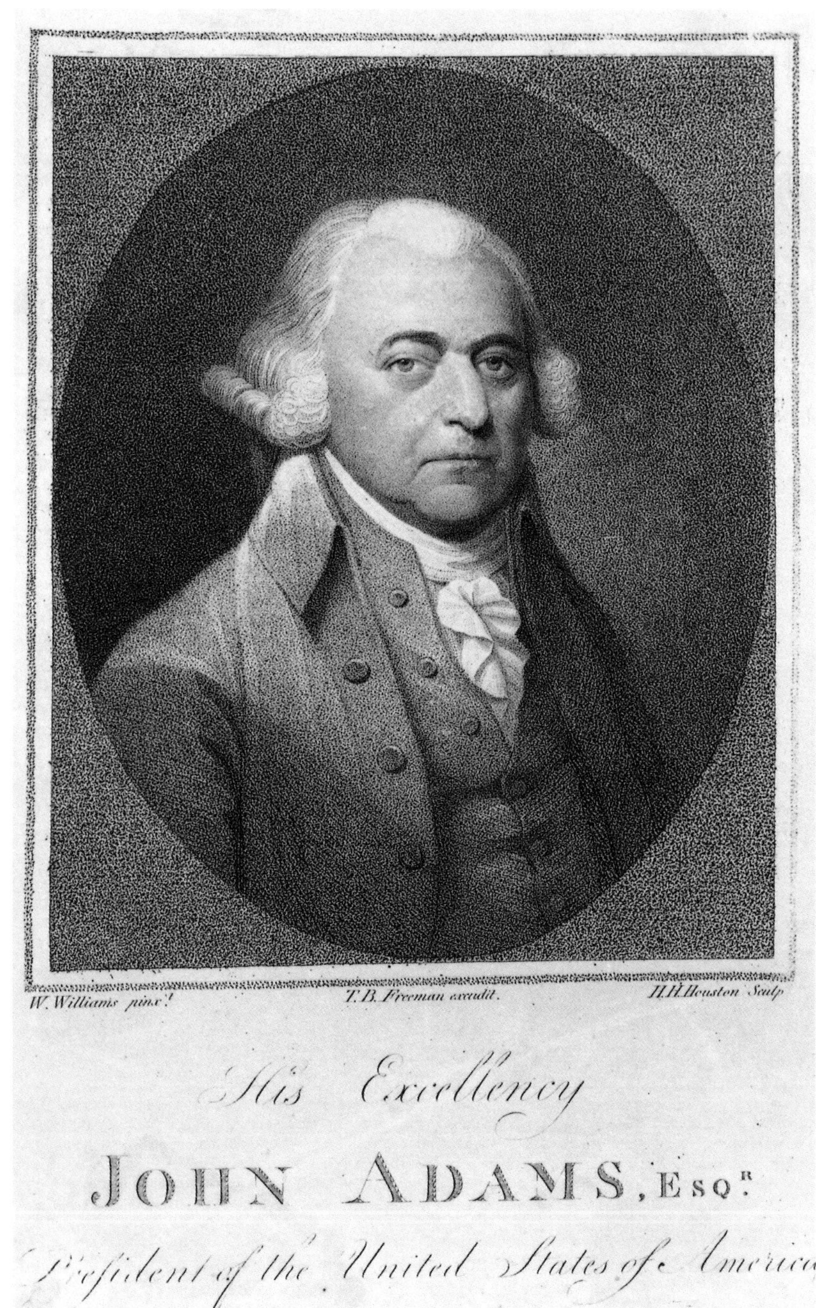
W. Williams pinx.t
T. B. Freeman excudit.
H. H. Houston Sculp
His Excellency
JOHN ADAMS, Esq.r
President of the United States of America

37.

H. H. Houston (w. in America 1796-1798), engraver
Tristram Bampfylde Freeman (w. in Philadelphia 1795-1842), publisher

His Excellency JOHN ADAMS, ESQR. President of the United States of America

Philadelphia, September 1, 1797
Stipple engraving and etching
Wove paper

Overall size: 22.3 x 16.8 cm
Platemark: (trimmed) x 14.5 cm
Image: 15.5 x 12.5 cm

76.53

Tristram Bampfylde Freeman envisioned a new American printmaking industry, one that would attract the best of European engravers to the United States, where they could produce images of superb quality and train native-born apprentices to work to the highest standards of the art. Houston was one of those English engravers who were attracted to the prospects of making prints unencumbered by systems long in place in Europe and dominated by a relatively few major figures.

Freeman advertised in the *Federal Gazette* on February 8, 1798, that he would have for sale on the following Monday (February12) likenesses of John Adams (1735-1826) and George Washington as engraved by two leading English artists. Black and white impressions could be purchased framed in the best burnished gold moldings and fitted with enamel glasses at six dollars for the pair. Impressions on white satin, printed in colors, were available for eight dollars.

Houston appears to have spent a very short time in Philadelphia, working there from 1796 to 1798. His departure, probably for England, coincides with the failing of Freeman's print publishing enterprise.

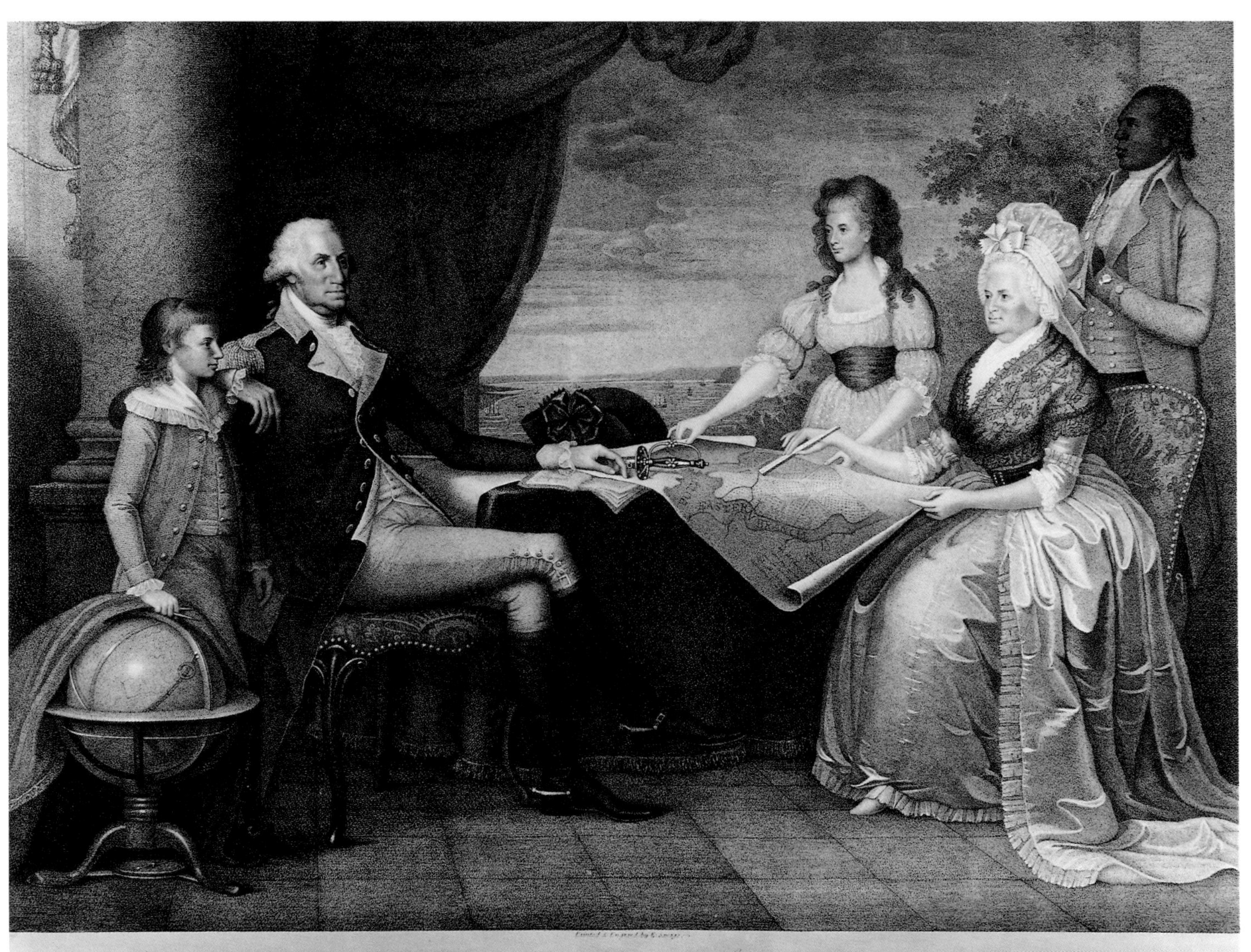
The WASHINGTON FAMILY.
George Washington his Lady, and her two Grandchildren by the name of Custis.
La FAMILLE de WASHINGTON.
George Washington Son Epoux, et Ses deux petits Enfants du Nom de Custis

38.

Edward Savage (1761-1817), artist and engraver of record
Edward Savage and Robert Wilkinson (n.a.), publishers

The WASHINGTON FAMILY. George Washington his Lady and her two grand-children by the name of Custis.

Philadelphia and London, March 10, 1798
Stipple etching and engraving
Wove paper, watermark of "1794 J WHATMAN" (twice)

Overall size: 55.0 x 68.4 cm
Platemark: 53.5 x 66.6 cm
Image: 46.9 x 62.7 cm

66.111
Gift of J. William Middendorf III

In London, Savage had an opportunity to see a variety of printmaking techniques, including a tedious but effective tonal process called stipple. Termed *crayon maniére* in France, where it was perfected, the technique was used as a basis for printing in colored inks before being adopted by English printmakers and printers.

On February 19, 1798, an announcement appeared in the *Gazette of the United States* (Philadelphia) inviting interested subscribers to M'Elwees Looking Glass Store to examine a proof print of George Washington and his family—his wife Martha, his step-grandchildren Patty and George Washington Custis, and his servant Billy Lee. A large print with an image measuring over twenty by twenty-six inches (50.8 by 66.0 cm), it required many hours of work to execute and develop dot by dot imperceptible changes of tone, from nearly black to the lightest gray. To the dismay of others working in his studio, Savage reportedly claimed complete credit for the work. In fact, he had supervised most of the translation of this image from his earlier painting of the Washington family and left the tedium of engraving to David Edwin (b. in England 1776, ac. in America 1797-d. 1841), who had recently arrived from London, and to other assistants.

References: John Hill Morgan and Mantle Fielding, *The Life Portraits of Washington and their Replicas* (Philadelphia: Privately printed for subscribers, 1931), 183-86; Advertisement of M'Elwee's Looking Glass Store, published in the *Gazette of the United States* (Philadelphia), February 19, 1798, as quoted in Prime, *Arts and Crafts in Philadelphia, 1786-1800*, 213; Wendy C. Wick, *George Washington, An American Icon: The Eighteenth Century Portraits* (Washington, D.C.: Smithsonian Institution Traveling Exhibition Service and The National Portrait Gallery, 1982), 122-24.

Hart 235; Stauffer 2754

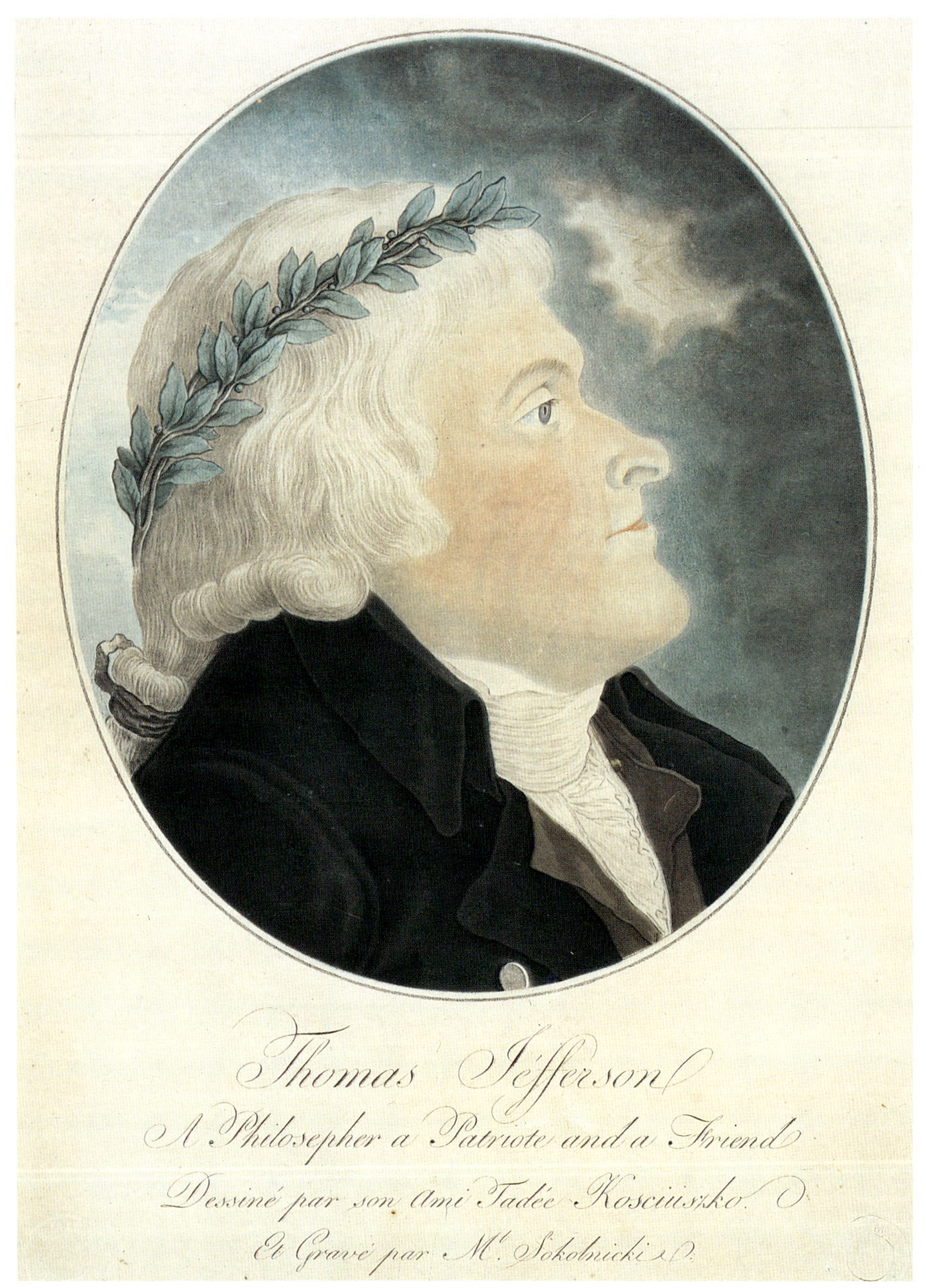
Thomas Jefferson
A Philosepher a Patriote and a Friend
Dessiné par son Ami Tadée Kosciuszko.
Et Gravé par Mr. Sokolnicki

39.

Thaddeus Kosciusko
(1746-1817), artist
Michel Sokolnicki
(1760-1816), engraver

Thomas Jefferson
A Philosopher a Patriote
and a Friend

Paris, 1798-99
Aquatint with some burin work,
watercolors
Wove paper

Overall size: 36.8 x 26.0 cm
Platemark: 35.5 x 25.3 cm
Image: 24.9 x 21.0 cm

65.79
Ex coll. B. Mastai Collection
(blind stamp)

Thomas Jefferson (1743-1826) was an emphatic supporter of men's rights to self-government, although he differed from many of his contemporaries over the issue of a strong central government. Polish officer Thaddeus Andrew Bonaventure Kosciusko, who had distinguished himself fighting for the Americans during the Revolutionary War, greatly respected Jefferson. During his visit to the United States in 1797-98, Kosciusko made a drawing of the statesman and took it to Paris to be engraved by Michel Sokolnicki.

Jefferson understood that the drawing as well as the print were made for Kosciusko's personal use. In 1802, he wrote to James Madison that he had received four copies from his friend, the only ones to come to America. Three remained in his family; the fourth he sent to the Madisons.

References: Alfred L. Bush, *The Life Portraits of Thomas Jefferson* (Charlottesville: Thomas Jefferson Memorial Foundation, 1962), 40-42; Letter from Jefferson to James Madison, May 5, 1802, *Jefferson Papers*, Library of Congress, Washington, D.C.

40

William Hogarth (1697-1764), artist, engraver, and publisher

John Wilkes Esqr.
Drawn from the life and etch'd in Aquafortis by Willm. Hogarth. Price 1 Shilling. Publish'd according to Act of Parliament May ye 16. 1763

London, May 16, 1763
Etching with some burin work
Laid paper, watermark of dovecote

Overall size: 34.6 x 21.9 cm
Platemark: 33.9 x 21.6 cm
Image: 31.1 x 21.6 cm

76.48

John Wilkes (1727-1797) believed in the cause and the rights of Britons, and that included vindicating American colonists, whom he considered as Englishmen abroad. He vigorously defended the colonial resistance to the Stamp Act of 1765, and for Americans the name Wilkes was synonymous with Liberty.

William Hogarth, too, believed in the inherent right of English people to freedom, yet he disagreed violently with Wilkes as to the extent to which Englishmen in pursuit of this freedom should refuse to recognize the orderly power of government. Wilkes had used issue number 17 of his own newspaper, the *North Briton*, for a sharp attack on Hogarth. In the forty-fifth issue, Wilkes turned his attentions to verbally assaulting both Lord Bute, who he believed to be guilty of duplicity, and George III, who he felt was covering up for Bute. That proved too much for Hogarth, who retaliated with this portrait of a sneering, devious man holding high the crumpled cap of LIBERTY. To the subject's right on a table are the issues of the newspaper, numbers 17 and 45, which the artist found most offensive.

Hogarth's dislike of Wilkes had little effect on the followers of either. Americans collected Hogarth's engravings with unbridled enthusiasm throughout the eighteenth and into the nineteenth centuries, and many a glass of punch raised in toast to Liberty was ladled from punchbowls that bore Wilkes' image as decoration (see cat. no. 87).

References: R. H. T. Halsey, *The Boston Port Bill as Pictured by a Contemporary London Cartoonist* (New York: Grolier Club, 1904), 95-122; British Library, *The American War of Independence, 1775-83* (London: British Library, 1975), 23, no. 14; Jarrett, *England in the Age of Hogarth,* 19; Paulson, *Hogarth's Graphic Works*, 1:256-59, 2:pl. 239; See punch bowl (60.503), cat. no. 87.

British Museum, *Satires*, 4050

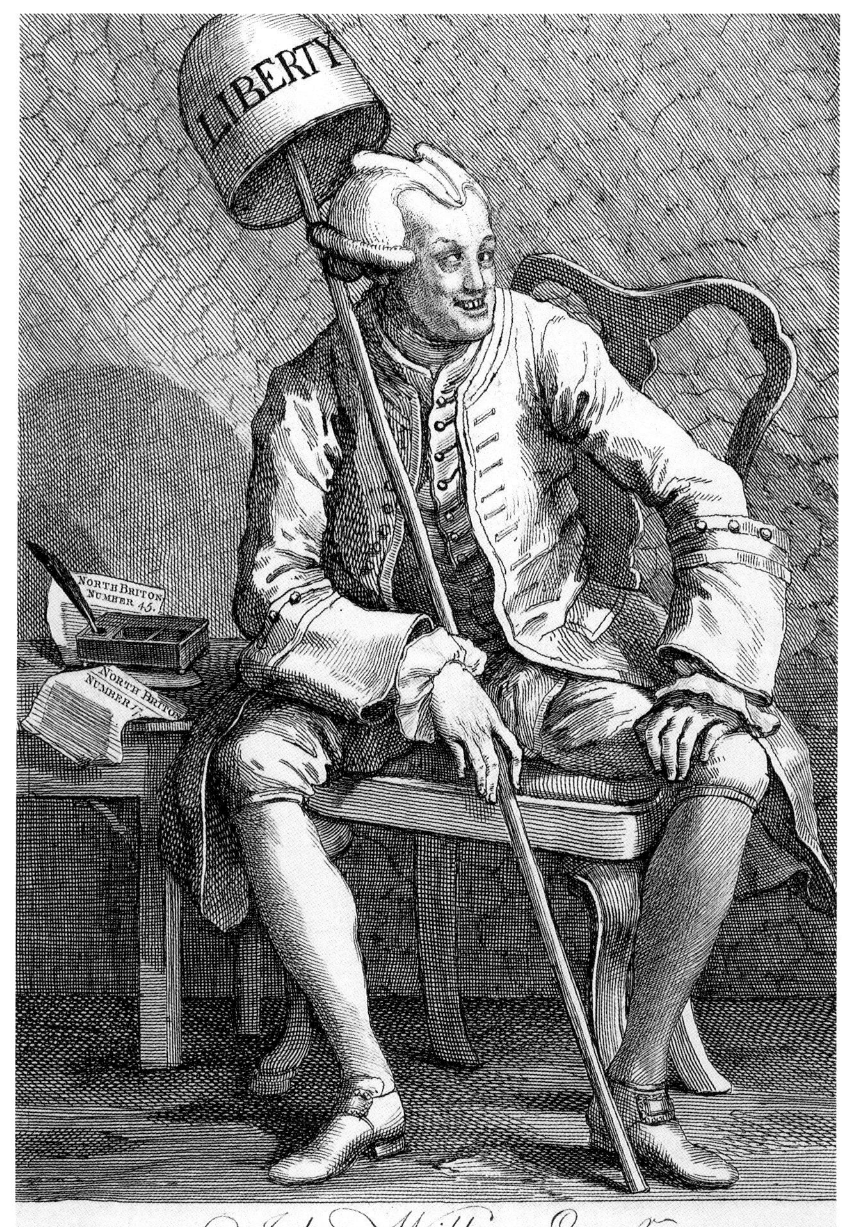
LIBERTY
NORTH BRITON NUMBER 45.
NORTH BRITON NUMBER 17
John Wilkes Esq.r
Drawn from the Life and Etch'd in Aquafortis by Will.m Hogarth,
Price 1 Shilling.
Publish'd according to Act of Parliament May ye 16. 1763.

41.

After Benjamin Wilson (1721-1788)

THE REPEAL or the Funeral Procession, of MISS AMERIC-STAMP

Over the Vault are placed two Skeleton Heads, Their elevation on Poles, and the dates of the two Rebellion Years, sufficiently shew what Party they espoused, and in what cause they suffered an ignominious Exit.

The reverend Mr. Anti-Sejanus who under that signature hackney'd his pen in support of the Stamps leads the procession as officiating Priest, with the burial service and funeral sermon in his hands.

Next follow two eminent Pillars of the Law, supporting, two black flags, on which are delineated the Stamps with the White Rose and Thistle interwoven: an expressive design, supposed to have been originally contrived on the 10 of June. The significative motto Semper Eadem is preserved: but the Price of the Stamp is changed to three farthings, an important sum taken from the Budget. The numbers 122 and 71 declare the minority which fought under these Banners.

Next appears the honourable Mr. George Stamp, full of Grief and despair, carrying his favourite Childs Coffin, Miss Americ Stamp, who was born in 1765, and died hard in 1766.

Immediately after, follows the chief Mourner Sejanus.

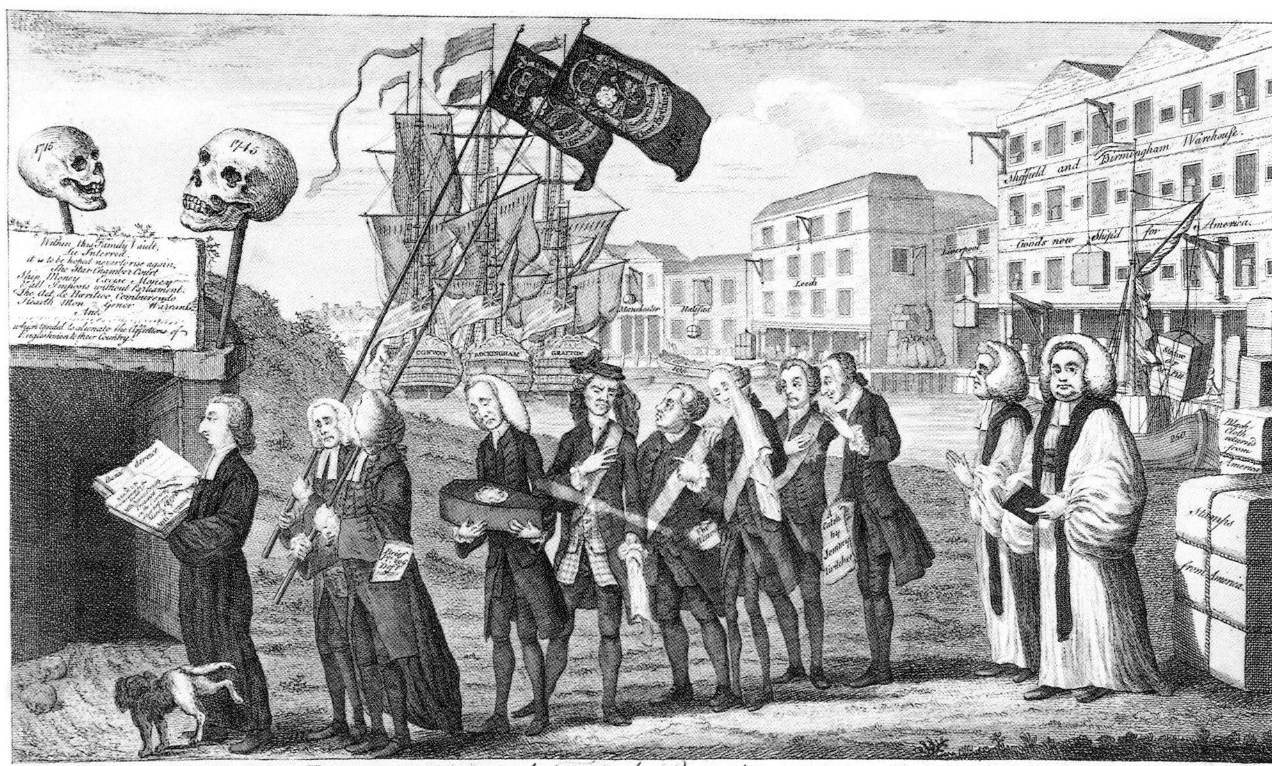

Then his Grace of Spital Fields, and Lord Gawkee.

After these Jemmy Twitcher, with a Catch, by way of funeral anthem, & by his side his friend and partner Mr. Falconer Donaldson of Halifax.

The rear is brought up by two right reverend Fathers of the Church.

These few mourners are separated from the joyful scene which appears on the River Thames, where three first rate ships are riding. VIZ. the Conway, Rocking-ham, and Grafton. Along the opposite Shore, stand open Warehouses, for the several goods of different manufactoring towns from which Cargoes are now shipping for America. Among these is a large Case containing the Statue of Mr. Pitt, which is heaving on board a Boat No. 250, there is another boat taking in goods nearer the first Rates, which is No. 105. These Numbers will ever be held in esteem by the true SONS of LIBERTY.

London, shortly after March 21, 1766
Line etching with engraved letters and details, watercolors
Laid paper, watermark of Strasburg lily and "L V G"

Overall size: 30.0 x 40.7 cm
Platemark: 25.1 x 35.1 cm
Image: 20.1 x 34.0 cm

57.1262

In February of 1765, George Grenville, prime minister to George III, suggested a tax be levied on specific colonial activities. Excise fees on papers relating to land transactions, court proceedings, and other legal documents, as well as newspapers, advertisements in newspapers, ship clearances, diplomas, and even dice, touched nearly every aspect of commerce and communication. Parliament passed the measure over great protests from within its own ranks and utter outrage from the colonists. Resistance in the colonies was both verbal and physical. Local stamp collectors resigned almost as soon as they were appointed. By the fall of 1765, twenty-seven colonial representatives met in New York City to declare formally that American colonists were deserving of the rights of Englishmen and should not to be taxed without due representation. To bolster their words, the colonists agreed not to import British goods. With control of the situation deteriorating, Parliament realized the tax could not be enforced, and on March 18, 1766, it repealed the Stamp Act.

Three days after repeal of the tax, Benjamin Wilson published a satire and broadside depicting England's futile attempt to gain revenues from the colonies. Englishmen and Americans alike found his work to their liking, and in a very short period Wilson earned some three hundred pounds for his effort, as well as the dubious compliment of numerous imitators.

This impression is one of two in the Winterthur Museum by unidentified engravers after Wilson. Like each of the other versions of *The Repeal*, it juxtaposes the drama of a somber procession of British ministers against a background of flourishing trade, suggesting that with the tax dead, business would continue as usual between the colonies and England.

One month after Wilson published his celebrated comment on the repeal, Benjamin Franklin sent copies from London to his wife in Philadelphia. A month later, the *Pennsylvania Staatsbote* for May 26, 1766, carried an advertisement announcing that within the week a Mr. Wilkinson would have for sale a reproduction of *The Repeal*. The advertisement included a detailed description of Wilson's invention.

References: Advertisement of Mr. Wilkinson, *Pennsylvania Staatsbote*, May 26, 1766, as quoted in Prime, *Arts and Crafts in Philadelphia, 1721-1785,* 32; Honour, *European Vision of America*, no. 228; Lillian B. Miller, *In the Minds and Hearts of the People: Prologue to the American Revolution: 1760-1774* (Greenwich, Conn.: New York Graphic Society, 1974), 81-103.

British Museum, *Satires*, 4140

42.

Paul Revere (1735-before 1818), engraver, printer, and publisher
Christian Remick (1726-after 1783), artist and colorist

A VIEW OF PART OF THE TOWN OF BOSTON IN NEW-ENGLAND AND BRITTISH SHIPS OF WAR LANDING THEIR TROOPS! 1768

Boston, Massachusetts, second state, first state published April 16, 1770
Line engraving, watercolors
Laid paper, watermark of lily on crowned shield with "GR"

Overall size, including period frame: 33.3 x 47.3 cm
Platemark: 25.8 x 40.1 cm
Image: 24.9 x 39.5 cm

58.2398

From the moment John Hancock's toughs boarded his ship, the *Liberty*, in Boston Harbor, restrained a British customs officer, and unloaded a cargo of wine due to be taxed under the Townshend Acts of 1767, the situation between British authorities and citizens in Boston quickly deteriorated into mob confrontations. Arrival of reinforcements of British soldiers was inevitable. On October 1, 1768, two British regiments landed, followed by two more in November.

No one appreciated the power of the print more than Paul Revere. Prominent in the secret organization of craftsmen, merchants, and friends who referred to themselves as the Sons of Liberty, he was among those who chose to keep the alleged atrocities of the British troops in Boston in the forefront of everyone's mind by any means available. With his skills of engraving on metal, Revere had the capacity to translate idea to image on copperplate, and then to reproduce those images any number of times for the benefit of another audience. A print could serve not just as a record of history but as propaganda. In this view of Boston with British troops landing, Revere was reporting an event that took place in October of 1768, nearly eighteen months before the engraving was available to the public.

Christian Remick gave notice in the *Boston Gazette* for October 1769 that he had lately arrived from Spain. His advertisement stated that he worked in watercolors and could provide customers with a wide variety of subjects. Apparently he had been in town for a year inasmuch as he invited any interested parties to see examples of his work, in particular "an accurate View of the Blockade of Boston, with the landing of the British Troops on the first of October 1768." On April 16, 1770, Revere placed a notice in the same newspaper announcing an engraving with a similar description and by the same title. There is a noticeable difference between Remick's watercolor (Massachusetts Historical Society) and the engraved version. This suggests that although Revere credited Remick with the drawing, the silversmith had a large hand in reworking any design to heighten the drama of the event and to add a gesture of disparagement towards British authority in the cartouche.

This engraving is known in two states: the first in which the date of the landing is marked as "fryday, Septr. 30th," and this second state, which bears corrected spelling.

References: Advertisement of Christian Remick, as quoted in Dow, *Arts & Crafts in New England*, 2-3; Shadwell, *American Printmaking*, 26-27, no. 31; Charles E. Goodspeed, *Yankee Bookseller, Being the Reminiscences of Charles E. Goodspeed* (Boston: Houghton Mifflin Co., and Cambridge, Mass.: Riverside Press, 1937), 112-13; Clarence S. Brigham, *Paul Revere's Engravings* (Worcester, Mass.: American Antiquarian Society, 1954), 48-49; Miller, *In the Minds and Hearts of the People*, 113-14.

Stokes and Haskell 1768—B-66; Stauffer 2676

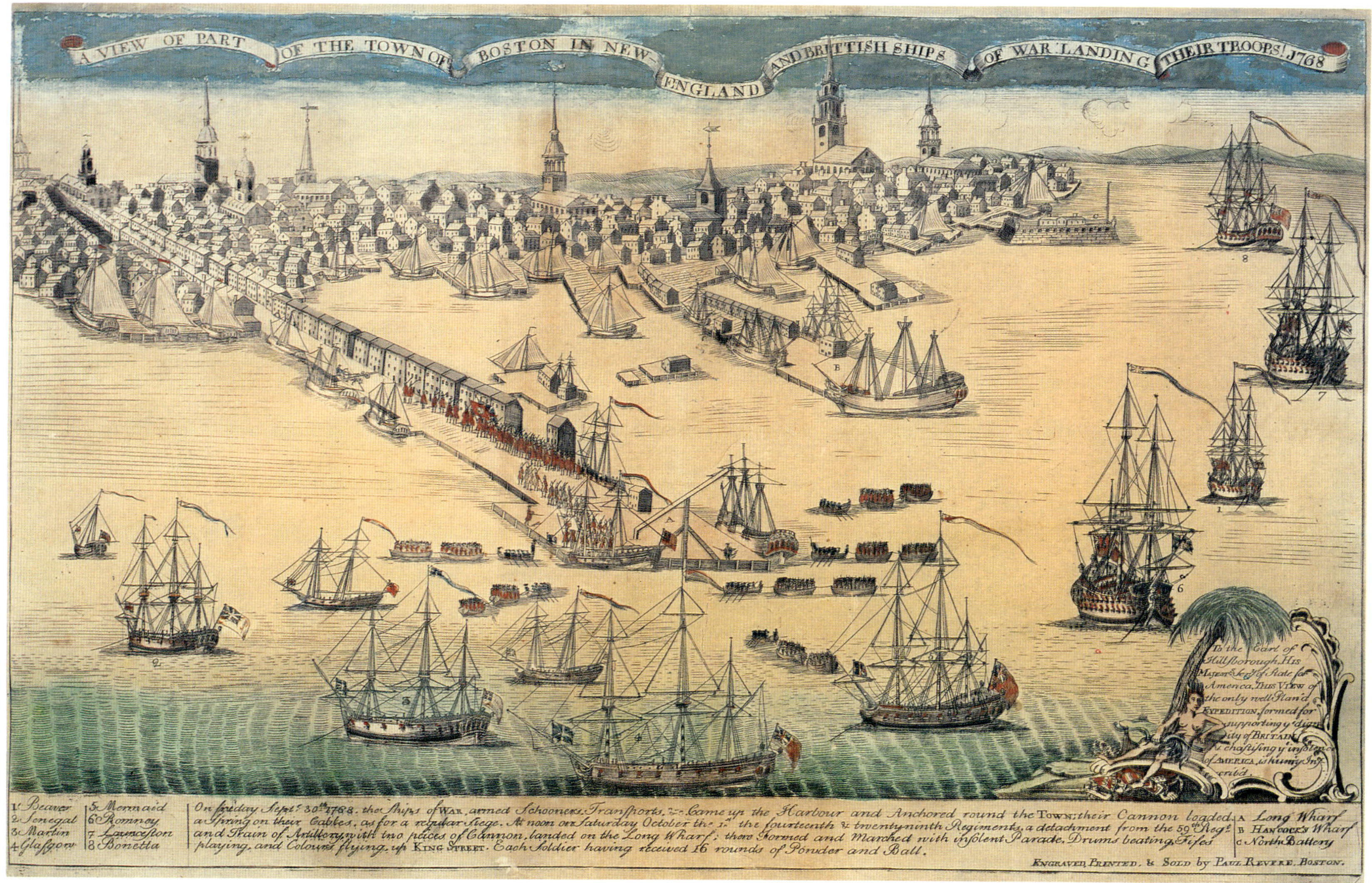
A VIEW OF PART OF THE TOWN OF BOSTON IN NEW-ENGLAND AND BRITTISH SHIPS OF WAR LANDING THEIR TROOPS! 1768
A
B
1
2
3
4
5
6
7
8
To the Earl of Hillsborough, His Majest's Secy of State for America, THIS VIEW of the only well Plan'd EXPEDITION, formed for supporting ye dignity of BRITAIN & chastising ye insolence of AMERICA, is hum^y Inscrib'd.
1 Beaver
2 Senegal
3 Martin
4 Glasgow
5 Mermaid
6 Romney
7 Launceston
8 Bonetta
On friday Septr 30th 1768. the Ships of WAR, armed Schooners, Transports, &c. Came up the Harbour and Anchored round the TOWN; their Cannon loaded, a Spring on their Cables, as for a regular Siege. At noon on Saturday October the 1st the fourteenth & twentyninth Regiments, a detachment from the 59th Reg^t and Train of Artillery, with two peices of Cannon, landed on the Long Wharf; there Formed and Marched with insolent Parade, Drums beating, Fifes playing, and Colours flying, up KING STREET. Each Soldier having received 16 rounds of Powder and Ball.
A Long Wharf
B HANCOCK'S Wharf
C North Battery
ENGRAVED, PRINTED, & SOLD by PAUL REVERE, BOSTON.

43.

Paul Revere (1735-before 1818), engraver
After Henry Pelham (1749-1806), artist

The BLOODY MASSACRE perpetrated in King—Street BOSTON on March 5th. 1770 by a party of the 29th REGT.

Boston, second state, 1770
Line engraving and etching, watercolors
Laid paper, watermark of Strasburg lily

Overall size: 27.5 x 23.8 cm
Platemark: 25.8 x (trimmed) cm
Image: 20.0 x 22.1 cm

55.500

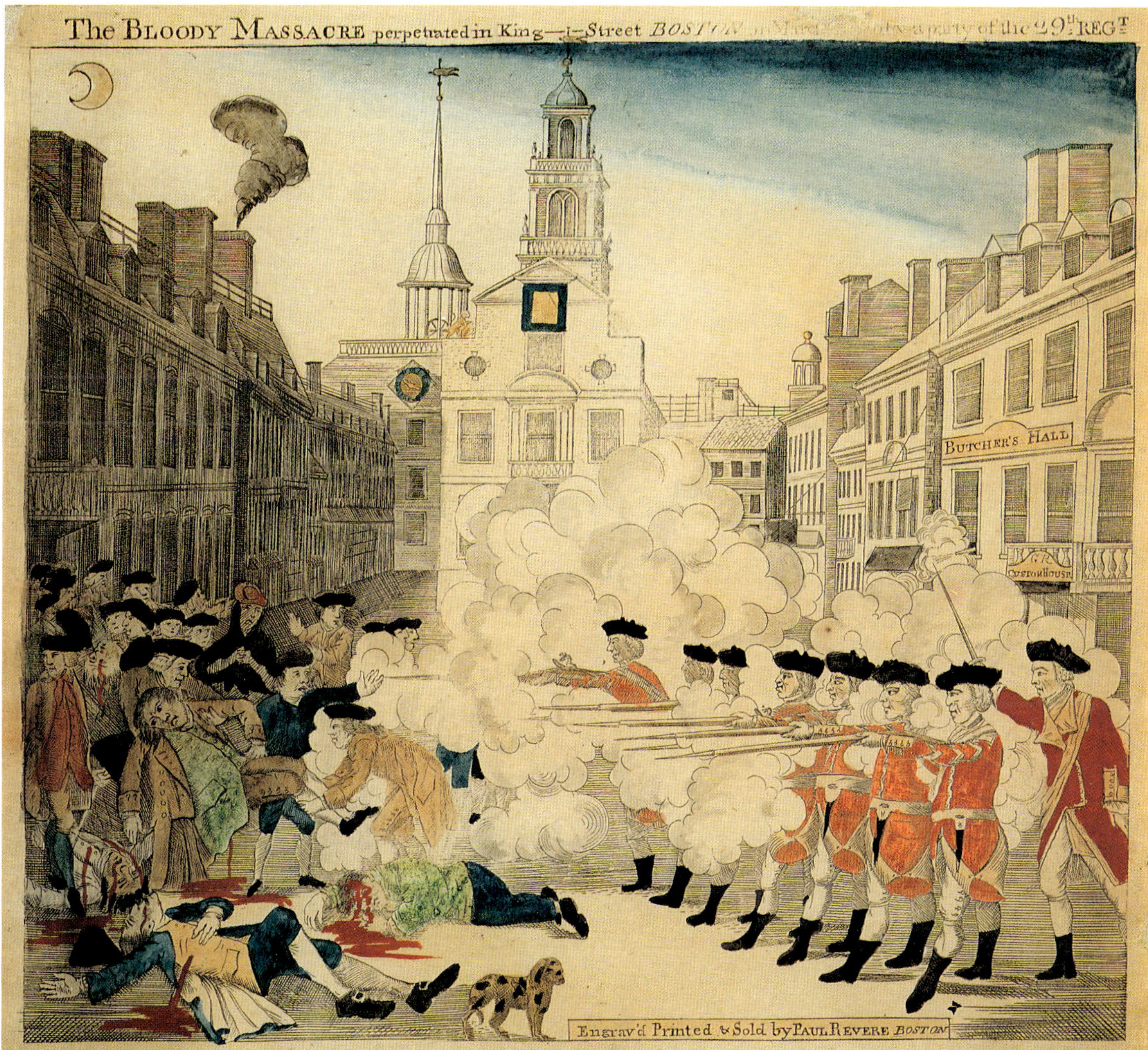

UnhappyBOSTON! ſee thy Sons deplore,
Thy hallow'd Walks beſmear'd with guiltleſs Gore:
While faithleſs P—n and his ſavage Bands,
With murd'rous Rancour ſtretch their bloody Hands;
Like fierce Barbarians grinning o'er their Prey,
Approve the Carnage, and enjoy the Day.

If ſcalding drops from Rage from Anguiſh Wrung
If ſpeechleſs Sorrows lab'ring for a Tongue,
Or if a weeping World can ought appeaſe
The plaintive Ghoſts of Victims ſuch as theſe;
The Patriot's copious Tears for each are ſhed,
A glorious Tribute which embalms the Dead.

But know, FATE ſummons to that awful Goal,
Where JUSTICE ſtrips the Murd'rer of his Soul:
Should venal C—ts the ſcandal of the Land,
Snatch the relentleſs Villain from her Hand,
Keen Execrations on this Plate inſcrib'd,
Shall reach a JUDGE who never can be brib'd.

The unhappy Sufferers were Meſs.rs SAM.L GRAY, SAM.L MAVERICK, JAM.S CALDWELL, CRISPUS ATTUCKS & PAT.K CARR *Killed. Six wounded; two of them* (CHRIST.R MONK & JOHN CLARK) *Mortally*

Jonathan Mulliken
(1746-1782), engraver
After Paul Revere (1735-before 1818) and Henry Pelham (1749-1806)

The BLOODY MASSACRE perpetrated in King—Street BOSTON on March 5th 1770 by a party of ye 29th REGT.

Newburyport, Massachusetts, probably 1770
Line engraving, watercolors
Laid paper

Overall size: 27.4 x 22.8 cm
Image: 20.0 x 21.0 cm
In original frame

55.501

With British soldiers throughout the city, frustration and hatred were felt by many Bostonians. Fiery orators such as Samuel Adams kept the situation at a pitch. One small confrontation was all that was needed, and that occurred on March 5, 1770. Hearing of a testy moment between several unemployed ropemakers and skittish British soldiers earlier in the day, a group gathered in front of the customs house that evening to confront a lone British sentry. The mob goaded a small British contingent of one officer and seven regulars who came to the sentry's rescue, until one fired. In the melee that followed, five civilians were killed, including a slave, two apprentices, and an employee of a maker of breeches.

Henry Pelham, John Singleton Copley's half-brother, began a copperplate illustrating that mortal hour under the title of *The Fruits of Arbitrary Power*. He made the mistake of taking it to Revere for criticism. Revere, instantly recognizing the commercial and political potential of so wanton an act of aggression against "unarmed" citizens, hastened to engrave a copy, which he published under his own name. In his hurry Revere inadvertently engraved the time on the town hall clock to show eight o'clock, an oversight that was soon corrected to the actual time of the incident, twenty minutes past ten.

Some weeks later, Henry Pelham managed to publish his original version, but it seemed to have little effect on the popularity of Revere's pirated design. Perhaps in a final act of justice, Jonathan Mulliken, a clockmaker from Newburyport, Massachusetts, published his literal borrowing of Revere's version. Like its prototype, Mulliken's *Bloody Massacre* survives in an eighteenth-century frame. An inscription on the reverse reads: "Ezra Morrill/ Salsbury/ Framd. & Glasd."

References: Miller, *In the Minds and Hearts of the People*, 116-18; Shadwell, *American Printmaking*, 28, nos. 34, 35; Brigham, *Paul Revere's Engravings*, 57; Ledger of Daniel Rea, painter of Boston, vol. 5 (1764-99), 82, entry dated March 15, 1770, "Stephen Whiting Picture Man, To Colourg. ye Prints of ye Massacre; @ 18, £0.4.8," Baker Library, Harvard University, Cambridge, Massachusetts.

Stokes and Haskell 1770—C-10; Stauffer 2675

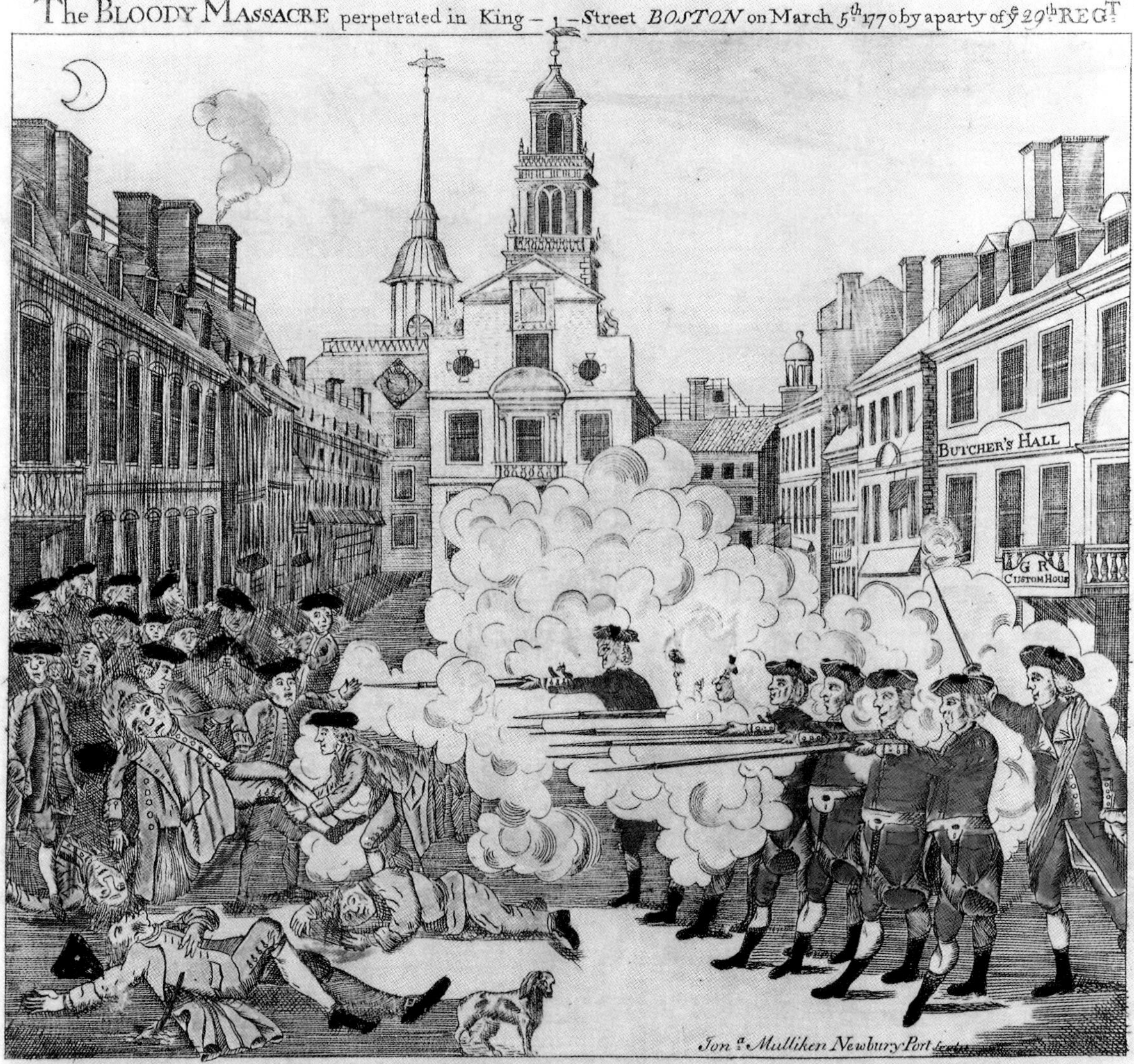
The BLOODY MASSACRE perpetrated in King-Street BOSTON on March 5th 1770 by a party of ye 29th REGT
BUTCHER'S HALL
G R
CUSTOM HOUSE
Jon.a Mulliken Newbury Port
Unhappy BOSTON see thy Sons deplore,
Thy hallow'd Walks besmear'd with guiltless gore
While faithless P—n and his savage Bands.
With murd'rous Rancour stretch their bloody Hands
Like fierce Barbarians grinning o're their Prey,
Approve the Carnage and enjoy the Day.
If scalding drops from rage from Anguish Wrung
If speechless Sorrows lab'ring for a Tongue
Or if a weeping World can ought appease
The plaintive Ghosts of Victims such as these
The Patriot's copious Tears for each are shed.
A glorious Tribute which embalms the Dead.
But know FATE summons to that awful Goal.
Where Justice strips the Murd'rer of his Soul.
Should venal C—ts the scandal of the Land.
Snatch the relentless Villain from her hand.
Keen execrations on this Plate inscrib'd.
Shall reach a JUDGE who never can be brib'd.
The unhappy Sufferers were Messs. SAML GRAY, SAML MAVERICK, JAMS CALDWELL, CRISPUS ATTUCKS, PATK CAR
Killed, Six wounded, two of them (CHRISTR MONK JOHN CLARK) Mortally

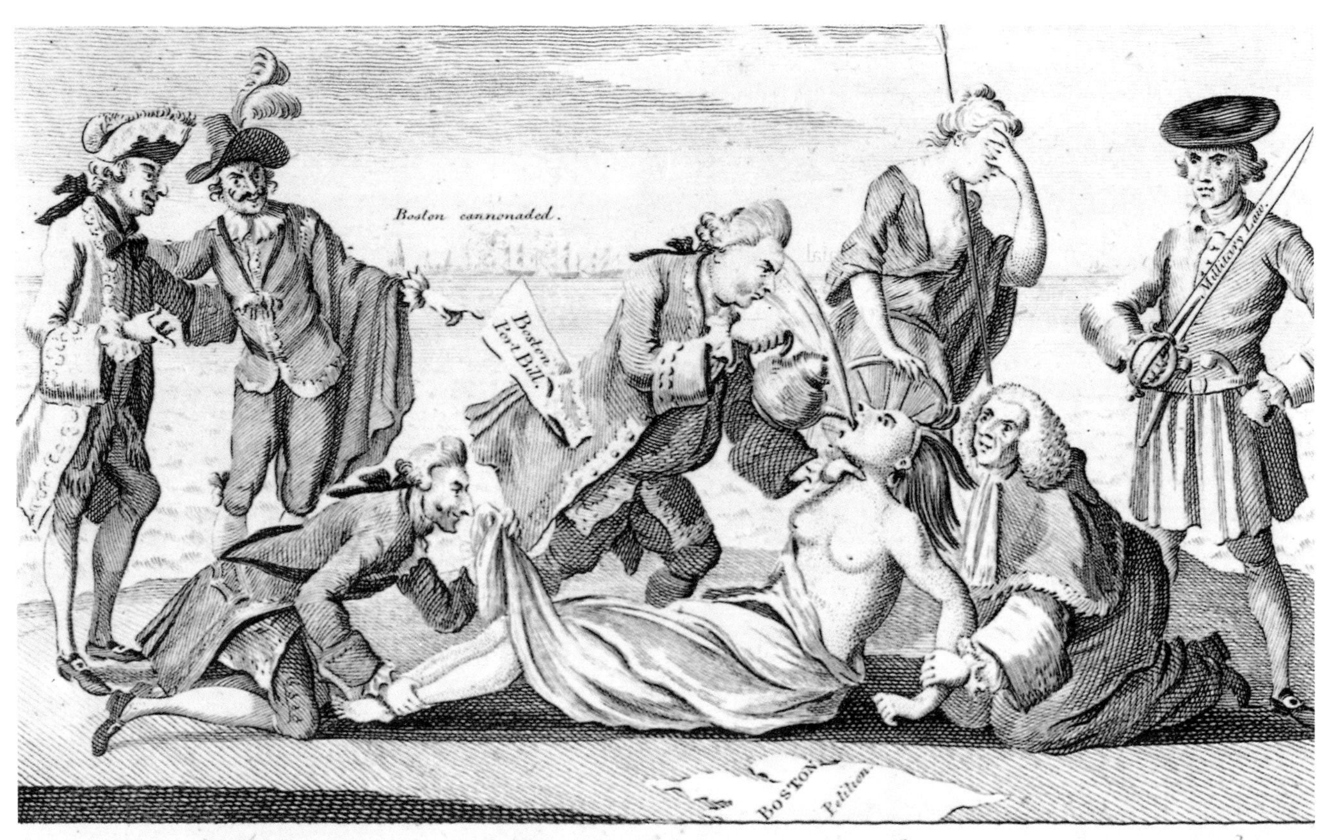

The able Doctor, or America Swallowing the Bitter Draught.

45.

Unknown

The able Doctor, or America Swallowing the Bitter Draught.

London, published in *London Magazine* (April 1774): 184
Line etching
Laid paper, watermark of partial fleur-de-lis

Overall size: 13.2 x 21.1 cm
Platemark: 11.1 x 18.4 cm
Image: 9.3 x 16.2 cm.

76.40

Like others of George III's ministers, Charles Townshend (1725-1767) was eager to rein in the strong-willed Americans and to squelch their prolonged euphoria over the defeat of the Stamp Act of 1765-66. In May of 1767, a proposed bill was brought before Parliament that would tax lead, printers' ink, and tea. Revenues collected in America were to pay the salaries and costs of keeping colonial governors and other officials. Ostensibly, such a tax was for Americans own benefit, although few colonists could forget that those officials being funded by this tax were royal appointees and that this was still a tax levied without due colonial representation in Parliament.

By any name the Townshend Acts of 1767 were not acceptable to Americans. The tax on tea became a rallying issue, and from New England to Edenton in North Carolina, patriots were refusing to buy the taxed goods. This resulted in English merchants losing in orders in one year almost three-quarters of a million pounds. With the boycott, Parliament repealed all the taxes except that on tea, which amounted to only three cents per pound of dry tea. Yet it was the tax's principle to which Americans objected, and the tea tax became the new symbol of England's refusal to grant colonists the basic rights of free Englishmen.

Some Britons abhorred this limited view of freedom. *The able Doctor, or America Swallowing the Bitter Draught* first appeared in *London Magazine* for April 1774. It shows America, naked to the waist, being held down at the ankles by William Murray, first earl of Mansfield, who seizes the opportunity to lift the victim's skirt. Lord Bute holds down her arms, while Lord North pours tea down her throat. Liberty hides her eyes in shame; France and Spain stand watching. Boston, under siege, is illustrated behind them, and John Montague, fourth earl of Sandwich, holds the threat of military law.

In May of 1775, a copy of the print was published in Dublin in *Hibernian Magazine.* In June of the same year, Paul Revere engraved a nearly identical copy of the image for the new *Royal American Magazine*, published in Boston. Revere's version differed only in his engraving of the word "TEA" on the pot.

Reference: Brigham, *Paul Revere's Engravings*, 85-86.

British Museum, *Satires*, 5226

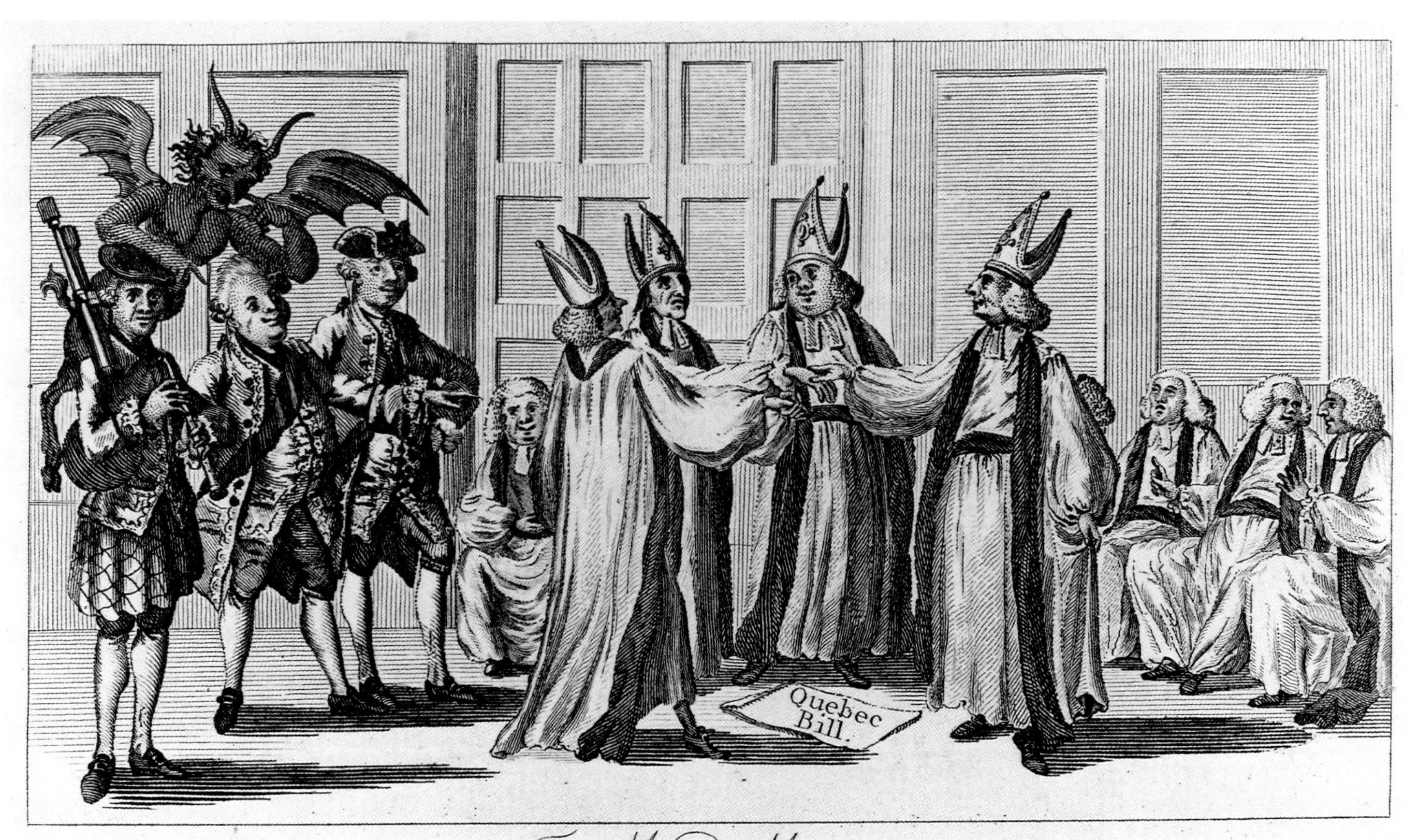

The Mitred Minuet.

46.

Unknown

The Mitred Minuet

London, May 1, 1774
Published in *London Magazine*
Line etching
Laid paper

Overall size: 13.3 x 21.3 cm
Platemark: 11.1 x 17.5 cm
Image: 9.2 x 16.2 cm

76.41

Five intolerable acts were passed by the British Parliament in the spring of 1774. The initial four Coercive Acts included three directed against Massachusetts—the Boston Port Bill, the Massachusetts Government Act, and the Administration of Justice Act—as well as the Quartering Act. Shortly after these came the Quebec Act. On the surface the Quebec Act was intended not to take away but to restore certain freedoms in British North America, in this case, the rights of Frenchmen in Quebec to practice Catholicism and the restoration of their legal and political institutions. What was supposed to be a decision based upon enlightenment backfired. Non-popery advocates in both England and the American colonies mounted a heated campaign.

William Pitt, first earl of Chatham, denounced the proposed bill on June 18, 1774. *The Mitred Minuet* was published a month earlier and featured four Catholic bishops, with hands cross-linked, dancing around a copy of the bill, while an audience of bishops without miters watches enthusiastically. Directing the dance are Lord Bute in his highland dress and Lord North, who points towards the participants. From above and behind the devil singles out North. Protestations aside, the bill was passed into law on June 22, 1774. The August issue of *Hibernian Magazine* featured *Mitred Minuet,* and in October 1774, colonial readers of *Royal American Magazine* (Boston) found in it Paul Revere's pirated version of the same subject.

British Museum, *Satires,* 5228

47.

Attributed to Philip Dawe
(ac. 1750-1785), engraver
Robert Sayer (b. 1725,
ac. 1751-d. 1794) and
John Bennett (ac. 1770-1784,
d. 1787), publishers

The PATRIOTICK BARBER of NEW YORK, or the CAPTAIN in the SUDS.

London, February 14, 1775
Mezzotint with minimal
burin work
Laid paper, watermark of "P.
TOMAS FIN DANGOUMOIS"

Overall size: 35.7 x 25.7 cm
Platemark: 35.4 x 25.3 cm
Image: 32.8 x 25.0 cm

57.1258.1

Determined to ignore resolutions of non-importation, British merchants with official encouragement sent ships loaded with tea into the port of Boston. Americans—merchants and consumers alike—were equally resolute. On December 16, 1773, a party of citizens seized a cargo of tea and threw it into Boston Harbor. As penalty, the British set up a naval blockade from Nahant Point to Alderton Point, making certain that vessels neither took on goods nor brought goods into the city. The blockade of Boston served more to strengthen the collective resolve of the colonists than to deny them provisions. Individuals and groups at some distance not only came to the aid of their compatriots but also waged their own acts of resistance. In one case, Jacob Vredenburgh, a New York barber, refused to finish shaving a customer when he learned that the man was actually the captain of a British transport.

In both England and America, barbershops were gathering places where gossip and politics shaped the topics for discussion. There is no mistaking barber Vredenburgh's political position in this image. Broadsides and portraits of William Pitt and Charles Pratt, Lord Camden (1714-1794), line the wall. Wig boxes of his customers fill the shelves and are piled on the floor, although only politically astute insiders would have recognized that these names represent members of the secretive Sons of Liberty.

Philip Dawe, to whose hand this engraving has been attributed, worked for the London printseller and publisher Robert Sayer. How the identities of New York patriots came to Dawe's attention is not known. It can certainly be assumed, however, that Sayer and his partner John Bennett were eager to ship any number of copies to markets abroad, as their catalogue for 1775 states.

Reference: Halsey, *Boston Port Bill*, 128-29, 142-54, 162-76, 212-22.

British Museum, *Satires*, 5284; Stokes and Haskell 1774—B-139

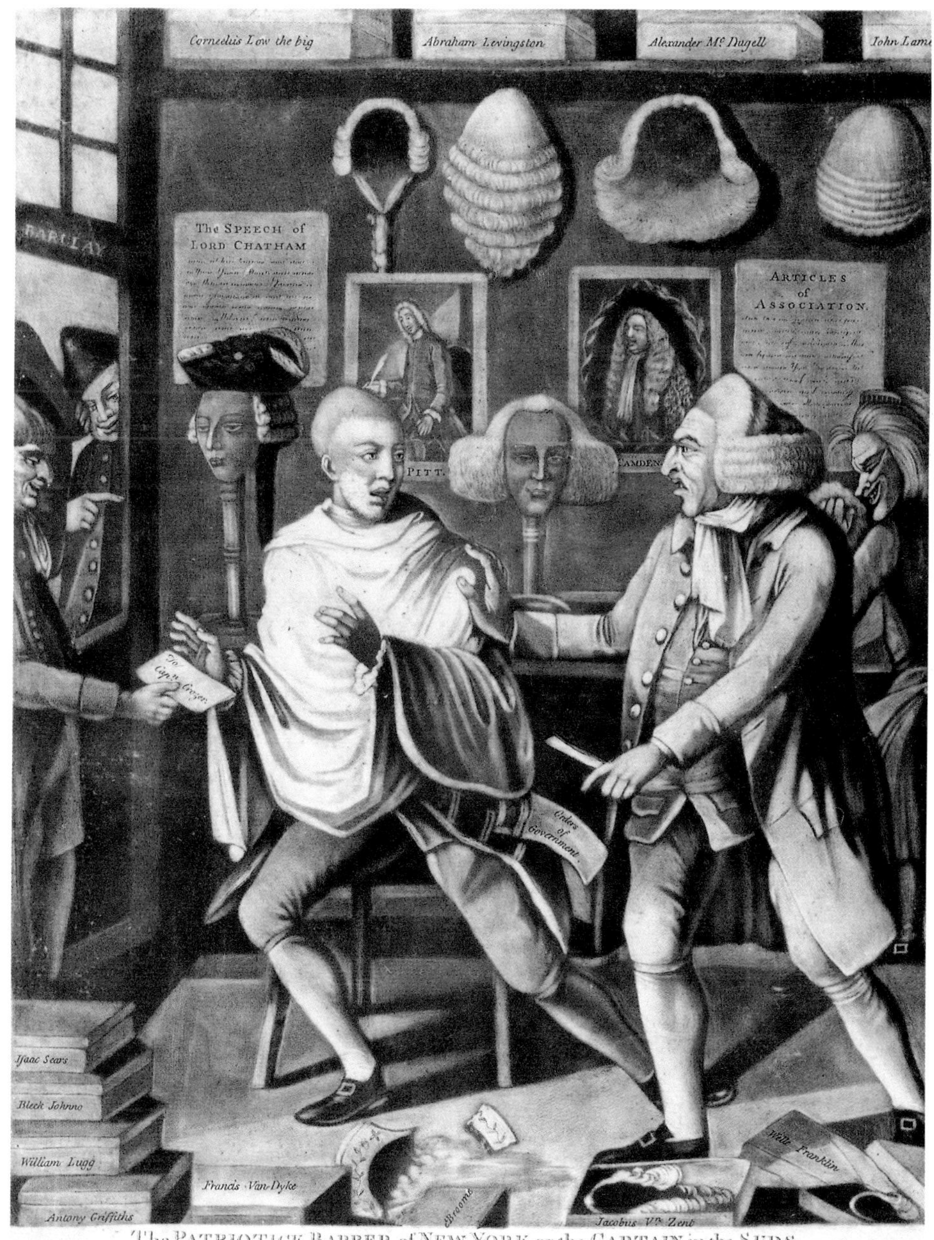

Plate III.

The PATRIOTICK BARBER of NEW YORK, or the CAPTAIN in the SUDS.

Then Patriot grand, maintain thy Stand,
And whilst thou sav'st America's Land,
Preserve the Golden Rule;

Forbid the Captains there to roam,
Half shave them first, then send 'em home,
Objects of ridicule.

London Printed for R. Sayer & J. Bennett No. 53 Fleet Street as the Act directs 14 Feb. 1775.

48.

Robert Sayer (b. 1725,
ac. 1751-d. 1794)
and John Bennett
(ac. 1770-1784,
d. 1787), publishers

A SOCIETY of PATRIOTIC LADIES, AT EDENTON in NORTH CAROLINA.

London, March 25, 1775
Mezzotint with minimal burin work
Laid paper, watermark of bend and lily

Overall size: 37.0 x 25.3 cm
Platemark: 35.4 x 25.3 cm
Image: 32.7 x 25.3 cm

57.1255

A group of fifty-one ladies in Edenton, recognizing that it was their patriotic duty to forgo any drinking of tea, decided to sign a petition pledging they would neither drink the brew nor wear dresses made of English fabrics. They were not alone in their sacrifice. On Tuesday, February 28, 1775, the Englishman Nicholas Cresswell on a trip to America wrote in his journal, "This is the last day Tea is allowed to be drank on the Continent by an act of Congress. The Ladies seem sad about it." Yet another observer noted that ladies of her acquaintance had burnt their stores of tea in a solemn ritual, but they had delayed until the sacrifice was "not very considerable, as I do not think any one offered above a quarter of a pound."

The women gathered in Edenton appear to be from different economic levels, and the engraver indulged in several amusing juxtapositions to heighten the humor of the situation. One dandy is more intent on an elegantly dressed young woman than the matron with gavel in hand would like. Behind them a woman guzzles the last flavorful drops as her scowling associate grabs for the bowl. There seems to be some urgency about the activity. In plain view through the door are representatives of the Committee of Correspondence, who were dispatched to collect the remaining tea.

References: Journal of Nicholas Cresswell, 1774-1777 (New York: Lincoln Macveagh, Dial Press, 1924), 58; Janet Schaw, *Journal of a Lady of Quality, Being a Narrative of a Journey from Scotland to the West Indies, North Carolina, and Portugal in the Years 1774 to 1776*, ed. Evangeline Walker Andrews and Charles McLean Andrews (New Haven: Yale University Press, 1923), 149, 155-56, 192-93; Halsey, *Boston Port Bill*, 311-22.

British Museum, *Satires*, listed following 5284

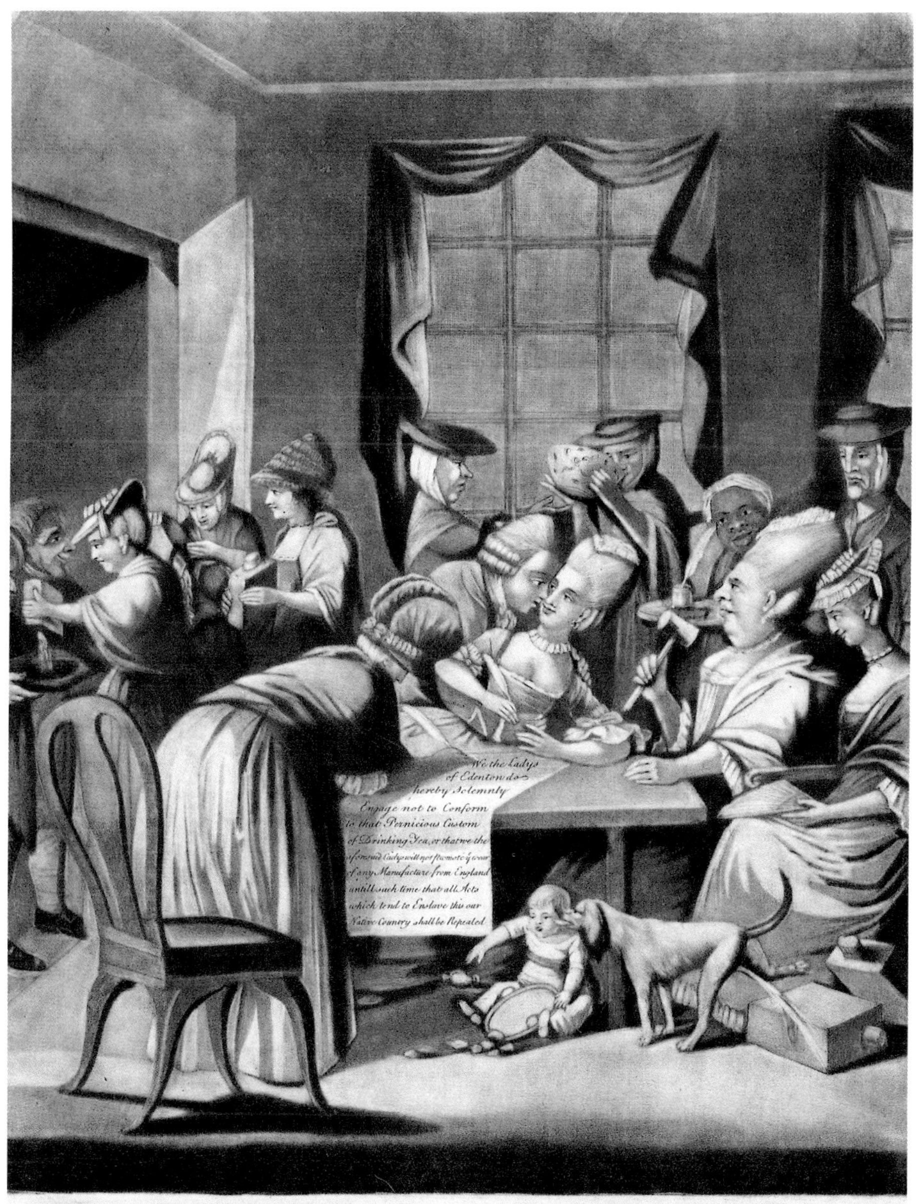

Plate V.

A SOCIETY of PATRIOTIC LADIES,
AT
EDENTON in NORTH CAROLINA.

London, Printed for R. Sayer, & J. Bennett, No 53 in Fleet Street, as the Act directs 25 March 1775.

377

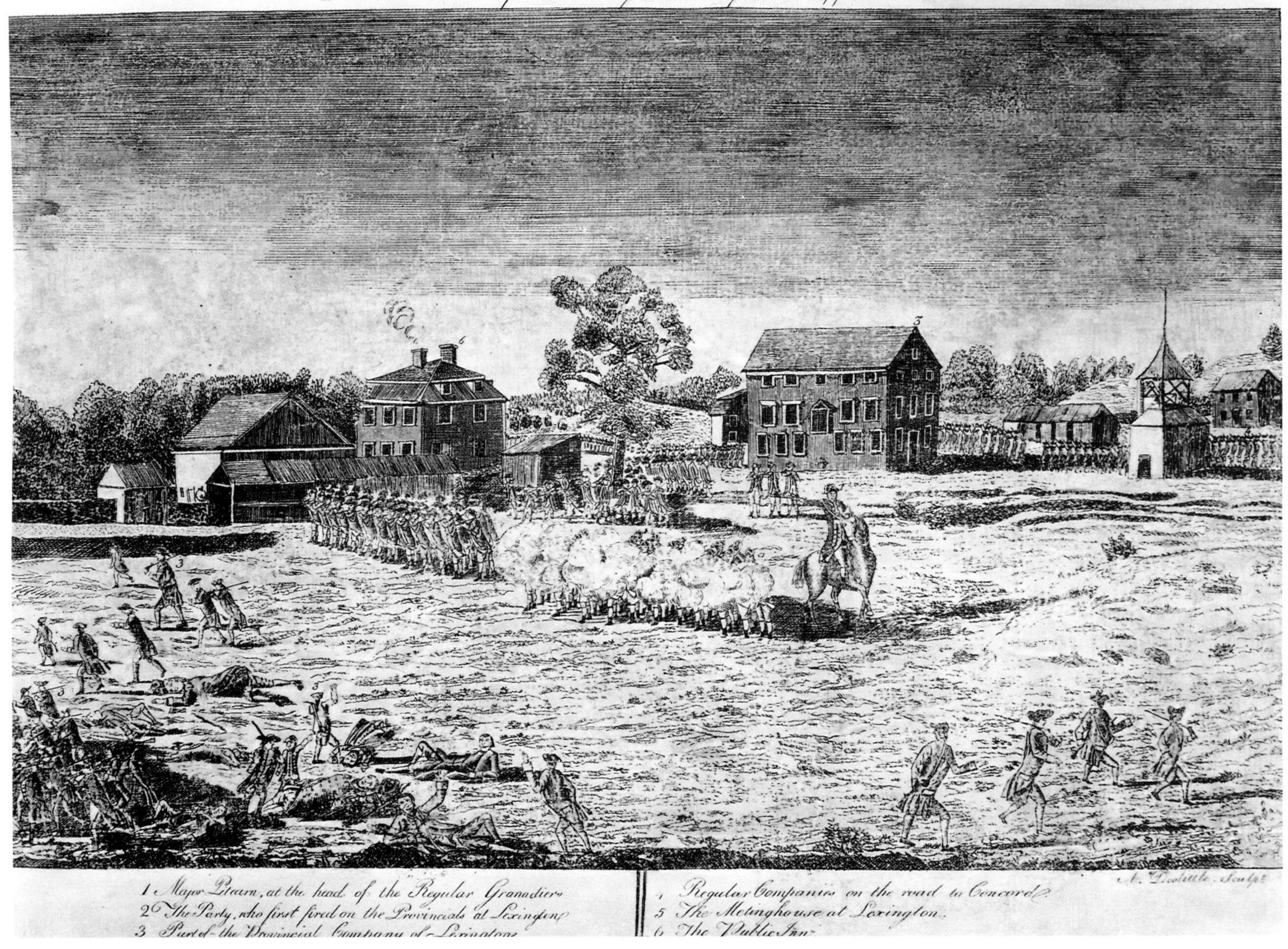
The Battle of Lexington, April 19th 1775. Plate I.
1 Major Pitcairn, at the head of the Regular Granadiers
2 The Party, who first fired on the Provincials at Lexington
3 Part of the Provincial Company of Lexington
4 Regular Companies on the road to Concord
5 The Metinghouse at Lexington
6 The Public Inn
A. Doolittle Sculpt.

49.

Amos Doolittle
(1754-1832), artist and engraver

The Battle of Lexington, April 19th. 1775. Plate 1

New Haven, Connecticut, 1775
Line etching with some burin work, watercolors
Laid paper

Overall size: 34.7 x 47.3 cm
Platemark: (trimmed) x 47.3 cm
Image: 29.7 x 44.9 cm

65.23

For all the injuries and indignities that time has brought to them, no images remain more prized in collections of eighteenth-century American historical prints than any or all of the four views engraved by Amos Doolittle following the clash of colonial militia and British regulars in the fields of Lexington and Concord, Massachusetts.

Doolittle was an eyewitness to the conflicts, and it is reported that he returned to the fields a few days later in the company of another colonial soldier, Ralph Earl (1751-1801), to reconstruct visually the recent events. Earl's paintings of the scenes have since been lost. In the relatively few complete sets and scattered individual plates from Doolittle's engravings of the Battles of Lexington and Concord, with their amateurishly executed and etched details and thick gouache colors, the intensity of that early moment in America's war for independence still lives.

In a time before cameras and television screens, before daily newspapers with front-page pictures, Doolittle and other eighteenth-century recorders of war scenes followed the convention of compressing into one image events that spanned several hours. Historians continue to search these images and written accounts from the period to better understand what really did transpire at Lexington and Concord.

Reference: Ian M. G. Quimby, "The Doolittle Engravings of the Battle of Lexington and Concord," in *Winterthur Portfolio* 4, 83-108.

Stokes and Haskell 1775-C-2; Stauffer 256

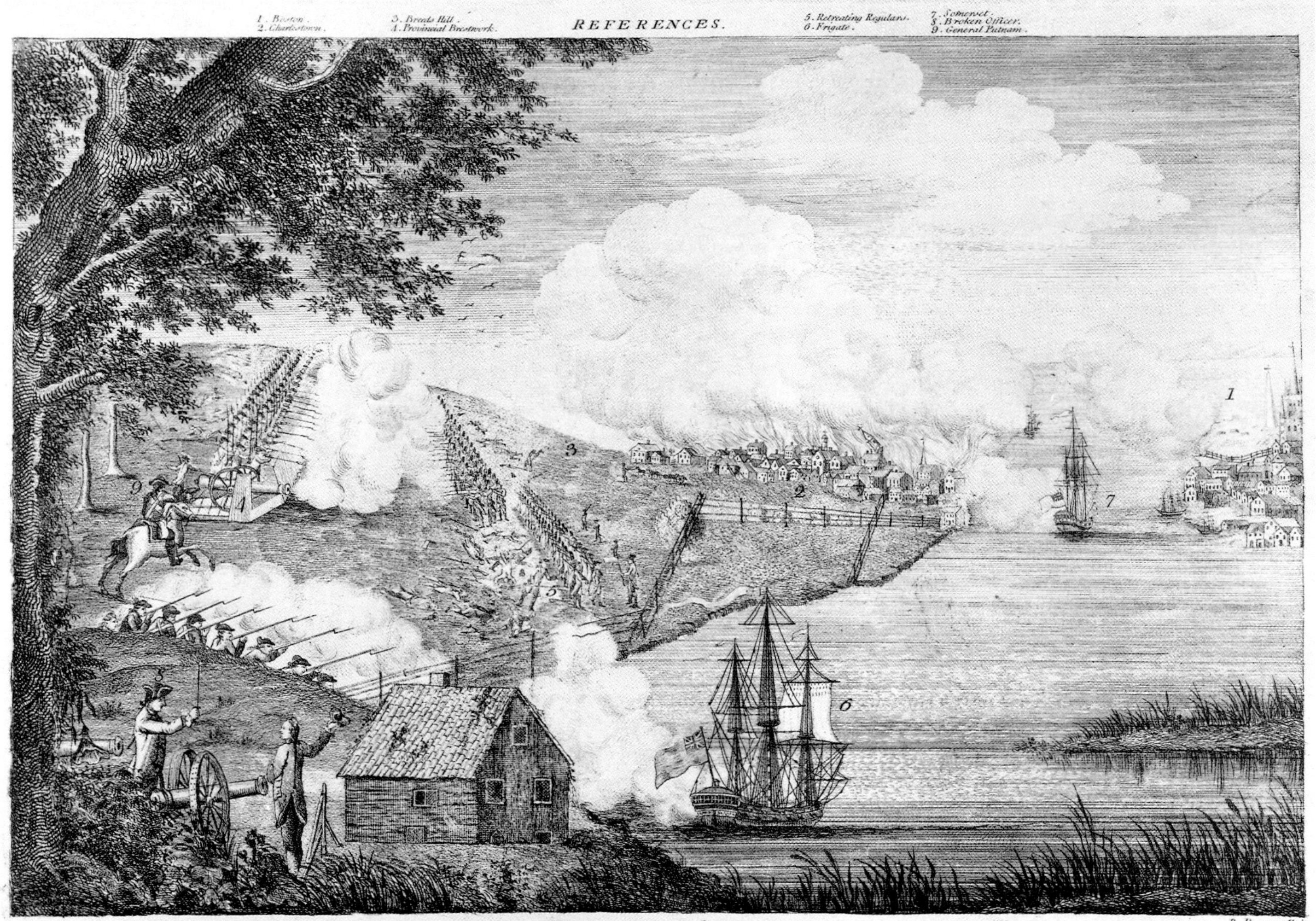
1. Boston.
2. Charlestown.
3. Breds Hill.
4. Provincial Brestwork.
REFERENCES.
5. Retreating Regulars.
6. Frigate.
7. Somerset.
8. Broken Officer.
9. General Putnam.
1
2
3
5
6
7
9
B. Romans Fecit.
AN EXACT VIEW OF THE LATE BATTLE AT CHARLESTOWN. JUNE 17TH 1775.
In which an advanced Party of about 700 Provincials, stood an Attack made by 11 Regiments & a Train of Artillery, & after an Engagement of 2 Hours Retreated to their Main Body at Cambridge. Leaving Eleven Hundred of the Regulars Killed and Wounded upon the Field.
London. Printed for Messrs. Wallis & Stonehouse, No. 16, Ludgate Street, as the Act directs. June A.

50.

Bernard Romans (b. ca. 1720, ac. in America from 1755, d. 1784), artist and engraver
Messrs. Wallis and Stonehouse, publishers

AN EXACT VIEW OF THE LATE BATTLE AT CHARLESTOWN, JUNE 17th 1775.

London, June 4, 1776
Line etching with burin work
Laid paper, watermark of a lily-crowned shield over "L V G"

Overall size: 32.6 x 44.5 cm
Platemark: 30.2 x 42.0 cm
Image: 27.5 x 40.0 cm

59.1550

Most news from the battlefields of the American war for independence reached the public through eyewitness accounts printed in local newspapers. These were then copied by other publishers in an ever widening circle. Pictures of the war's events were a rarity, and those that were prepared as prints frequently appeared long after the fact. When an image was at last available, it was often full of inaccuracies—deliberate or unintentional—as several hands translated and edited it from rough drawing to finished engraving.

Most armies took surveyors and topographical artists with them. Bernard Romans was trained in England as a mapmaker, engineer, surveyor, engraver, and botanist. Skilled as an observer and draftsman, Romans was with the colonial troops on Breed's Hill on June 17, 1775. Because he was present at the battle at Charlestown, his original publication bore an unusual level of truth. Romans' engraving was published in September, as was a smaller but similar version offered by Robert Aitken (1734-1802) for the September issue of *Pennsylvania Magazine; or American Monthly Museum*. Robert Sause advertised in New York that a view of the battle at Charlestown could be purchased either "elegantly colored" for eight shillings or in a frame and glazed for twenty shillings. What seems to be a third version of Romans' view was published in London in June of the following year. This version, undoubtedly copied from one of Romans' first editions, seems to reproduce the original in both its execution and its naivete.

References: Advertisement of Nicholas Brooks in the *Pennsylvania Gazette*, November 1, 1775, notes, "Likewise to be had at the above Place, a large exact View of the late Battle at Charlestown, elegantly coloured at 7 s. 6d. or put in a double carved and gilt Frame, 20 by 16 inches with Crown Glass at 18s. 6d.," as quoted in Prime, *Arts and Crafts in Philadelphia, 1721-1785*, 16-17; Notices to the public in the *Pennsylvania Gazette*, September 30, 1775, as quoted in Prime, *Arts and Crafts in Philadelphia, 1721-1785*, 34-35; Advertisement of Richard Sause in the *New York Gazette and Weekly Merchandizer*, January 15, 1776; Shadwell, *American Printmaking*, nos. 54, 55.

51.

Unknown

[Regarding the state of the English Nation, in the Year 1778]

Holland, 1780
Etching with burin work
Laid paper

Overall size: 22.3 x 30.4 cm
Platemark: 19.5 x 26.0 cm
Image: 17.2 x 25.7 cm

57.1263

France and Spain, usually personified as elegant courtiers and often accompanied by Holland in the dress of a burgher, were frequent characters in satirical tableaux that illustrated England's confrontations with America. The nature of their presence was never more succinctly delineated than in *A Picturesque View of the State of the Nation for February 1778*, which first appeared in *Westminster Magazine* for February 1778. By the time of the publication of this image of an American Indian dehorning the British cow as the royal lion sleeps, British military and naval forces in the colonies were suffering severe losses. England's continental neighbors were taking advantage of the situation. France and Spain joined to support the American army with equipment and technical assistance. Holland seized the time to build her trade with the East Indies.

The original English design of this print was borrowed by many. This copy, made in Holland in 1780, originally carried the title "Wegens de Staat der Englische Natie, in't Jaar 1778." In its uncropped state, it included an explanatory text set in type. This particular etching is nearly twice the size of that first image published in *Westminster Magazine*. A second version in the Winterthur collection, in reverse and smaller, was also published in 1780 and carries the French title "Mal Lui Veut Nal Lui Torne Dit Le Bon Homme Richard."

Other engravings after this subject were prepared for transfer onto mugs and pitchers. Referred to as the "Cow Caricature," it is judged to have been as widely reproduced as any of the Revolutionary War satires (see cat. no. 86).

References: Joan D. Dolmetsch, *Rebellion and Reconciliation: Satirical Prints on the Revolution at Williamsburg* (Williamsburg: Colonial Williamsburg Foundation, 1976), 94-95; Willard E. Keys, "The Cow and the Sleeping Lion," *Antiques* 39, no. 1 (January 1941): 25-27.

British Museum, *Satires*, 5726A

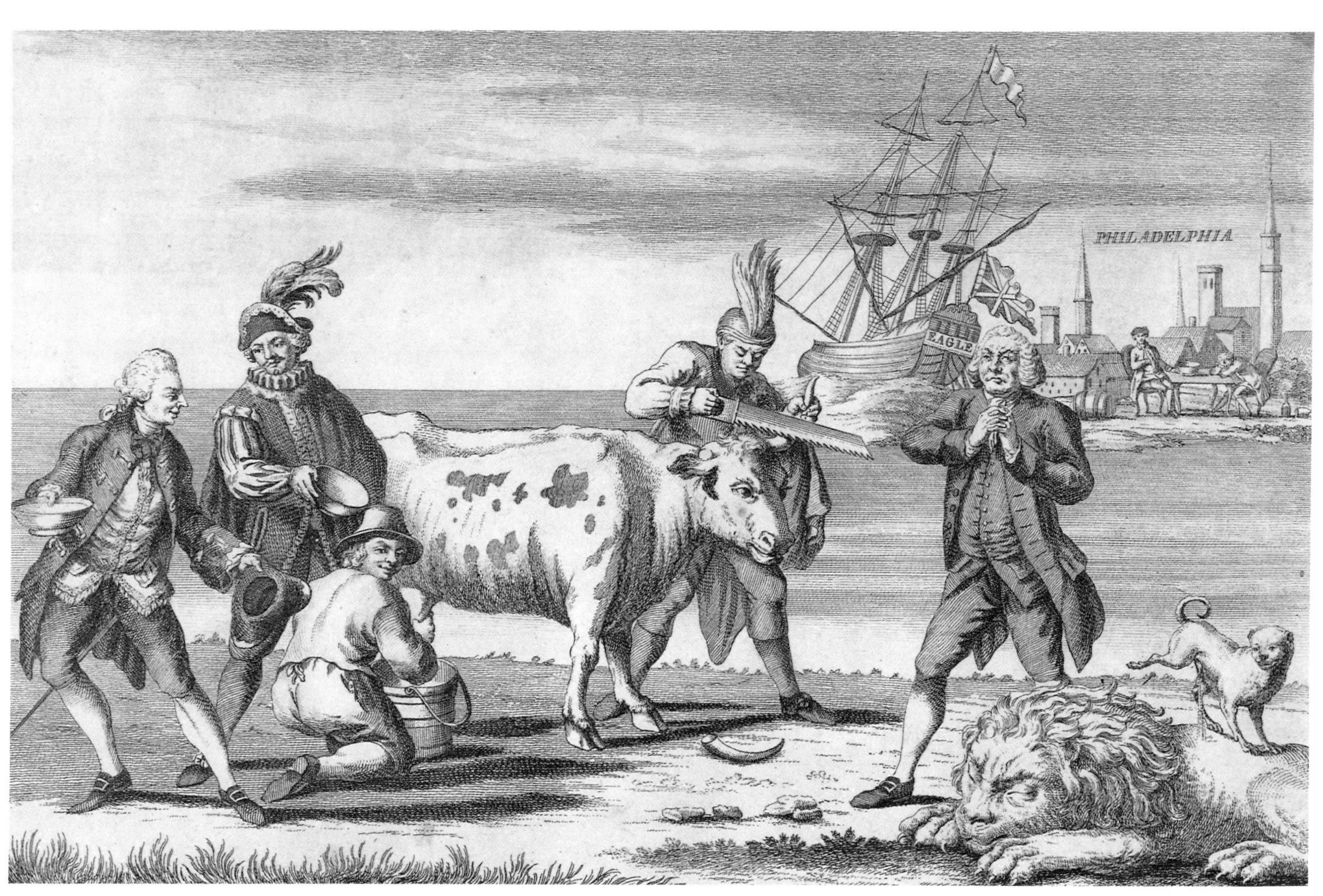
PHILADELPHIA
EAGLE

52.

Unknown

THE ALLIED DESPOTS. OR THE FRIENDSHIP of BRITAIN for AMERICA.

Philadelphia, Pennsylvania,
February 20, 1794
Line etching
Laid paper

Overall size: 26.3 x 42.5 cm
Platemark: 20.6 x 29.8 cm
Image: 17.1 x 28.2 cm

62.189

On the surface, satire and allegory are most successful when the viewer can instantly recognize and understand the messages conveyed through a sort of pictorial shorthand. Both intend to raise an emotional response, but the enjoyment of allegorical subjects can be a more studied experience. In satire, the message must be quickly understood if the work's humor—its major element—is to be appreciated. To the contemporary observer accustomed to the quick one-liners of today's political cartoonist and the exaggerated but highly recognizable features of often photographed subjects, it may take a bit of searching to see any humor in many eighteenth-century offerings.

The bite of satire and its humor then depended less on caricature or distortion of an individual's features and more on grotesque detail and shocking contrasts in behavior. Like many of today's most successful editorial cartoons, eighteenth-century satires utilized double entendres. Most colonial Americans who had seen a portrait of George III would recognize him, with all his royal trappings, in *The Allied Despots.* Fewer would have recognized Mustapha IV (1779-1808) as the sultan of Turkey, but with George's gesture to a British man whipping another in chains and to a few turbaned ruffians beating men and women in bondage, the comparison of the two rulers is clear. Suggesting that history repeats itself, another scene in the left distance illustrates savage Indians flinging babies into the woods while scalping the parents.

Published in Philadelphia at a time when American sailors were being captured and imprisoned for refusing to serve in the king's navy, this satire focused on an issue that ultimately led to the War of 1812. Few American businessmen, such as Nicholas Cruger or John Murray of New York and Thomas Dobson of Philadelphia, or families of seamen would disagree with "Valentine Verax's" assessment of the situation.

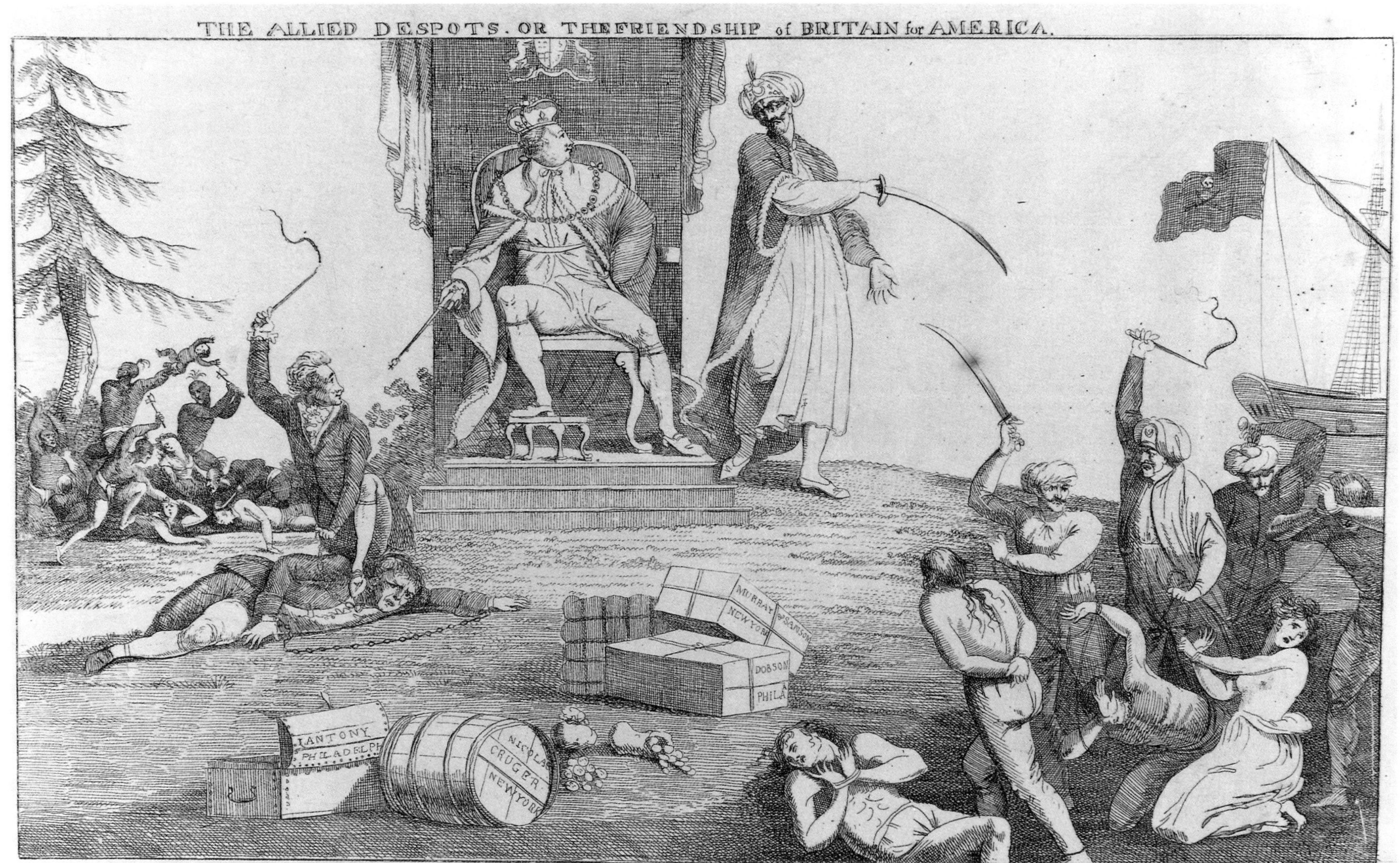
THE ALLIED DESPOTS. OR THE FRIENDSHIP of BRITAIN for AMERICA.
MURRAY & SAMSON NEW YORK
DOBSON PHILA
IANTONY PHILADELPH
NICOLA CRUGER NEW YORK
Valentine Verax fecit Philadelphia Feb.y 20 1794
The Imperial George instructeth his good Ally & Cousin Mustapha, in the misteries of regal policy—Sheweth him as a proof of their efficacy, how Billy manageth John Bull—Relateth with Delight the depredations which his allies the Savages by his instigation make on the sons of Liberty—Exorteth him to annoy them by Sea, as implacably, as the Savages do by land—Which Mustapha performeth—Then sheweth his Royal preceptor how prompt a pupil he is.

53.

Anthony van Dyke (1599-1641), artist
Richard Earlom (1743-1822), delineator
John Miller (ac. 1760-?), engraver
John Boydell (1719-1804), publisher

The CONTINENCE of SCIPIO

London, February 1, 1766
Line etching with burin work
Laid paper, watermark of a dovecote and a partial countermark of "DUPUY FIN AUVERGNE 1742"

Overall size: 46.9 x 62.5 cm
Platemark: (trimmed) x 60.4 cm
Image: 40.5 x 57.7 cm

60.729 a

John Boydell's greatest contribution to his country's printmaking was his entrepreneurial achievement in bringing the work of English engravers out from the shadow of continental productions. He openly sought work from the best line engravers in London, and he bought paintings with themes from history and literature from leading artists as subjects for the engravers' burins.

Because Boydell carefully supervised his publications, thus assuring that they met the highest standards, the popularity of his offerings made him a fortune and brought fine examples of art to those far from London. Boydell hired Richard Earlom, an exceptional engraver in both mezzotint and line, to copy Anthony van Dyke's interpretation of *The Continence of Scipio* (1620-21). Long a favorite subject for artists, this scene recalls the emotional moment when the Roman general Scipio refuses his own passions to hold true to his word. According to Dr. Alexander Hamilton (1712-1756), who saw a copy of Nicholas Poussin's painting of the subject in John Smibert's Boston studio, Scipio the Younger (185-129 B.C.) "delivers the lady to the Prince to whom she had been betrothed.…But what I admired most is an image of the phantom of chastity behind the solium upon which Scipio sits, standing on tip-toe to crown him."

Robert Kennedy of Philadelphia may have been referring to this very print in his advertisement in the *Pennsylvania Chronicle* for December 12, 1768, when he offered prints "glazed in the present English taste… amongst which are scriptural, historical… and miscellaneous designs." This impression came into the Winterthur collection, mounted on canvas stretched over wood strainers, with the trade card of Robert Kennedy affixed directly to the canvas (see cat. no. 54).

References: Calloway, *English Prints for the Collector*, 81-82; Oliver Millar, *Van Dyck in England* (London: National Portrait Gallery, 1982), 43-44; Alexander Hamilton, *Gentleman's Progress: the Itinerarium of Dr. Alexander Hamilton 1744*, ed. Carl Bridenbaugh (Chapel Hill: University of North Carolina Press for the Institute of Early American History and Culture Press, 1948), 114, 237 n. 262; Advertisement of Robert and Thomas Kennedy, as quoted in Prime, *Arts and Crafts of Philadelphia, 1721-1785*, 33.

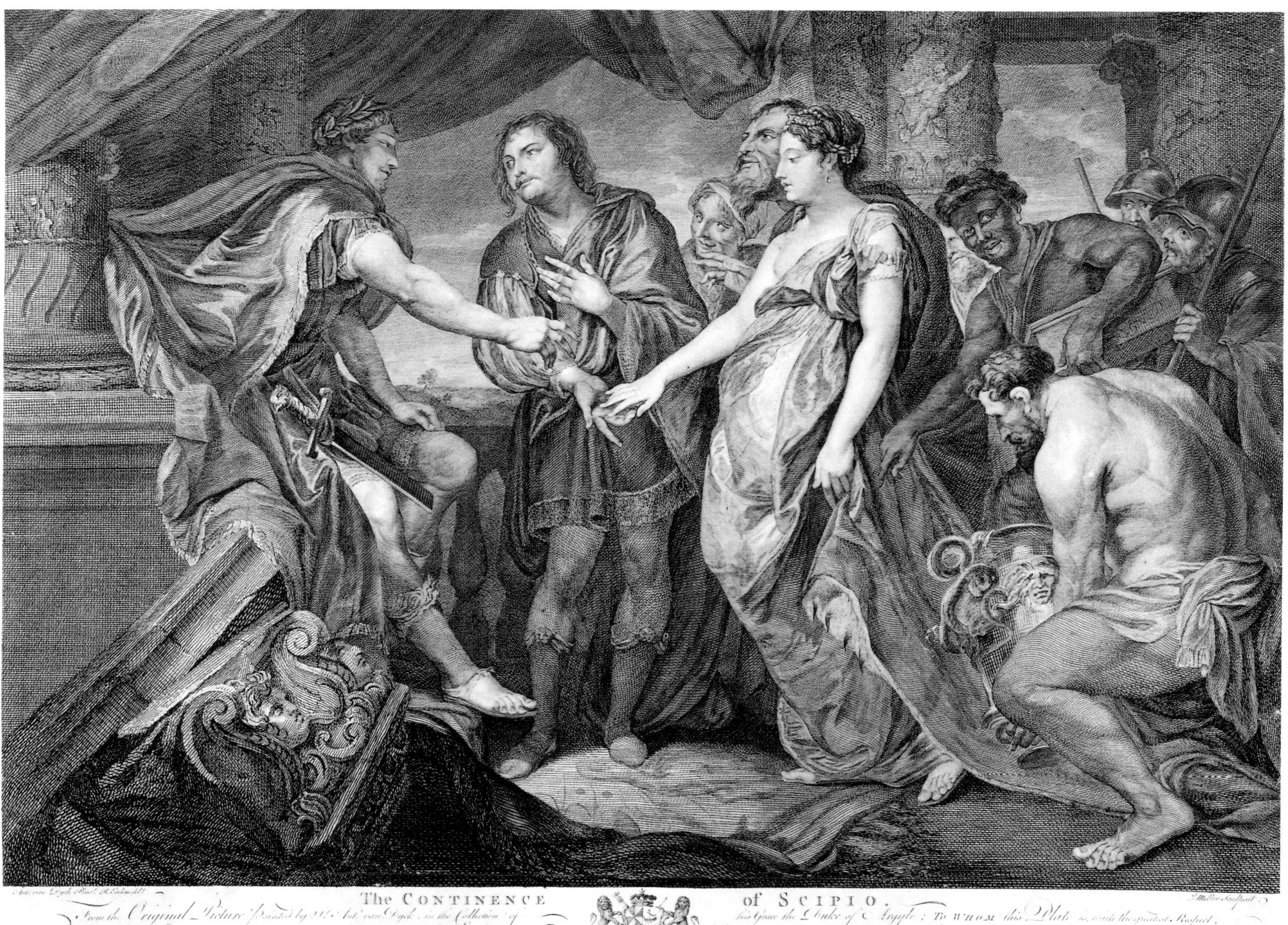
Ant. van Dyck Pinx. R. Eadom delt.
The CONTINENCE of SCIPIO.
J. Miller Sculpsit.
From the Original Picture painted by Sr. Ant. van Dyck, in the Collection of his Grace the Duke of Argyle; To WHOM this Plate is, with the greatest Respect, most humbly Dedicated, By his Grace's most Obliged and most Obedient humble Servant,
No. 28.
Published according to Act of Parliament Feb. 1st 1766.
By J. BOYDELL Engraver, in Cheapside LONDON.
J. BOYDELL

54.

James Smither (d. 1797), engraver

Trade card for Robert Kennedy at WESTHEAD in Second Street below Walnut Street—PHILADA.

Philadelphia, Pennsylvania, ca.1768
Line engraving
Laid paper

Overall size: 26.4 x 21.3 cm
Platemark: 25.3 x 18.4 cm
Image: 24.9 x 18.4 cm

60.729 c

Trade cards, billheads, labels, handbills and advertising broadsides, and bookplates, as well as official jobs such as making dies and seals, or plates for currency, continued to occupy the larger part of the American engraver's trade into the last years of the eighteenth century. For those who aspired to follow in the paths of leading London engravers, or for the English-trained engravers who came to America, the realities of commerce and the necessities of earning a living often dictated the kind of work that was held in dismal contrast to the great pictorial essays being produced in European capitals.

Some, such as James Smither, who came to Philadelphia from England, seem to rise above the pedestrian and bring to ordinary jobs an elegance and beauty that carried an everyday assignment into the extraordinary. Advertising in the *Pennsylvania Journal* of 1768, Smither executed two grand trade cards: one for Benjamin Randolph, a leading cabinetmaker in Philadelphia; and this one for Robert Kennedy, who in no uncertain terms promoted his business as catering to those ladies and gentlemen who possessed the most elegant taste.

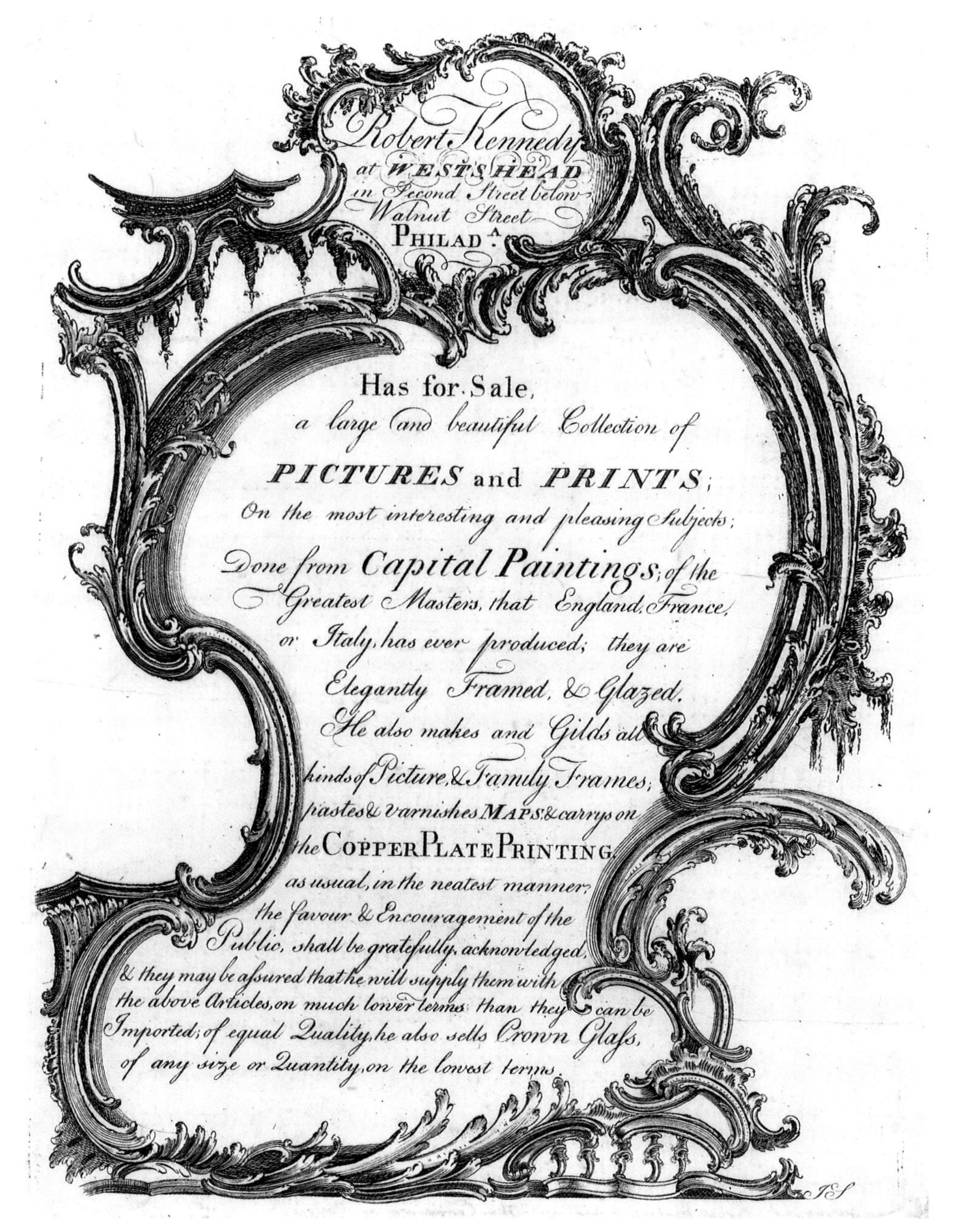
Robert Kennedy
at WEST'S HEAD
in Second Street below
Walnut Street
PHILAD^A.
Has for Sale,
a large and beautiful Collection of
PICTURES and PRINTS;
On the most interesting and pleasing Subjects;
Done from Capital Paintings, of the
Greatest Masters, that England, France,
or Italy, has ever produced; they are
Elegantly Framed, & Glazed.
He also makes and Gilds all
kinds of Picture, & Family Frames;
pastes & varnishes MAPS & carrys on
the COPPER PLATE PRINTING
as usual, in the neatest manner,
the favour & Encouragement of the
Public, shall be gratefully acknowledged,
& they may be assured that he will supply them with
the above Articles, on much lower terms than they can be
Imported; of equal Quality, he also sells Crown Glass,
of any size or Quantity, on the lowest terms.
I.S.

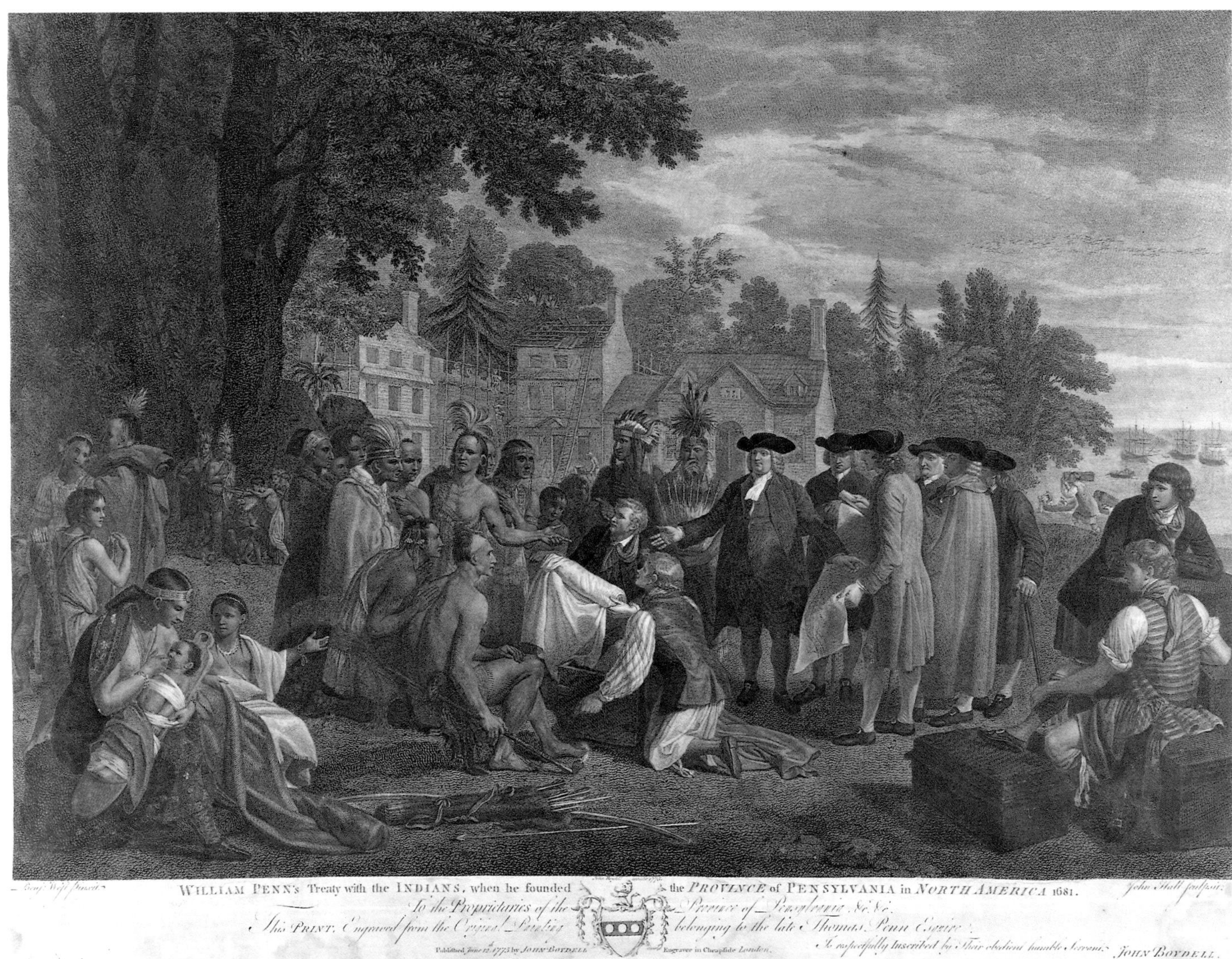
Benj: West pinxit
WILLIAM PENN's Treaty with the INDIANS, when he founded the PROVINCE of PENSYLVANIA in NORTH AMERICA 1681.
John Hall sculpsit.
To the Proprietaries of the Province of Pensylvania &c. &c.
This PRINT, Engraved from the Original Painting belonging to the late Thomas Penn Esquire;
Is respectfully Inscribed by Their obedient humble Servant, JOHN BOYDELL.
Published June 12th 1775 by JOHN BOYDELL Engraver in Cheapside London.

55.

Benjamin West (1738-1820),
artist
John Hall (1739-1797),
engraver
John Boydell (1719-1804),
publisher

WILLIAM PENN'S Treaty with the INDIANS, when he founded the PROVINCE OF PENSYLVANIA in NORTH AMERICA 1681.

London, June 12, 1775
Line etching with minimal burin work, watercolors
Laid paper

Overall size: 55.2 x 67.6 x 3.5 cm
Platemark: 48.0 x 61.7 cm
Image: 42.5 x 58.5 cm
In original frame

58.2878

While ancient struggles between virtue and vice had long been a subject for artists, John Boydell was well aware of new currents in London that chose to celebrate the honor and valor of modern men. Benjamin West, an American artist who had adopted London as his home a decade earlier, was now historical painter to George III and praised for his 1770 painting of the battlefield scene outside Quebec as General James Wolfe lay dying on September 13, 1759.

Recreating history demanded the distant artist's ingenuity as well as his general familiarity with written accounts of the subject. From England in 1772, West painted his interpretation of William Penn's 1683 signing of a treaty with the Indians under a tree in Kensington, near Philadelphia. Boydell advertised to subscribers in January of 1773 that he was engaging John Hall to prepare a copperplate after the painting. This engraving was to be a companion to the artist's *Death of General Wolfe,* which William Woollett had just begun to engrave.

Pulling impressions as orders warranted, Boydell kept both of the copperplates in his inventory until his death. This particular impression retains its original framing and is mounted in an alternate manner to the etching of *Scipio* (cat. no. 53), in that it was put on a support of paper, not canvas, and drawn over strainers. When dry and taut, the print was painted with watercolors.

References: Ellen Start Brinton, "Benjamin West's Painting of Penn's Treaty with the Indians," *Bulletin of Friends' Historical Association* 30 (1941): 147; Snyder, *City of Independence,* 249-54.

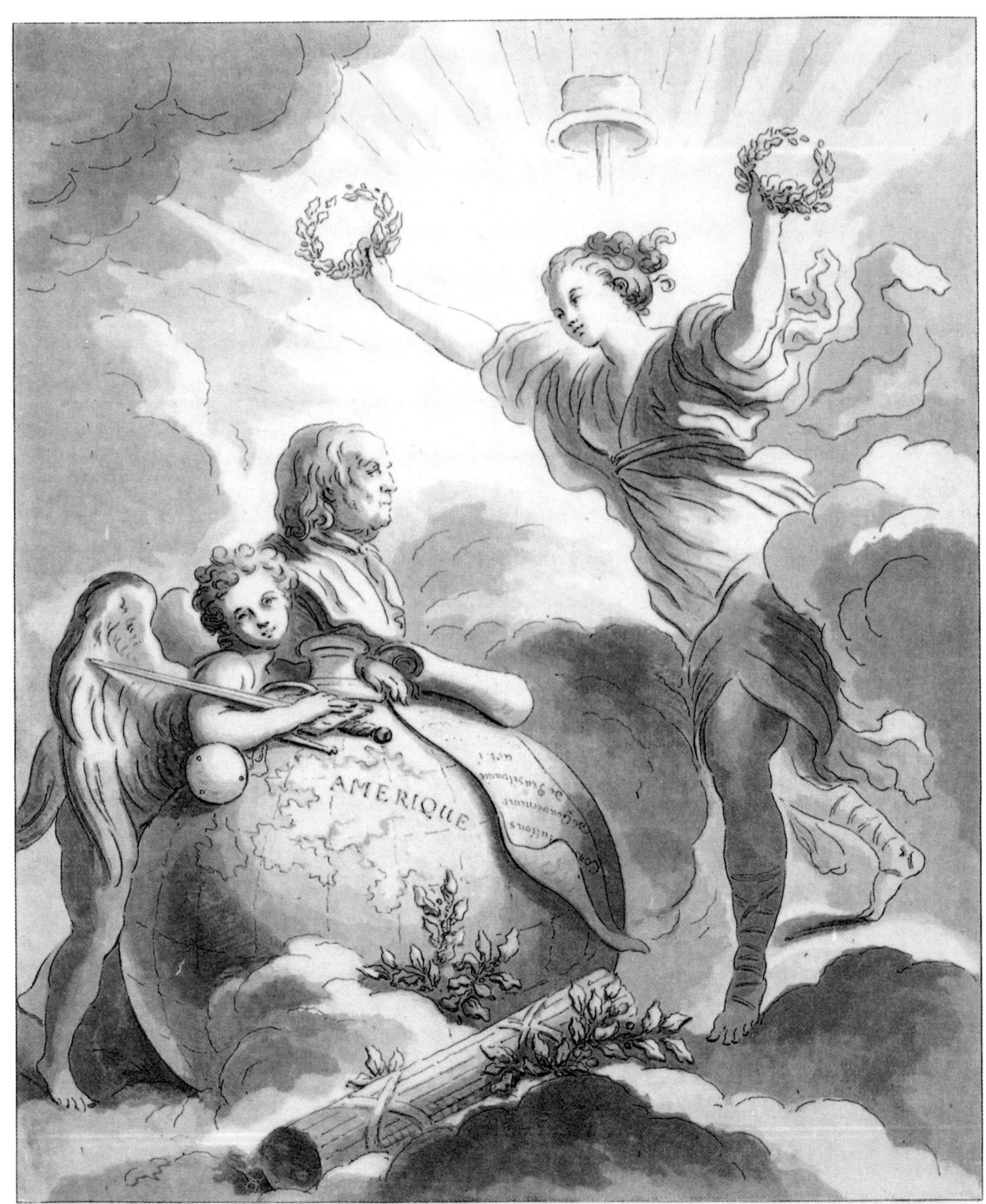

Le Docteur Francklin Couronné par la Liberté .

56.

Jean Claude Richard,
Abbé de Saint Non
(1727-1791), engraver
Jean-Honoré Fragonard
(1732-1806), artist

Le Docteur Francklin Couronné par la Liberté

Paris, spring of 1778
Aquatint, line etching with a minimum of burin work
Laid paper

Overall size: 36.2 x 30.1 cm
Platemark: 24.3 x 20.3 cm
Image: 23.2 x 19.0 cm

77.209

In the cause for American independence a number of the country's best men traveled to Europe to secure aid and support. Benjamin Franklin, with his quick wit, his "Poor Richard" common sense, and his simple dress, was the most respected and admired of all. His easy manner and his passionate belief in Americans' right to those same liberties won for Englishmen with the Magna Charta captured the attention of powerful figures on the Continent, while his scientific genius and deep interest in technical matters won for him the approval of the intellectual community.

Jean Jacques Caffiére (1725-1792) sculpted a bust of Franklin from life in 1777. Early in 1778, Jean-Honoré Fragonard made a sepia wash drawing of the bust, adding to it the figures of Liberty descending from the clouds to crown the bust with two wreaths and a youthful angel to hold the bust steady atop a large globe. Abbé de Saint Non, who had been experimenting with a new method of preparing a copperplate for printing in tones, took Fragonard's sketch to a luncheon attended by Franklin. He planned to use it as a model to demonstrate to the elder statesman an innovative technique of etching. Aquatint was an astonishingly quick process, so much so that a plate could be completed in the short span of a morning or during a luncheon.

Abbé de Saint Non presented Franklin with the first impression and with others for friends and family. He was apologetic, however, believing that he had worked too fast and had caused some areas to be over bitten, particularly that of the liberty cap. It is known that he worked to minimize these faults, and this impression was printed from a subsequent state of the plate.

Reference: Charles Coleman Sellers, *Benjamin Franklin in Portraiture* (New Haven: Yale University Press, 1962), 284-86, 197-98, pl. 17.

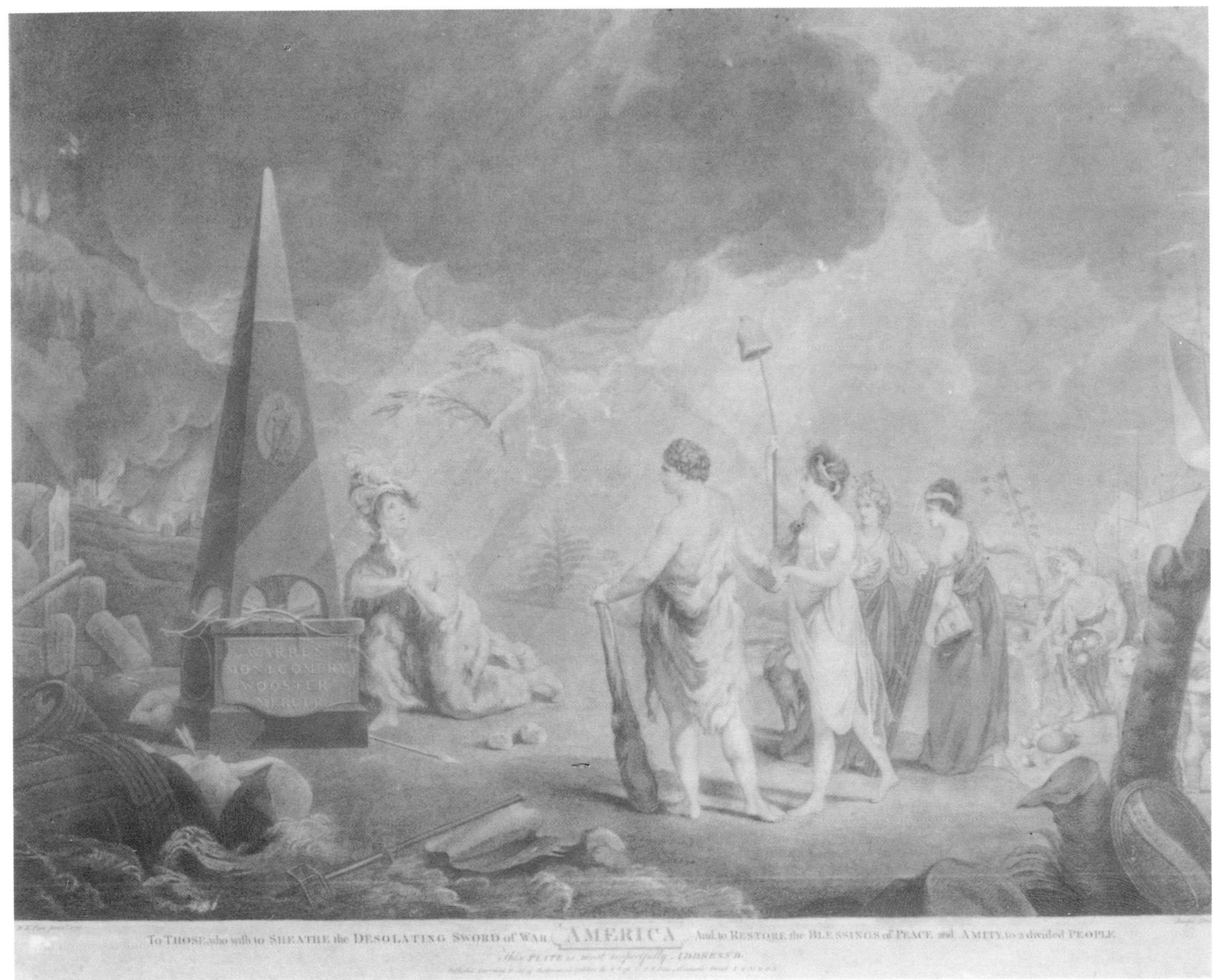

CARRE[illegible]
MONTGOMERY
WOOSTER
To THOSE, who wish to SHEATHE the DESOLATING SWORD of WAR, AMERICA And, to RESTORE the BLESSINGS of PEACE and AMITY, to a divided PEOPLE.
This PLATE is most respectfully ADDRESSED.

57.

Joseph Strutt (1749-1802), engraver
Robert Edge Pine (ca. 1730-1788), artist and publisher

AMERICA TO THOSE, who wish to SHEATHE the DESOLATING SWORD OF WAR. And to RESTORE the BLESSINGS of PEACE and AMITY, to a divided PEOPLE.

London, October 6, 1781
Stipple and line etching, printed in sepia
Laid paper, watermark of "DUPUY FIN AUVERGNE 1742"
Mounted on linen backing

Overall size:
61.9 x 75.0 x 3.2 cm
Platemark: 48.3 x 60.8 cm
Image: 44.8 x 60.0 cm
In original frame

61.499 a-d

Respected in England as a painter of historical and theatrical subjects, Robert Edge Pine left for the United States in 1784. He, like others to follow, was convinced that an important market for his work waited in America. Upon his arrival in Philadelphia he opened a gallery where he exhibited a selection of his portraits and history paintings. Among these works was his allegory of 1778, which addressed the issues of the prevailing division among Englishmen and its most imminent and sad resolution, the Revolutionary War. When he finished the painting, Pine probably contacted Joseph Strutt, a London publisher, in a plan to have the painting engraved for the popular market both at home and abroad in America. A delay of nearly three years between the completion of the canvas and the publication of the print is not readily explained, except that the technique used—stipple—is a tedious process of developing tones dot by dot. It is well documented that images of this large size could require two or more years to complete.

Pine died before the fortune he had envisioned in America could be realized. Impressions of *America,* however, continued to carry his fame throughout the United States. This one found its way to a Boston shop on Milk Street, where at the sign of the vase, a Mr. Dearborne mounted it on canvas and stretched it over strainers. He also affixed his label and a copy of the "Explanation" of the allegory, which was designed to be pasted on the back of all framed copies.

References: Prime, *Arts and Crafts in Philadelphia, 1786-1800,* 26-29; Stauffer, *American Engravers Upon Copper and Steel,* 2:90.

58.

Johan Gotthard Müller (1747-1830), engraver
Antonio C. de Poggi (n.a.), publisher
John Trumbull (1756-1843), artist

THE BATTLE OF BUNKER'S HILL

Stuttgart and London, scratch letter proof 1786-98, published February 1798
Line etching and engraving
Wove paper

Overall size: 67.7 x 102.3 cm
Platemark: 58.2 x 79.8 cm
Image: 50.35 x 75.6 cm

89.5

John Trumbull, assigned to the garrison at Roxbury, Massachusetts, could hear the distant retort of rifles coming from Charlestown on June 7, 1775, as colonial militia met the British troops on Bunker's Hill. The evening's news brought reports of the death of Major-General Joseph Warren and the sad events of the day. It was not until 1786, after spending months in London studying with Benjamin West, that Trumbull finished a small, detailed painting of the subject. Encouraged by West, he approached Antonio de Poggi, a leading London publisher of prints, to assist him in putting his painting in the hands of an accomplished engraver and to join him in the venture of producing the print. After failing to find a suitable engraver in Paris and Amsterdam, Trumbull and Poggi engaged a Stuttgart engraver, Johan Gotthard Müller, in July of 1788 to prepare the copperplate. Müller took his time, much to Trumbull's dismay. The plate was finally ready in July of 1797.

In November of that year Poggi began to pull impressions. The first trial proofs were taken when the title and publication lines were only lightly etched or scratched onto the copperplate. This impression (with its history of remaining in the artist's collection until it passed to his nephew, Professor Benjamin Silliman, Jr.) bears the date "Feby. 1798" in the publication line. In the first published state with closed letters, the publication date appears as *March* 1798.

Not everyone appreciated Trumbull's interpretation of the scene on Bunker's Hill. American artist William Dunlap (1766-1839) in his *History of the Arts of Design* (1834) observed that the painting focused on the humane gesture of a British officer, Major John Small, who deflects the left arm of a British regular attempting to bayonet the dying Mercer. One of Dunlap's correspondents in the compiling of the *History* wrote of an artist's obligation to truth. "When a man becomes a 'graphic historiographer,' he has a duty to fulfil which cannot be dispensed with. If the historian or the 'graphic historiographer' cannot tell the whole truth, he must not at least violate the known truth." As Irma B. Jaffe has carefully noted, Trumbull, who was familiar with the code of the gentleman and officer, intended a deeper meaning: conditioned behavior would prevail even in the heat of battle. Trumbull was not, as Dunlap supposed, celebrating a British officer in the battle scene but recording the code of virtue and honor that all gentlemen, whatever their politics, were expected to uphold.

References: William Dunlap, *A History of the Rise and Progress of the Arts of Design in the United States,* comp. Frank W. Bayley and Charles Goodspeed, rev. and enl. ed. (New York: Benjamin Blom, 1965), 2:33-35, 37; Irma B. Jaffe, *John Trumbull: Patriot-Artist of the American Revolution* (Boston: New York Graphic Society, 1975), 89.

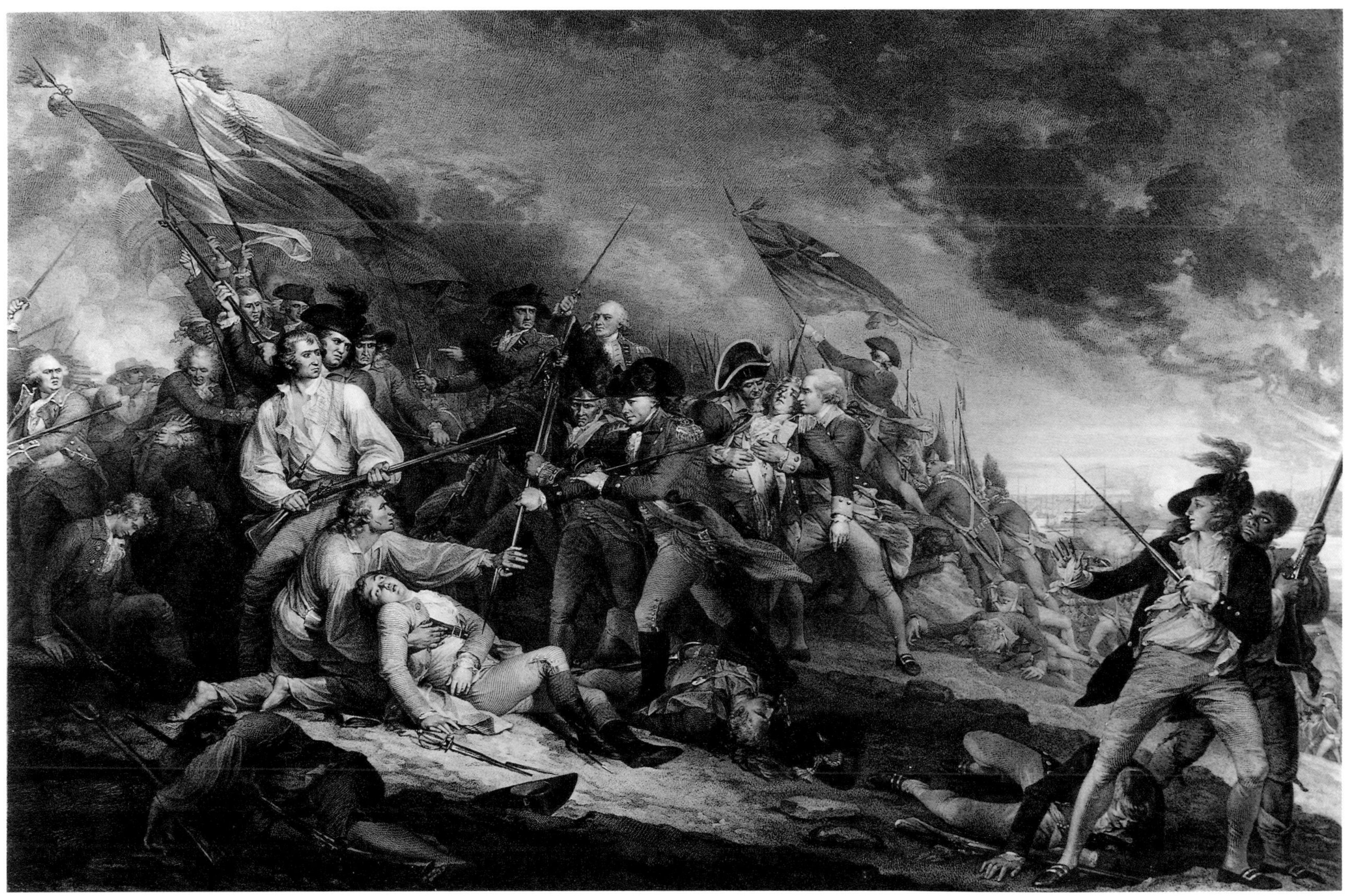

59.

Johan Frederick Clemens (1749-1790/1), principal engraver
Luigi Schiavonetti (1765-1810), etcher of figures
Wilson Lowry (1762-1824), engraver of background, foreground, and firearms
Antonio C. de Poggi (n.a.), publisher
John Trumbull (1756-1843), artist

DEATH OF GENERAL MONTGOMERY

London, scratch letter proof, April 4, 1794
Line etching and engraving
Wove paper

Overall size: 68.2 x 91.5 cm
Platemark: 58.5 x 76.9 cm
Image: 50.9 x 76.9 cm

89.6

Upon completion of *The Battle of Bunker's Hill* early in 1786, John Trumbull turned to the next subject in his series of salutes to the American Revolution. His painting of *The Death of General Montgomery,* finished in three consecutive months in that year, shows Major-General Richard Montgomery at the battle of Quebec in December 1775, dying of wounds as his aides-de-camp, Captain Jacob Chessman and Captain John MacPherson, lie dead before him. Lieutenants Matthias Ogden and John Humphries support the collapsing leader, as soldiers from Virginia, Pennsylvania, and Connecticut move forward.

Intended to be engraved as a companion piece to *The Battle of Bunker's Hill, The Death of General Montgomery* was turned over to Poggi, who looked to the pool of engravers in London for production of the plate. Subscriptions for the set were advertised at six guineas.

Under direct supervision, the London engravers worked at a faster rate than the distant Müller. Judging from the date given in scratch letters in the proof state, it is evident that plans were to release the set as early as 1794. And yet, the first published state of *The Death of General Montgomery* bears the date of 1798 to coincide with the issue of Trumbull's *Bunker's Hill.* Such a delay gives some insight into the mechanics of late eighteenth-century picture publishing.

Reference: Jaffe, *John Trumbull,* 82, 95-96, 141-44, 147.

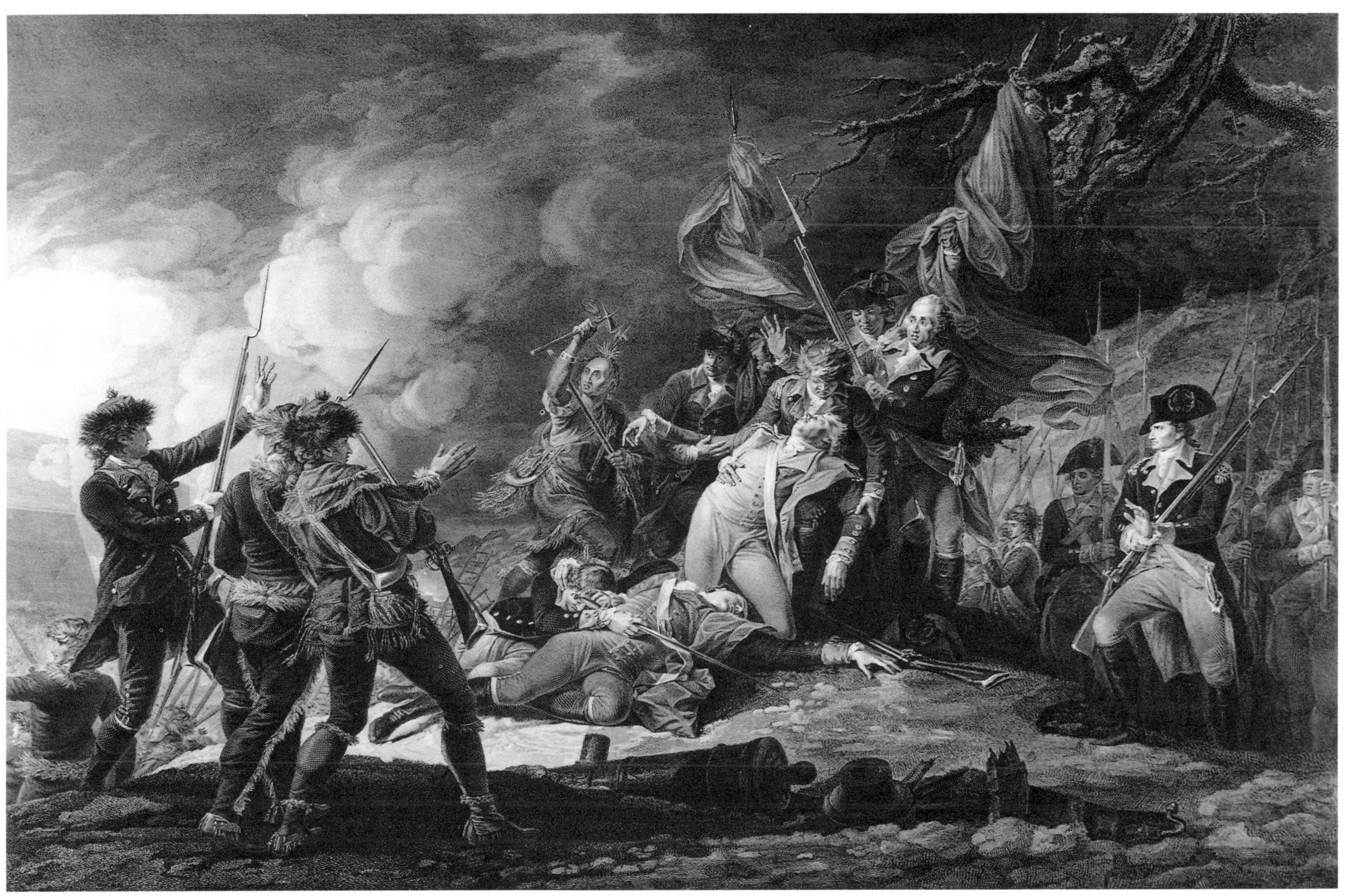

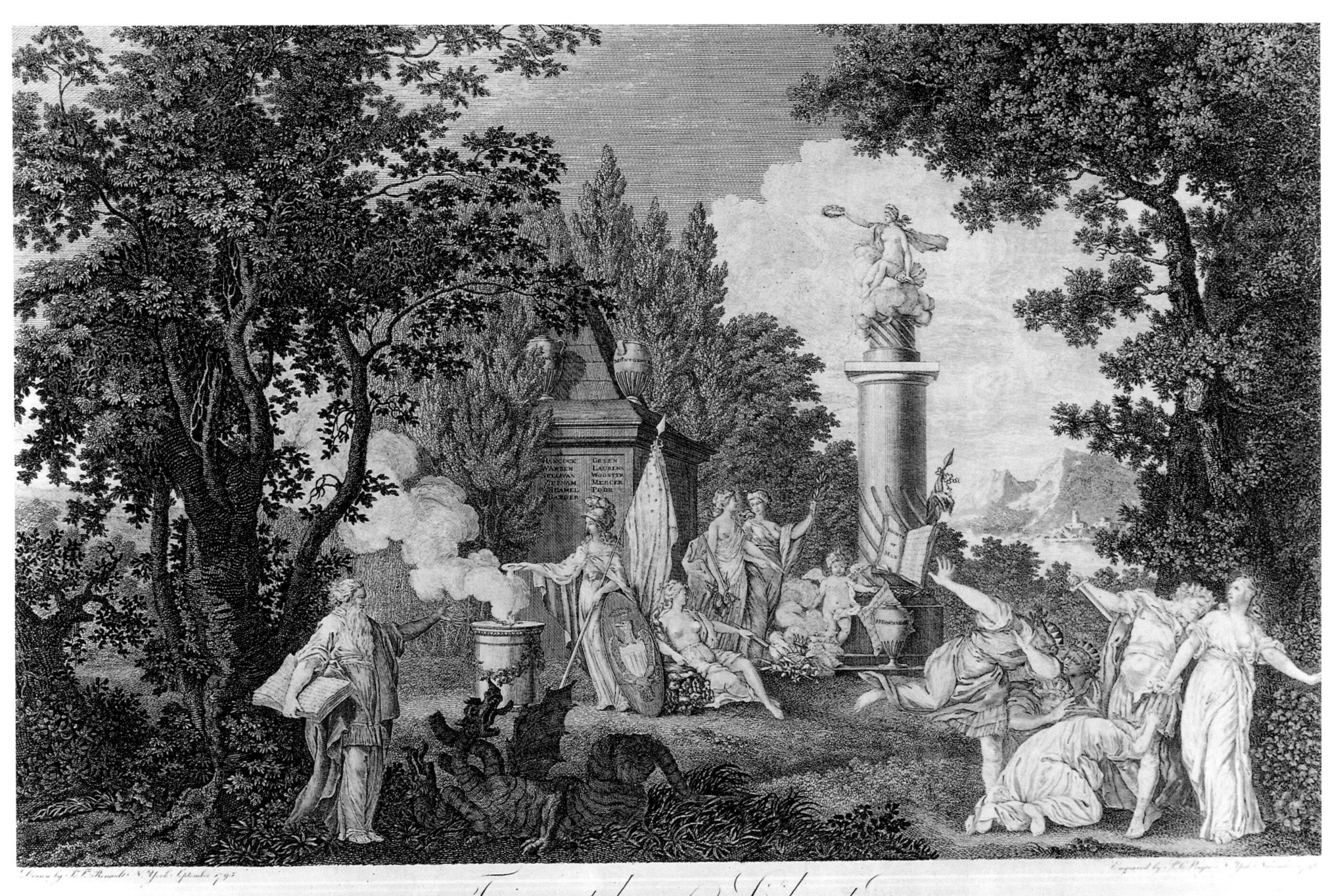

Triumph of Liberty
Dedicated to its Defenders in America

60.

Peter C. Verger (ac. in America 1795-1805/6), engraver
John Francis Renault, Sr. (ac. in America 1781-1819), artist and publisher

Triumph of Liberty

New York and Paris,
first state, 1797
Line etching and engraving
Laid paper, with double chain lines at 2.5 cm

Overall size: 41.3 x 54.6 cm
Platemark: 38.1 x 53.0 cm
Image: 30.0 x 46.8 cm

58.48

61.

John Francis Renault, Sr. (ac. in America 1781-1819), publisher

Prospectus of an Allegorical Picture of the Triumph of Liberty

New York, January 6, 1797
Letterpress
Laid paper

Overall size: 33.6 x 20.1 cm

58.48b

In the seventeen years from the end of the Revolutionary War to the end of the eighteenth century, numbers of foreign engravers and print publishers were attracted to the United States. Some, such as English engraver H. H. Houston, found the climate less than they had expected and returned home. Others stayed to find employment in the businesses of printing books and securities. Still others who sought both temporary and permanent respite from the upheavals of the French Revolution brought with them a formality of execution and an allegorical tradition that was quite different from the English genre generally available in book and printsellers' shops.

John Francis Renault, Sr., wished to honor his adopted country and pay homage to its heroes with an appropriate allegory. Although the design was executed in New York, it was wholly French, with only the names of colonial patriots to give the proper national identity, as promised in the title. Considering a statement by the authors that they had spared no "expense to procure the best paper and engraving," it is probable that the copperplate was actually engraved in France. The final production, however, was entirely American. In an early advertisement Renault and Verger assured subscribers that this undertaking would be printed on American paper made especially for the project by Messrs Kollack and Kinnan of Springfield, New Jersey.

Many Americans would have instantly recognized Minerva, cast in the role of America with the flag and shield of the United States, as she pours incense on the eternal flame before the monument to her defenders. Few would have grasped the iconography of the monument to French Liberty, with its urn containing the ashes of Jean Jacques Rousseau (1712-1778), and the open book of law bearing "The Rights of Man." For the larger audience, Renault and Verger issued a prospectus that detailed the subject and served as a tutorial, explaining the image's more subtle meanings.

When acquired by the Winterthur Museum in 1958, this impression was mounted on strainers and in its original frame. Affixed to the reverse was a prospectus, which for purposes of conservation and preservation was subsequently removed.

References: Advertisement of Renault and Verger, as quoted in Rita Susswein Gottesman, *The Arts and Crafts in New York 1777-1799,* (reprint, New York: New-York Historical Society, 1954), 100-101; Stauffer, *American Engravers Upon Copper and Steel,* 1:281-83, 2:551-52.

Stauffer 3344

PROSPECTUS

OF AN ALLEGORIGAL PICTURE

OF

THE TRIUMPH OF LIBERTY.

IN the right of the picture is the GODDESS OF LIBERTY, riſing to the ſkies on an obeliſk, preſenting a crown of oak, to which all the heroes, filled with her ſublime ſentiments, are worthy to aſpire.

The Book of the Law is ſupported by a cube of the obeliſk, pointing to t ſolidity of that moral, "The Rights of Man."

On the ſide is a little Genius preſenting to view the Marſeilles Hymn.

On one of the ſteps of this monument is an urn containing the aſhes of John James Rouſſeau.

At a little diſtance are the three Divinities, the attendants on Liberty, (namely, JUSTICE, holding the Scales and Sword; PEACE, preſenting an Olive Branch, and PLENTY with a horn full of fruit, an emblematical preſage of the happineſs of the people) ſhe burns crowns, ſceptres, croſſes of Saint Louis, ſpears and titles of nobility, cemented and writ with the blood of the human race.

On the ſide of the obeliſk, are the Kings, who are inimical to Liberty; they have all a particular expreſſion of countenance, that indicates the rage and deſpair that rankles in their hearts: One appears to be on the point of throwing himſelf headlong down a precipice; another on the earth; a third is juſt going to ſtab himſelf, having the different paſſions of grief, rage and deſpair depicted in his countenance; and near him is a Queen, who, by the expreſſion of her eyes viſibly diſcovers the fury with which her ſpirits are agitated.

In the left is a grand tomb, encloſing the manes of thoſe American Heroes, who have ſerved and died in defence of Liberty and their Country, and thoſe who have deſerved well of it, ſuch as FRANKLIN, WARREN, MONTGOMERY, GREEN, LAURENS, HANCOCK, SULLIVAN, PUTNAM, SCAMEL, BARBER, MERCER, WOOSTER and POOR; near which is the GENIUS OF THE COUNTRY, in the habit and helmet of Minerva, bearing the colours of the nation, and at her ſide an Eagle, emblematical of AMERICA; incenſe is continually burning at the foot of the tomb, where a bard is diſcovered ſinging hymns, in praiſe of thoſe illuſtrious heroes. At the bottom of the picture is a ſeven headed Hydra, or Deſpotiſm tumbling into ruin.

Dedicated to the defenders of Liberty in America; BY RENAULT, SEN. Author of the Work.

I, the underſigned, having taken all the neceſſary ſteps for the engraving, paper and printing of the impreſſion of the picture of the TRIUMPH OF LIBERTY, in conjunction with Mr. RENAULT, SEN. Author of the above work, we this day open a ſubſcription at the rate of three dollars for each copy, or engraving without frame. And we can with confidence aſſure the public that we have ſpared neither trouble nor expenſe to procure the beſt paper and engraving. No money is required till the delivery of the picture to the ſubſcriber.

RENAULT & VERGER.

JANUARY 6, 1797.

62.

William Hogarth (1697-1764), artist, engraver, and publisher

A MIDNIGHT MODERN CONVERSATION

London, second state, first issued March 1, 1733
Line etching with some burin work
Laid paper

Overall size: 34.4 x 42.2 cm
Overall platemark: trimmed
Image: 32.7 x 45.6 cm

75.219
Gift of Gordon A. Rust

William Hogarth may have viewed himself as a chronicler of his times, a moralist, and a painter of contemporary history, but his deftness at delineating the essence of the human character gave image to a world that in some way touched everyone. Eighteenth-century England, particularly London, comes alive in his work, and the engravings that he made, or had made after his paintings with the clear motive of profit, were as vigorously collected in the colonies as they were in Great Britain.

In 1731-32, Hogarth painted members of a London drinking club as they sought their entertainment in the grape. Ten characters reflect different stages of drunkenness, from the casual raising of the glass in toast to unconsciousness. The hour is four o'clock and the punchbowl is filled to the rim; so, too, are most of the glasses. Certainly many other punchbowls had been full. One man lets the melted wax of the burning candle that lit his pipe drop onto his coat. Another falls to the floor, broken wine bottle in hand. And in the corner is a small covered pot that allows any and all to accommodate human nature without leaving the room and the revelling.

Hogarth offered the engraving of *A Midnight Modern Conversation* in December of 1732 at a subscription price of five shillings. Publication was promised for the following March or possibly earlier. Its success was immediate, and pirated copies appeared for framing, fan mounts, snuff boxes, and punch bowl decoration. Within two years Hogarth would be spearheading protective legislation that would make illegal the pirating of an artist's original design. He won the law with the Copyright Act of 1735, which forbade the copying of a work for a period of fourteen years, but he did not win the war against imitators.

Reference: Paulson, *Hogarth's Graphic Works,* 1:150-52, no. 128.

British Museum, *Satires,* 2122

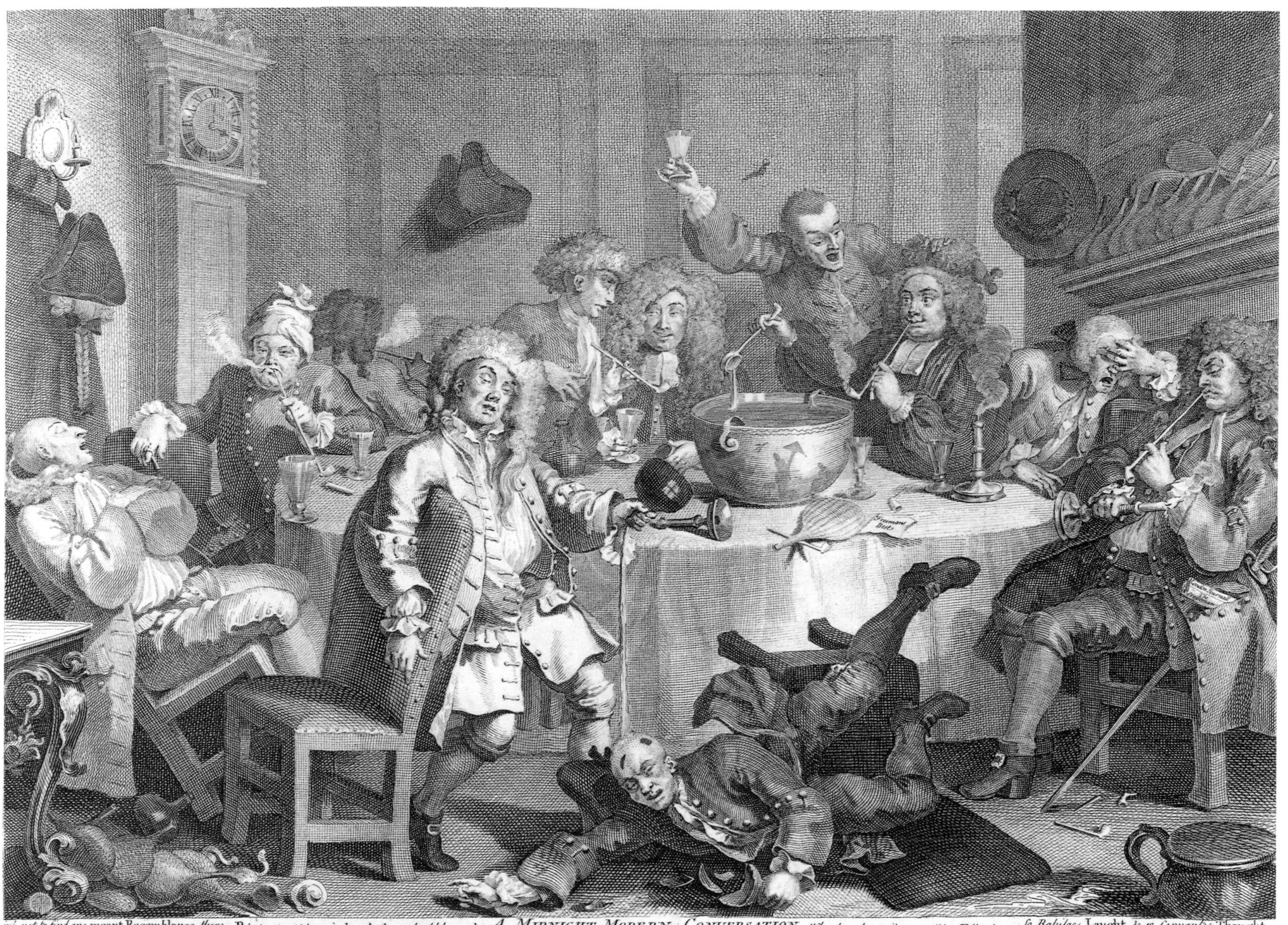

ink not to find one meant Resemblance there
lash the Vices but the Persons spare
Prints should be prizd as Authors should be read
A MIDNIGHT MODERN CONUERSATION
Wm. Hogarth Inv. Pinxt & Sculpt.
Who sharply smile prevailing Folly dead
So Rabilaes Laught, & so Cervantes Thought
So Nature dictated what Art has Taught.

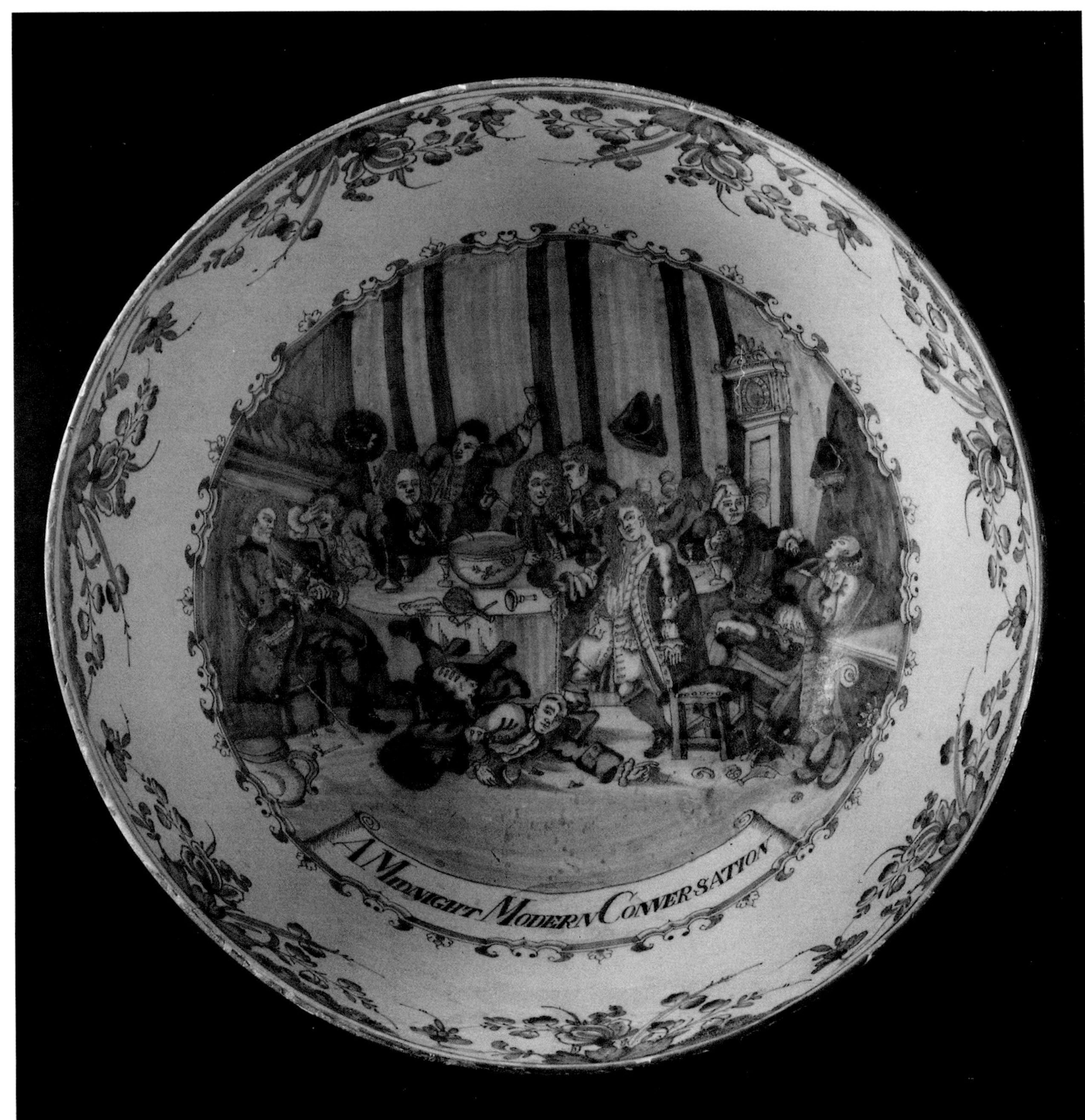
A MIDNIGHT MODERN CONVERSATION

63.

Punch bowl

Liverpool, England, ca. 1750
Tin-glazed earthenware with design featuring Hogarth's "A Midnight Modern Conversation" painted in blue inside and center

15.2 x 26.0 cm (6 x 10 1/4 in.)

84.30

Hogarth's engraving of *A Midnight Modern Conversation* was a perennial favorite in the colonies. It appears from Massachusetts to Virginia in newspaper advertisements and inventories of the eighteenth century. While there is no mention of fans behind which ladies could titter or of mugs from which the hearty could drink in keeping with its image, at least one punchbowl is described, which when emptied revealed the lesson of too much alcohol. Dr. William Bentley (1759-1819) recorded a meeting in his diary for June 20, 1810, when a gentlewoman of many years shared with him one of her most prized possessions. It was, as he recorded, "a punch bowl of Delft [that] had within Hogarth's Midnight modern conversation."

Reference: The Diary of William Bentley D.D. Pastor of the East Church, Salem, Massachusetts. . ., 4 vols. (Salem, Mass.: Essex Institute, 1904-1905), 3:524-25.

64.

Bowles and Carver (firm ac. 1793-ca. 1806), publishers

SETTLING the AFFAIRS of the NATION

London, 1794-1800
Line etching with some burin work
Laid paper, watermark of fleur-de-lis and countermark of "IV"

Overall size: 36.2 x 50.2 cm
Image: 34.3 x 50.2 cm

73.561

Pictures of eighteenth-century English or American taverns, ordinarys, or alehouses are few, and those that feature interior scenes are fewer still. The diaries and letters of contemporary travelers are filled with notations on the cleanliness or, more generally, the filth of such establishments. Some describe in detail the quality of food—the fatty meats, dried breads, and diluted punches. On occasion others remark of poor sleeping conditions, where drivers shared beds with passengers and bed linens remained unchanged for long periods of time.

The English tavern or ordinary in *Settling the Affairs of the Nation* would seem to disprove the eyewitness accounts of many. The setting in which a pretty, well-attired barmaid fills a glass for a customer appears to be immaculate. It is decorated for a festive occasion, most likely Christmas or Boxing Day in view of the generous use of evergreens in the windows and the great bunch of mistletoe hanging from the ceiling.

A young man drowsy from the heat of the fireplace sits to the far left, undisturbed by the remarks made by the soldier to an attentive group of three elderly gentlemen. Above the entrance door hangs a recent portrait of John Wilkes as a reminder that gathering places such as this were a public forum for political ideas.

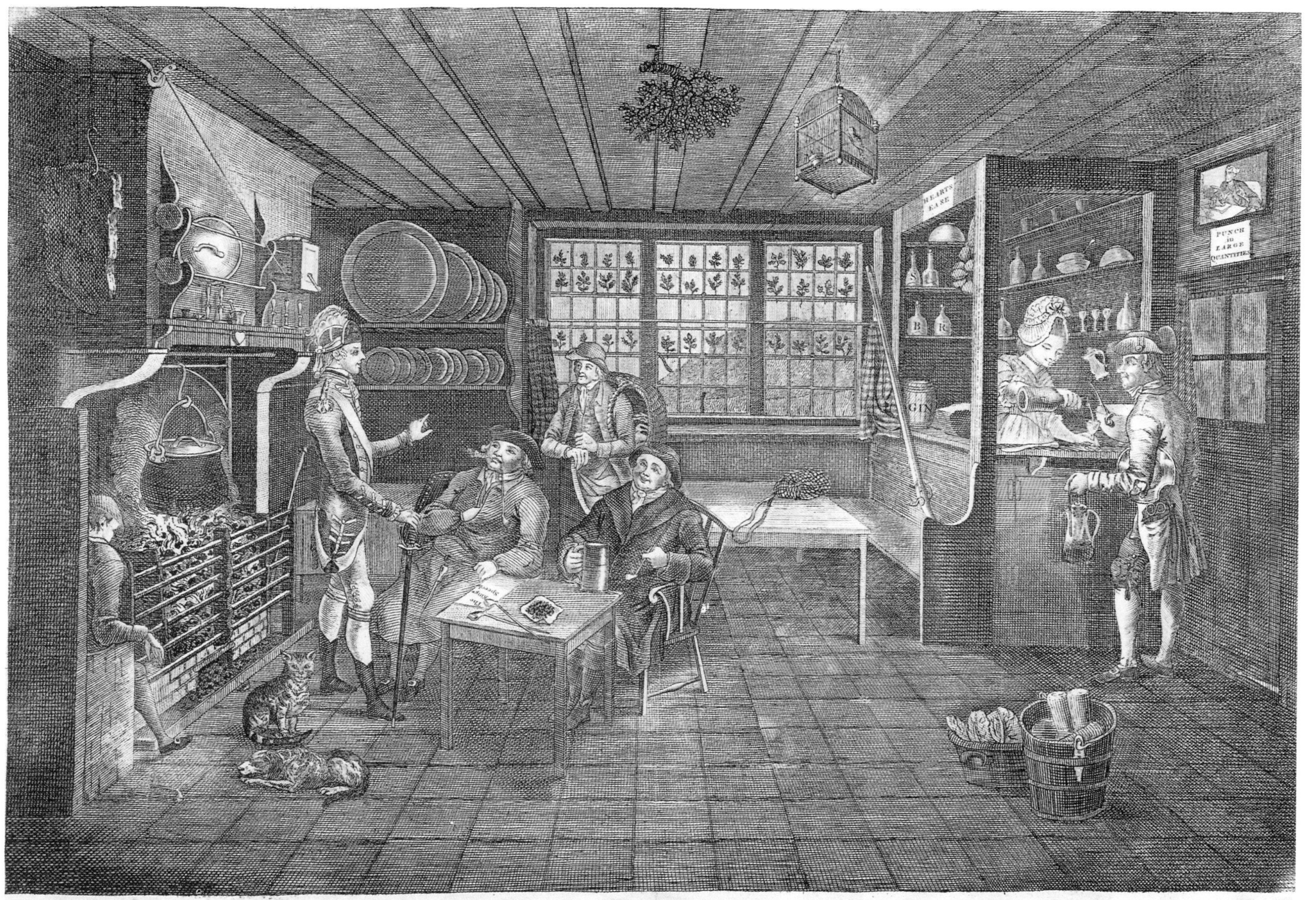

Printed for & Sold by BOWLES & CARVER, at their Map and **SETTLING the AFFAIRS of the NATION.** Print Warehouse, No. 69 in St. Paul's Church Yard, LONDON.

65

Matthew Darly
(ac. 1750-1778), publisher

THE PREPOSTEROUS HEAD DRESS, or the FEATHERD LADY

London, March 20, 1776
Line etching
Laid paper, watermark of fleur-de-lis

Overall size: 34.7 x 24.6 cm
Platemark: 52.2 x 37.7 cm
Image: 47.3 x 36.1 cm

59.98.20

Printmakers and print publishers were looking constantly for new subjects and new ideas that would keep customers coming into their shops. They displayed recent releases of prints in the individual lights or panes of their shop windows. Portraits, usually of religious leaders, were fitted in the uppermost windows, with rows below filled with portraits of the beautiful or subjects from history. Satirical essays on the most current topics of debate or gossip were more likely found in the rows of panes closer to eye level.

When a group of young men, recently returned from their Grand Tours of Europe, adopted an affected manner of dress and demeanor in the 1760s, printmakers gained a topic that would last for nearly two decades. It may be impossible to determine who was most responsible for the longevity of this fad: the young fops who dressed in silk, ribbons, lace, and butterfly bows; the printmakers who celebrated them with weekly issues of their latest exploits; or the young ladies who seized the opportunity to be daringly different.

Like the young gentlemen, these ladies wore an abundance of bows and outrageously oversized corsages, but they concentrated their attentions on achieving the most fantastic of hair designs. Reports circulated that some of these creations reached nearly half the bearer's height. To wear them required an act of careful balance, and constant caution was necessary when navigating doors and approaching lighted chandeliers.

A schoolgirl in Boston who was quite familiar with English prints wrote to her mother on January 17, 1772, of her experience with a modified version of the fashionable headdress. "The famous roll is not made wholly of a red Cow Tail, but is a mixture of that & horsehair (very coarse) & a little human hair of yellow hue...my aunt...hopes a little fals[e] English will not spoil the whole with Mamma. Rome was not built in a day."

Reference: Diary of Anna Green Winslow: A Boston School Girl of 1771, ed. Alice Morse Earle (Boston and New York: Houghton Mifflin & Co., and Cambridge, Mass.: Riverside Press, 1894), 71.

British Museum, *Satires,* 5370

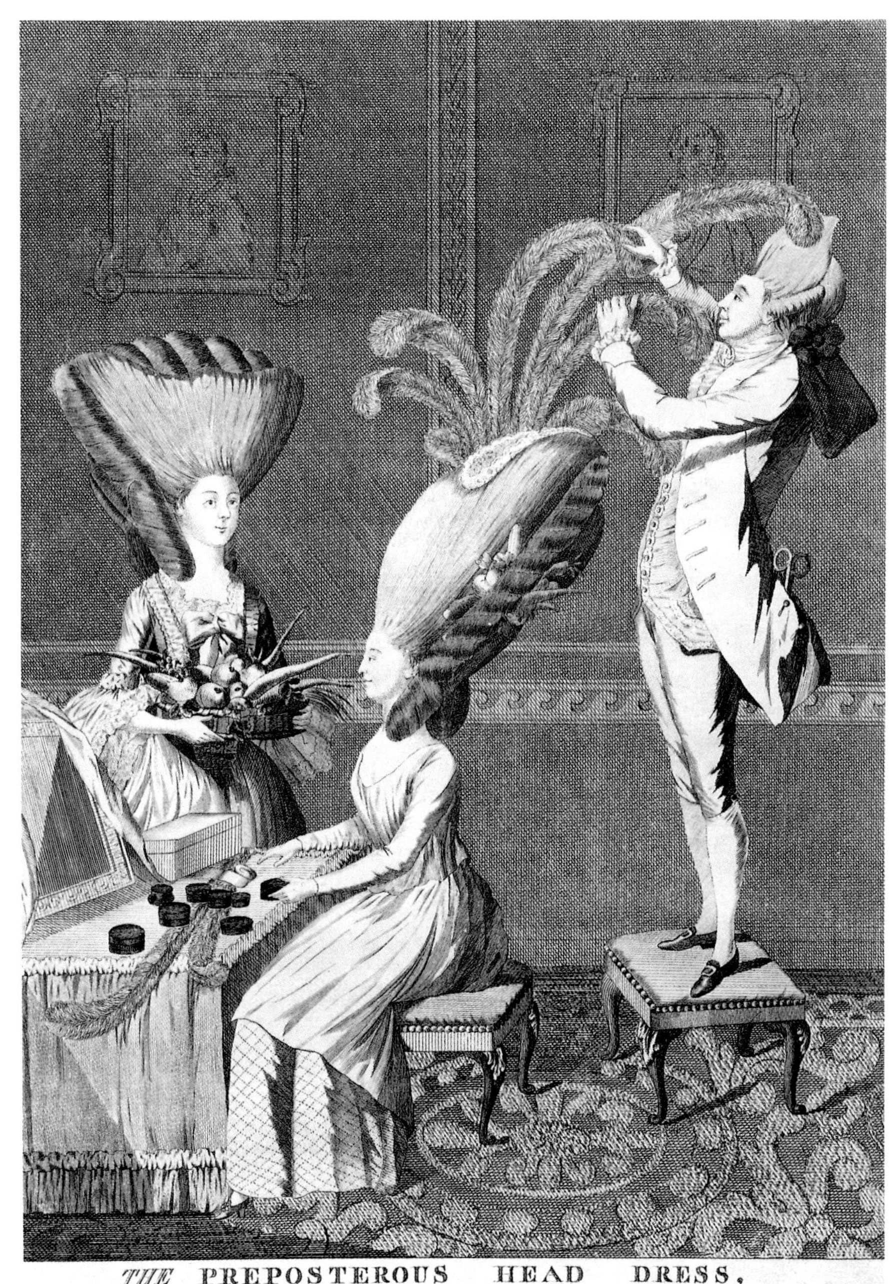

THE PREPOSTEROUS HEAD DRESS,
or the FEATHERD LADY.

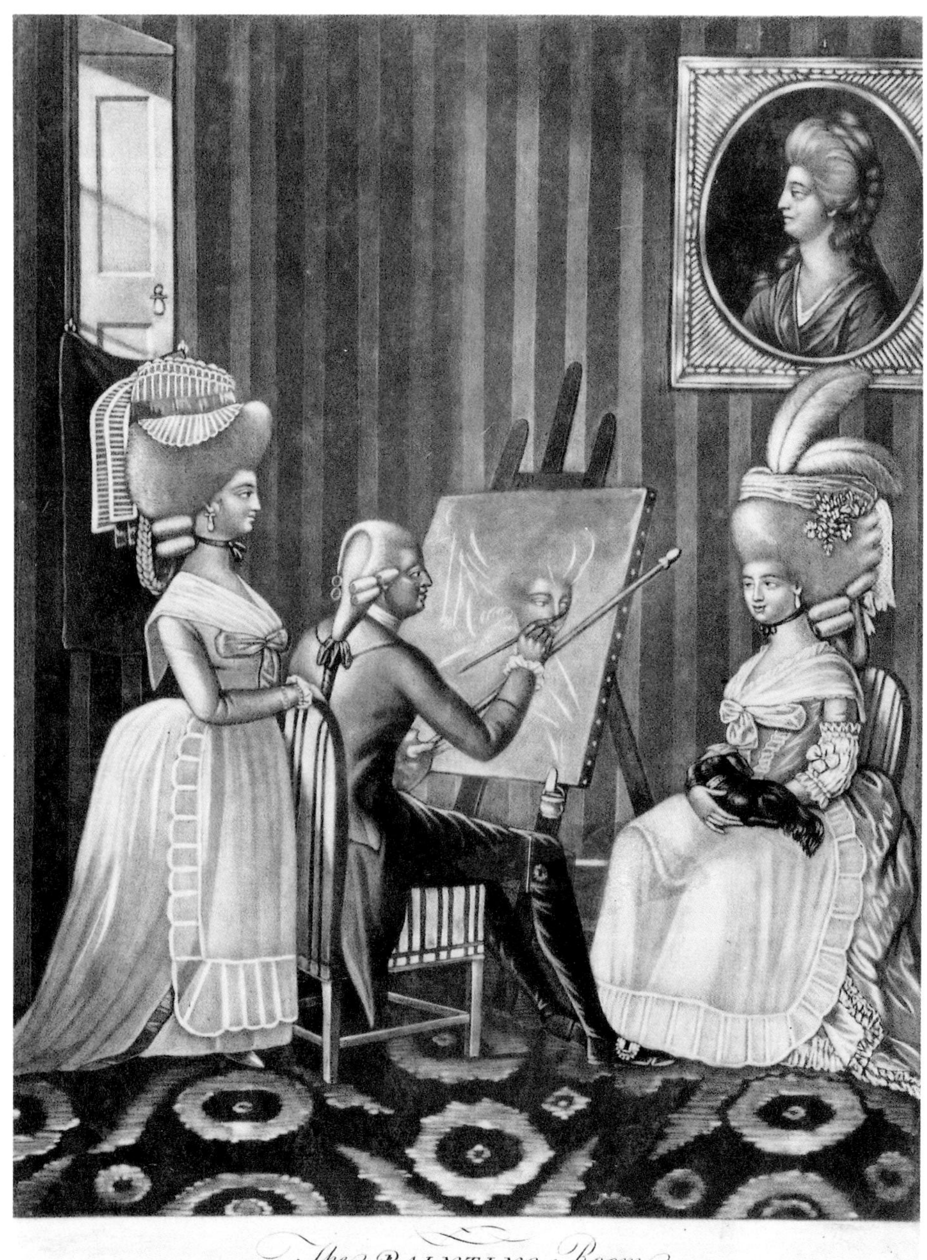
The PAINTING Room.
London, Printed for R. Sayer & J. Bennett, Map, Chart & Printsellers, No. 53, Fleet Street, as the Act directs, 8 Jany. 1782.

66.

Robert Sayer (b. 1725, ac. 1751-d. 1794) and John Bennett (ac. 1770-1784, d. 1787), publishers

The PAINTING Room.

London, January 8, 1782
Mezzotint with roulette and burin work
Laid paper, watermark of a bunch of grapes in a single circle similar to those used by Dupuy's mill at Auvergne

Overall size: 37.9 x 27.3 cm
Platemark: 35.5 x 26.1 cm
Image: 32.9 x 25.0 cm

65.2987

News of the Macaroni, or English dandies, reached the colonies through Americans returning from tours abroad, through magazines and newspapers, and most engagingly, through the colorful images imported by American printsellers. For older generations in England and America, it was a relief when the sons they sent to Europe managed to return to their native country being "neither Fop or Coxcomb."

On a more serious level, fashion-conscious young Britons fresh from their European travels were determined to saturate their lives with culture and to expand upon their firsthand experience with the arts, architecture, sculpture, and literature. Following the assumption that if one practiced drawing he or she could better understand art, these amateur artists sketched, drew, and painted members of their families and their friends. They frequented galleries and the painting rooms of artists for whom they sat and from whom they sought to understand the mysteries of the craft.

Neither satire nor true genre, prints such as *The Painting Room* found an enthusiastic market in the second half of the eighteenth century. Particularly popular issues remained in printsellers' catalogues and inventories for years, an indication that the copperplates were stored and printed on demand.

Reference: Susan Turner Norton to John Hatley Norton, Winchester, Virginia, postmarked London, October 13, 1783, as quoted in *John Norton & Sons: Merchants of London and Virginia: Being the Papers from their Counting House for the Years 1750-1795,* ed. Frances Norton Mason (Richmond, Vir.: Deitz Press, 1937), 456.

67.

Robert Sayer (b. 1725, ac. 1751-d. 1794) and John Bennett (ac. 1770-1784, d. 1787), publishers

CONJUGAL PEACE London, Printed for R. Sayer and J. Bennett, Map and Printsellers, No. 53, Fleet Street, as the Act directs, 14. Feb. 1782

London, February 14, 1782
Mezzotint with roulette and burin work, opaque watercolors
Laid paper

Overall size: 47.1 x 30.6 cm
Platemark: 35.4 x 25.2 cm
Image: 32.2 x 25.0 cm

55.14.1

Under the heading of "Miscellaneous and Humorous Subjects," printsellers such as Robert Sayer and John, Thomas, and Carington Bowles, who dealt in large volume for the popular market, listed hundreds of titles containing a sentimental or genre reference. As an example, the Sayer and Bennett catalogue for 1775 listed 162 fourteen-by-ten-inch (35.5 by 25.4 cm) mezzotints at one shilling each. These included such subjects as "The *Batchelor's* curse, its companion...the *Humours* of the Pantheon, its companion...The *Smoaker,* its companion...The happy *Smoakers*...The studious *Yawner*...The drowsy *Dame*...The *Cobler* at *Work* ... Four agreeable prints of a *Country Life,*" and this little domestic scene as number 183, "Conjugal *Happiness.*" Another ninety-two titles were listed for mezzotints of half that size and offered at half the price. In many respects, including the choice of subjects and the use of large and small formats, this focus of the eighteenth-century London printseller's business was a precursor to the highly successful American firm of Currier and Ives in the next century.

From a number of sources, including the surviving prints, it is known that many of these eighteenth-century popular subjects were intended to be watercolored. This example, which remained protected in folio over the years, presents clearly the brilliant colors that were originally favored.

Reference: Sayer and Bennett, *Catalogue of Prints for the year 1775,* 15-25, 31-33.

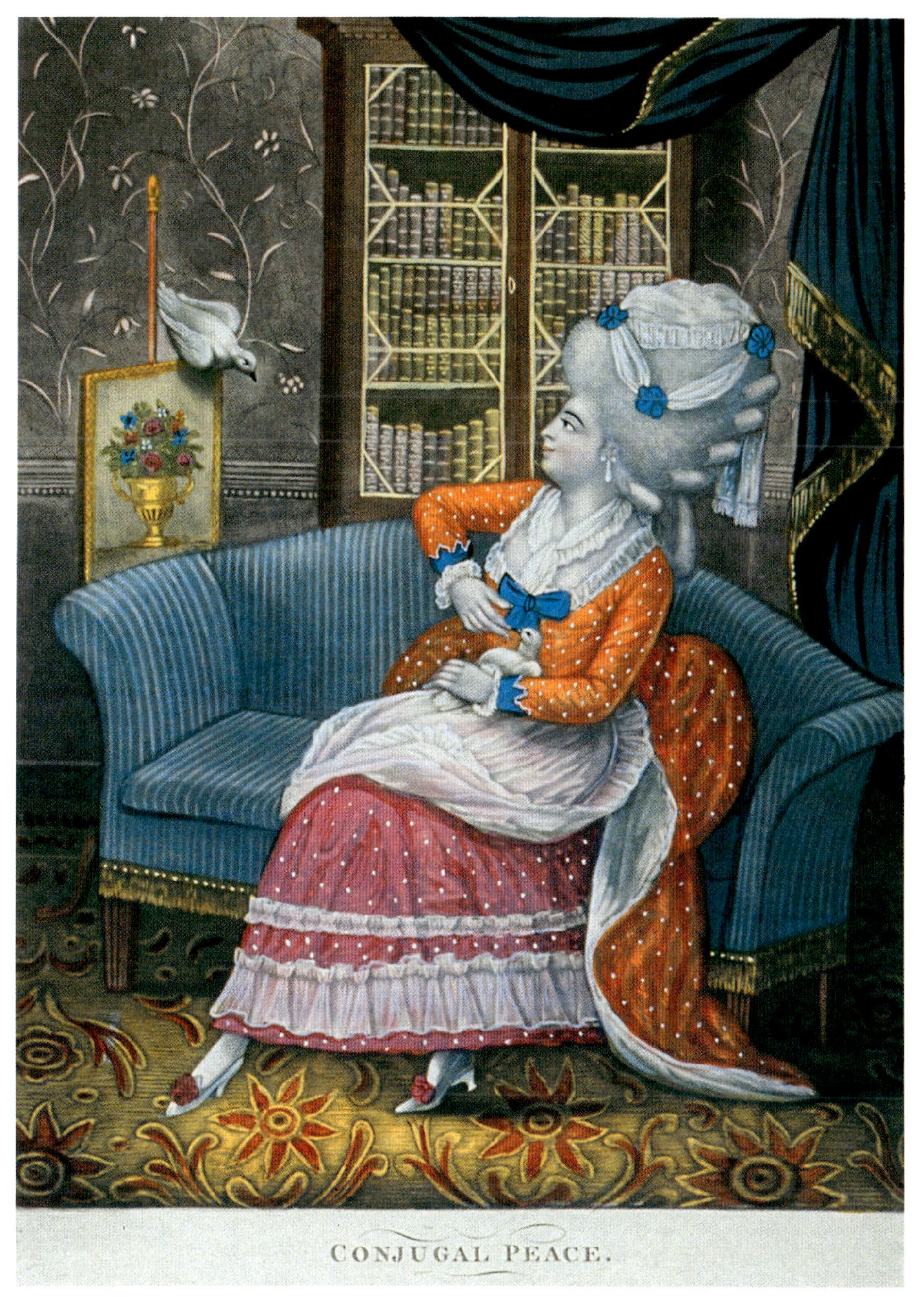
CONJUGAL PEACE.

68.

John Boydell (1719-1804), delineator and engraver

A North View of Denbigh Castle, in North Wales
This noble ancient Castle (one adorn'd with lofty Towers) is partly situated on a high Rock; and was one of the frontier Garrisons of Wales, before that Country became subject to England.

London, 1750
Line etching with burin work
Laid paper

Overall size: 40.9 x 54.8 cm
Platemark: 29.8 x 44.8 cm
Image: 28.0 x 43.3 cm

77.214

John Boydell was apprenticed to the engraver William H. Toms (see cat. no. 5) about 1738 or 1739. At the time Toms was working on Bishop Roberts' perspective of Charleston, South Carolina. These were the early years of the great era of English topographical prints, a body of images that balance somewhere between perspective plans of the terrain and the romantic landscape of late eighteenth-century painting. Through the engraved works of Wenceslas Hollar and Johannes Kip (d. 1722), Boydell became familiar with the aerial or bird's-eye view, a format that concentrated on architecture and garden design but was largely devoid of human scale or interest.

Boydell engraved a series of views of country seats and towns in the mid-eighteenth century. In this view of Denbigh Castle, the scene is brought into the viewer's plane. At first glance the subject would appear to be genre, not architecture, although with horses and dogs running across the landscape in a hobby-horse gait, Boydell cannot be credited with understanding the mechanics of motion. That comprehension would come a century later, after the invention of the camera and with the work of artists such as Thomas Eakins (1844-1916).

Whether or not the gait of the horses was artificial, engravings of horses are mentioned in eighteenth-century American advertisements and inventories. Americans frequently wagered pence or pounds on whose horse was the faster. Impromptu races down straight roads and organized matches on fields were held from New York to the Carolinas. Blooded and registered stallions and mares that descended from the great English Arabians were being imported into the colonies at enormous expense. In 1745, Mrs. Sarah Dolbear of Boston owned a picture of the duke of Bolton's horse. A Baltimore inventory of 1770 lists nineteen small horse prints in the house of Christopher Caran, and Philip Fithian described twenty-four pictures of the day's most celebrated horses that he saw on the dining room walls in the Virginia home of the Tayloe family in 1773-74.

References: F. L. Wilder, *Sporting Prints* (New York: Viking Press, 1974), 7-20, 24, 218-24; *Journal and Letters of Philip Vickers Fithian 1773-1774: A Plantation Tutor of the Old Dominion,* ed. Homer Dickinson Farish (Charlottesville: University Press of Virginia, 1957), 95; Alexander Mackay-Smith, *The Colonial Quarter Race Horse: America's First Breed of Horses. . .* (Richmond, Vir.: Whittet & Shepperson, 1983).

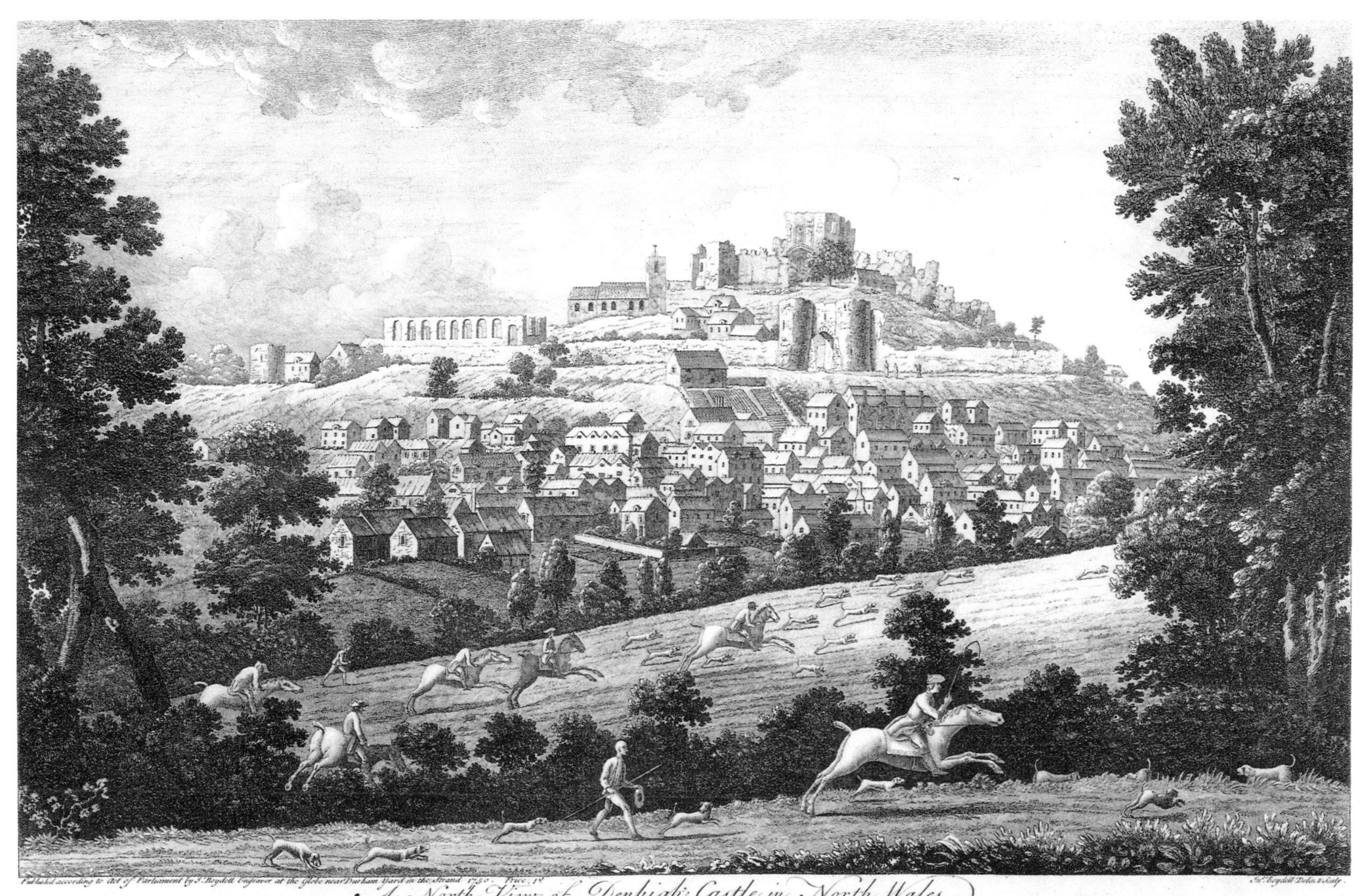

Published according to Act of Parliament by J. Boydell Engraver at the Globe near Durham Yard in the Strand 1750. Price 1s

Jn. Boydell Delin. & Sculp.

A North View of Denbigh Castle, in North Wales.

This noble antient Castle (once adorn'd with lofty Towers) is partly situated on a high Rock; and was one of the Frontier Garrisons of Wales, before that Country became subject to England.

58

69.
Remi Parr (b. 1723), engraver
John Bowles (1701-1779), publisher

FLORA Or a curious collection of ye. most BEAUTIFUL FLOWERS as they appear in their greatest Perfection each Month of the Year.

London, 1744 or 1745
Line etching with some burin work, watercolors
Laid paper, watermark of lily or fleur-de-lis in crowned shield with "4" and "L V G"

Overall size: 36.7 x 26.7 cm
Platemark: 35.1 x 25.3 cm
Image: 33.6 x 24.4 cm

66.1049

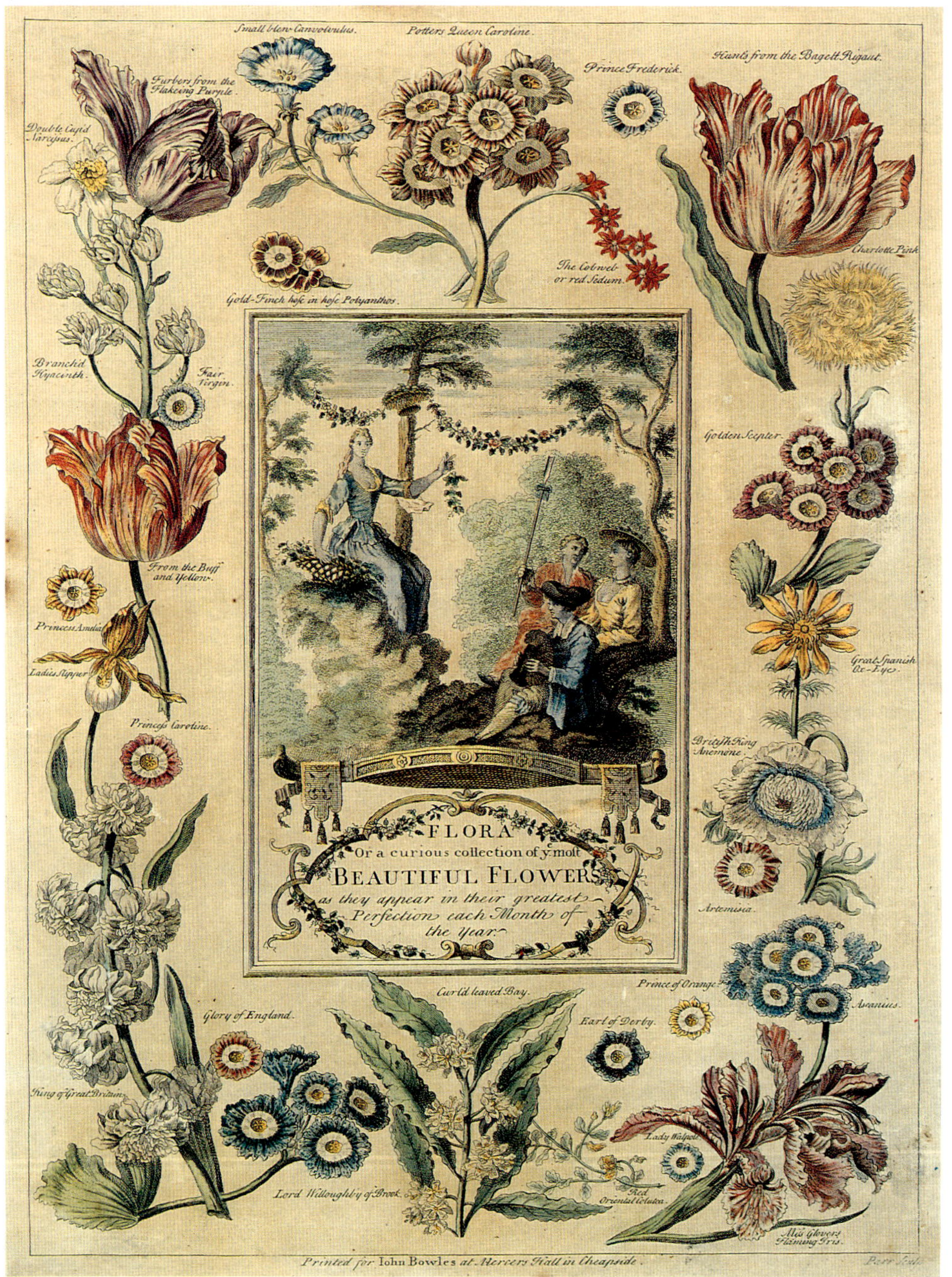

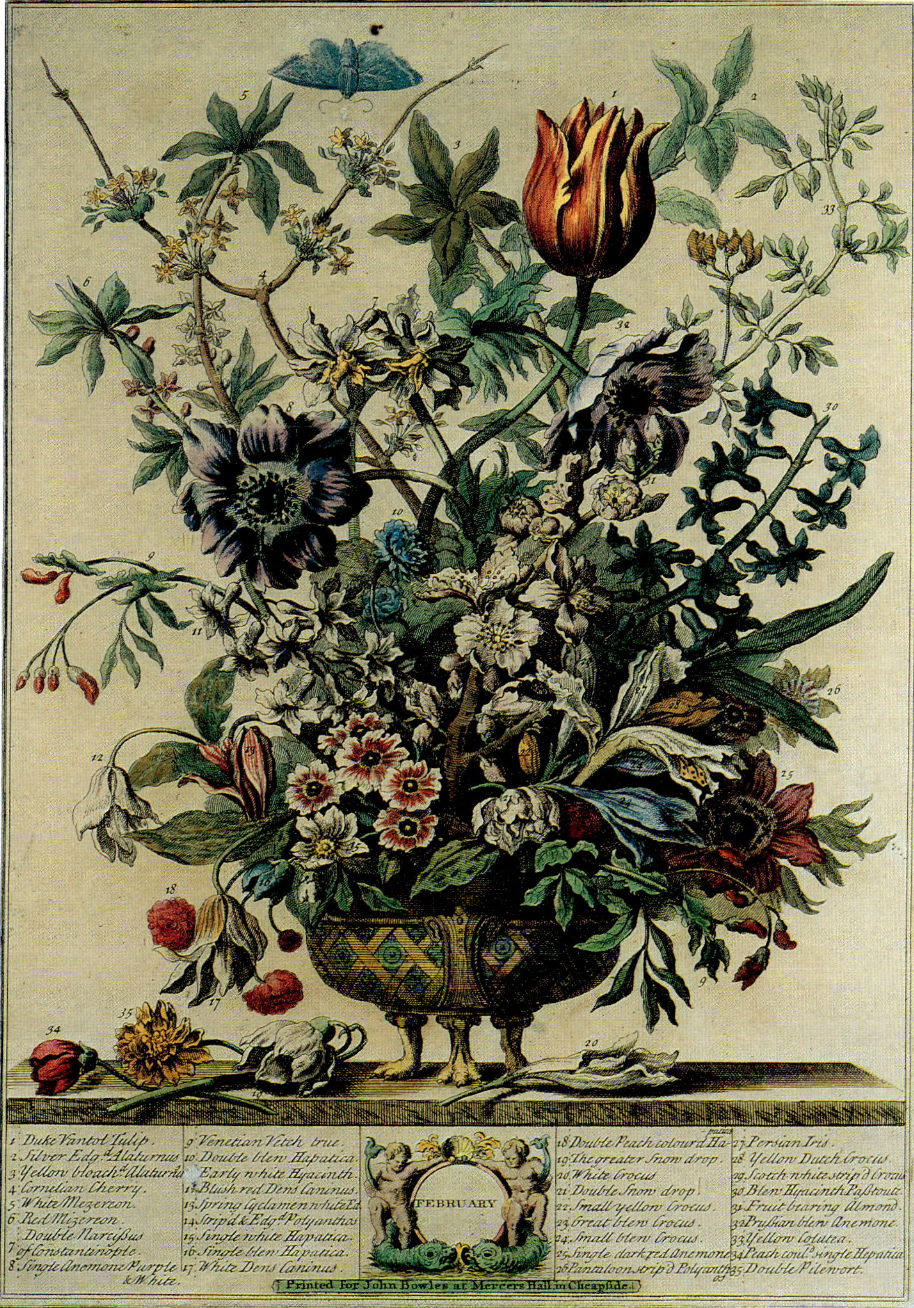

70.

Probably Thomas Bowles II (b. 1712), engraver
John Bowles (1701-1779), publisher

FEBRUARY

London, 1744 or 1745
Line etching with some burin work, watercolors
Laid paper, watermark of a lily in a rounded shield with "4" and "L V G" below and countermark of "IV"

Overall size: 36.4 x 24.4 cm
Image: 34.4 x 26.2 cm

66.1048.2

71.

Remi Parr (b. 1723), engraver
John Bowles (1701-1779), publisher

NOVEMBER

London, 1744 or 1745
Line etching with some burin work, watercolors
Laid paper

Overall size: 36.7 x 26.7 cm
Platemark: 34.7 x 25.3 cm
Image: 33.8 x 24.5 cm

66.1048.11

Robert Furber's (ac. 1724-1732) remarkable set of the twelve months in flowers, published in 1730, is among the most sought after of eighteenth-century sets of framing prints. Its success was immediate both in England and America. An engraved and watercolored set of the flowers was recorded in Williamsburg in 1734, and sets of flower prints appear in American inventories throughout the century. One inventory in particular, that of the household goods of Andrew Belcher, Esquire, taken in Boston in 1771, noted "13 Flower Pieces of the Seasons" hanging in the south upper chamber. It is possible that Mr. Belcher liked the subject of flowers and the seasons and managed to put together all or parts of several sets of four, but in all probability the clerks who recorded that inventory were referring to a particular set of the twelve months.

More than a decade after Furber's months in flowers were published as engravings from paintings by the Dutch artist Pieter Casteels (1684-1749), John Bowles engaged Remi Paar, a former apprentice, to engrave a quarto-size version. To the twelve plates representing the months he added a handsome title page that illustrates the joys of the garden, thus making it a set of thirteen.

Paar's name as engraver appears on the title page and in the lower right-hand corner above the engraved border on plates representing *July, September,* and *November* in the Winterthur set. The plate for *January* has "T. Bowles Sculp." below the border at right, and "Bowles, Sc" is seen below the border at right for *December.* The name of a third engraver, "J. Clark Sculp," appears within the border at lower right for the month of June. All the months (except August) carry the publication line "*printed for* John Bowles *at Mercers Hall in Cheapside*" or a slight variation thereof. Although the opportunity to mix and match prints among sets is suggested in printseller's catalogues of the time, the probability that this particular set was assembled in the nineteenth century is reinforced by the use of cadmium yellow to strengthen the fugitive yellows in the eighteenth-century watercolors.

Bowles' set of the months in flowers is just one of at least six eighteenth-century quarto-size versions. In 1775, Robert Sayer's catalogue for that year announced that he was prepared to sell in London or to ship overseas "A Collection of Curious Flowers, painted by P. Casteels...Coloured from nature." Sayer assured his buyers that his plates were complete with botanical terms and that they were "the most beautiful furniture for dining rooms, banqueting rooms, closets" or were useful as patterns for the ladies' embroidery. In fact, Sayer went so far as to offer designers and embroideresses less expensive sets in black and white.

References: Gordon Dunthorne, *Flowers and Fruit Prints of the 18th and 19th Centuries* (Washington, D.C.: Published by the author, 1938), 199; Dolmetsch, "Prints in Colonial America," 65; Abbott Lowell Cummings, *Rural Household Inventories Establishing the Names, Uses and Furnishings of Rooms in the Colonial New England Home, 1675-1775* (Boston: Society for the Preservation of New England Antiquities, 1964), 245.

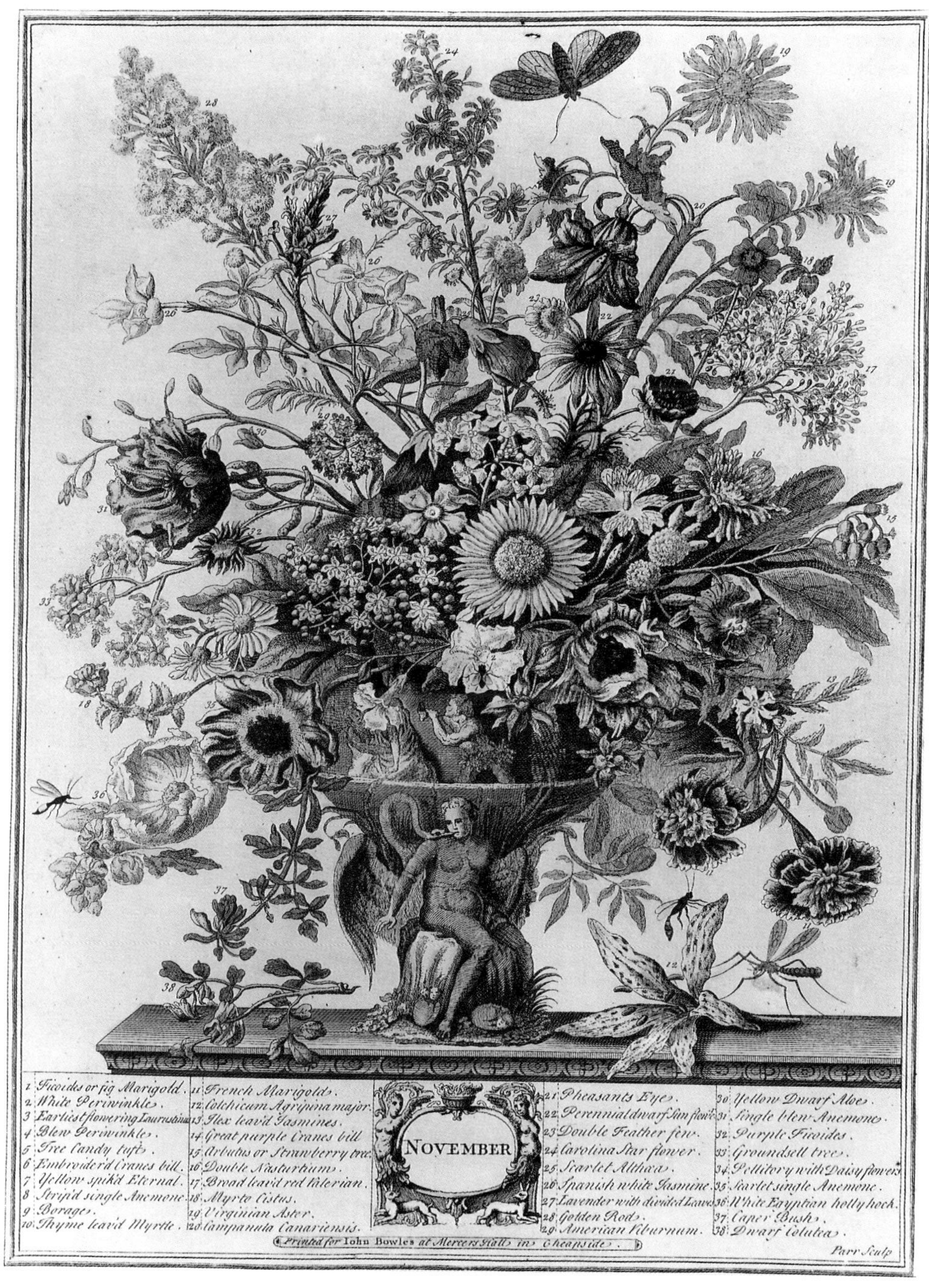
1 Ficoides or fig Marigold.
2 White Periwinkle.
3 Earliest flowering Laurustinus
4 Blew Periwinkle.
5 Tree Candy tuft.
6 Embroider'd Cranes bill.
7 Yellow spik'd Eternal.
8 Strip'd single Anemone.
9 Borage.
10 Thyme leav'd Myrtle.
11 French Marigold.
12 Colchicum Agripina major.
13 Ilex leav'd Jasmines.
14 Great purple Cranes bill
15 Arbutus or Strawberry tree.
16 Double Nasturtium.
17 Broad leav'd red Valerian.
18 Myrto Cistus.
19 Virginian Aster.
20 Campanula Canariensis.
NOVEMBER
21 Pheasants Eye.
22 Perennial dwarf Sun flower
23 Double Feather few.
24 Carolina Star flower.
25 Scarlet Althæa.
26 Spanish white Jasmine.
27 Lavender with divided Leaves
28 Golden Rod.
29 American Viburnum.
30 Yellow Dwarf Aloe.
31 Single blew Anemone.
32 Purple Ficoides.
33 Groundsell tree.
34 Pellitory with Daisy flowers
35 Scarlet single Anemone.
36 White Egyptian holly hock.
37 Caper Bush.
38 Dwarf Colutea.
Printed for John Bowles at Mercers Hall in Cheapside.
Parr Sculp

72.

Richard Purcell, alias Charles Corbutt (1736 -1765/6), engraver
Robert Pyle (d. ca. 1763), artist
Robert Sayer (b. 1725, ac. 1751-d. 1794), publisher

Summer

London, 1755-65
Mezzotint, roulette with minimum of line engraving, watercolors
Laid paper, watermark of "T. Dupuy Fin AUVERGNE 1742"

Overall size: 35.4 x 25.7 cm
Image: 31.2 x 24.8 cm

59.74.10

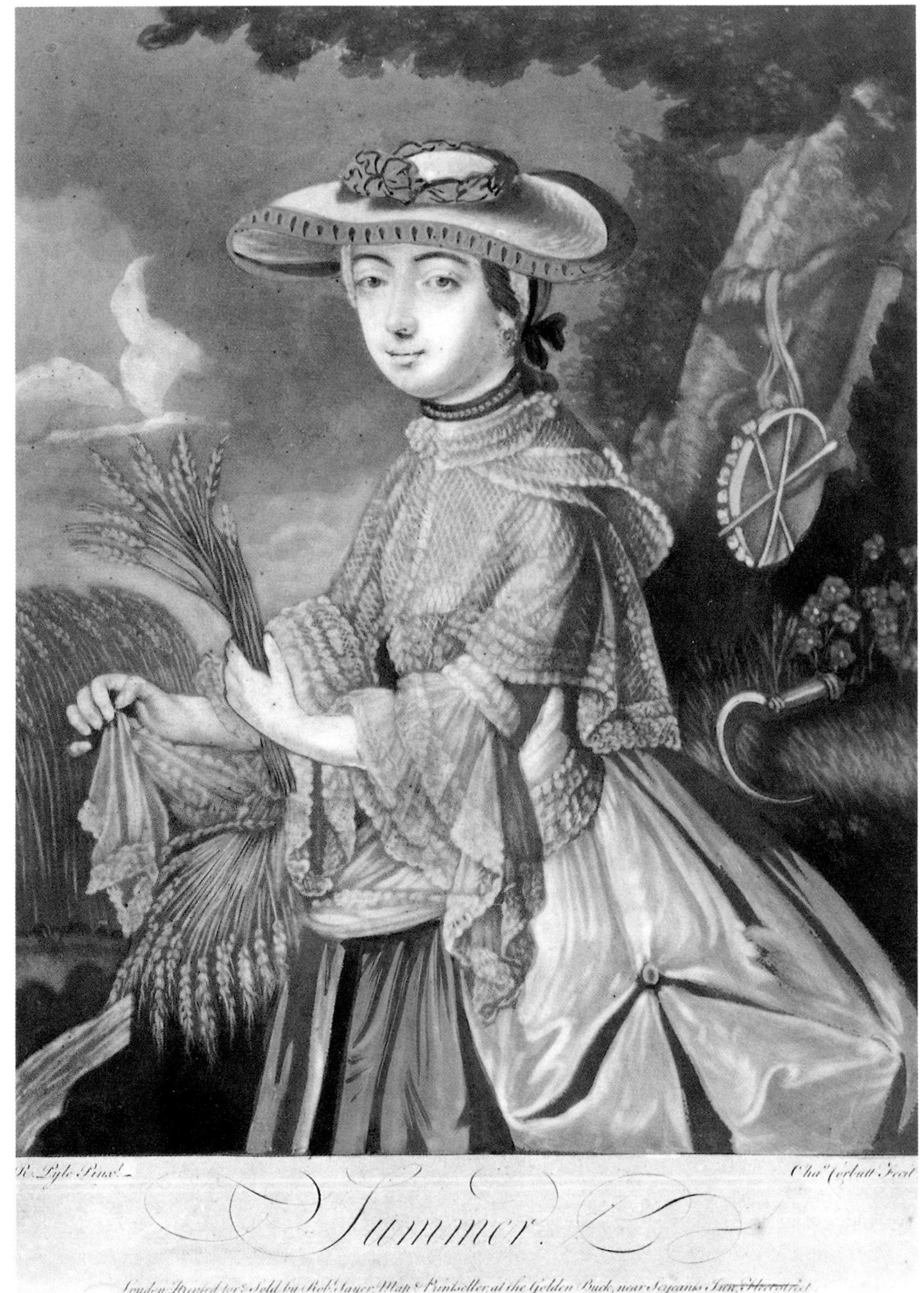

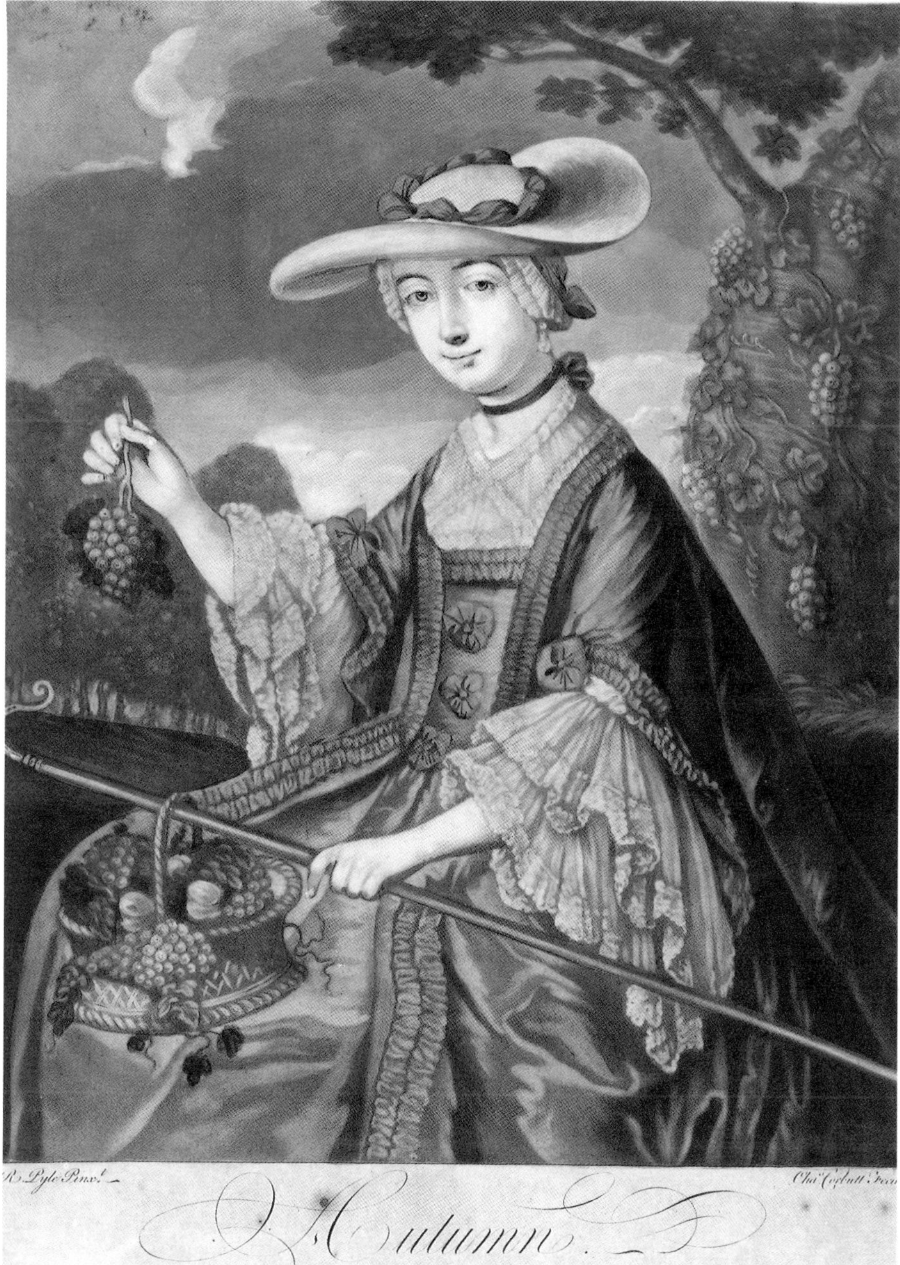

73.

Richard Purcell, alias
Charles Corbutt (1736-1765/6),
engraver
Robert Pyle (d. ca. 1763), artist
Robert Sayer (b. 1725, ac.
1751-d. 1794), publisher

Autumn

London, 1755-65
Mezzotint, roulette with
minimum of line engraving,
watercolors
Laid paper

Overall size: 36.8 x 26.5 cm
Platemark: 35.4 x 25.1 cm
Image: 31.5 x 24.9 cm

59.74.11

74.

Richard Purcell, alias
Charles Corbutt
(1736-1765/6), engraver
Robert Pyle (d. ca. 1763), artist
Robert Sayer (b. 1725, ac. 1751-d. 1794), publisher

Winter

London, 1755-65
Mezzotint, roulette with minimum of line engraving, watercolors
Laid paper

Overall size: 36.7 x 26.6 cm
Platemark: 35.4 x 25.2 cm
Image: 31.2 x 25.1 cm

59.74.12

75.

Richard Purcell, alias
Charles Corbutt
(1736-1765/6), engraver
Robert Pyle (d. ca. 1763), artist
Robert Sayer (b. 1725, ac. 1751-d. 1794), publisher

Spring

London, 1755-65
Mezzotint, roulette with minimum of line engraving, watercolors
Laid paper

Overall size: 36.5 x 26.2 cm
Platemark: 35.4 x 25.4 cm
Image: 31.5 x 25.1 cm

59.74.9

Of the numbers of European engravers and etchers who left the Continent for England in the seventeenth century, Wenceslas Hollar was of particular and lasting influence. In 1641, he etched a set of four three-quarter length portraits of beautiful young women, each dressed exquisitely and representing a season of the year. Favorable reception was sufficient to encourage him to execute two additional sets, one in 1643 featuring half-length figures, and another the next year using full-length figures. In each Hollar placed his subjects against a detailed scene, and in so doing he established a formula for sets of seasons and months that remained popular to the end of the eighteenth century.

When the household of Abiah Holbrook of Boston was inventoried in 1769, it included "four pictures of the seasons." Advertisements, accounts, inventories, and personal papers attest to the appeal of sets of the seasons throughout America in the eighteenth century. To meet the demand in 1775, Robert Sayer offered three different sets to his customers in London and abroad: one of rural scenes taken from paintings by François Boucher (1703-1770); and two engraved by Richard Purcell, who often used the alias Charles Corbutt. This set, being one of the latter, was engraved in the popular posture size.

In view of their eighteenth-century popularity, a surprisingly small number of complete sets of the seasons survive. Of those that do, many show the results of long exposure to light and an accumulation of airborne pollutants and insect stains, naturally occurring changes that at once veil their original brilliance and reveal their continued use as decoration.

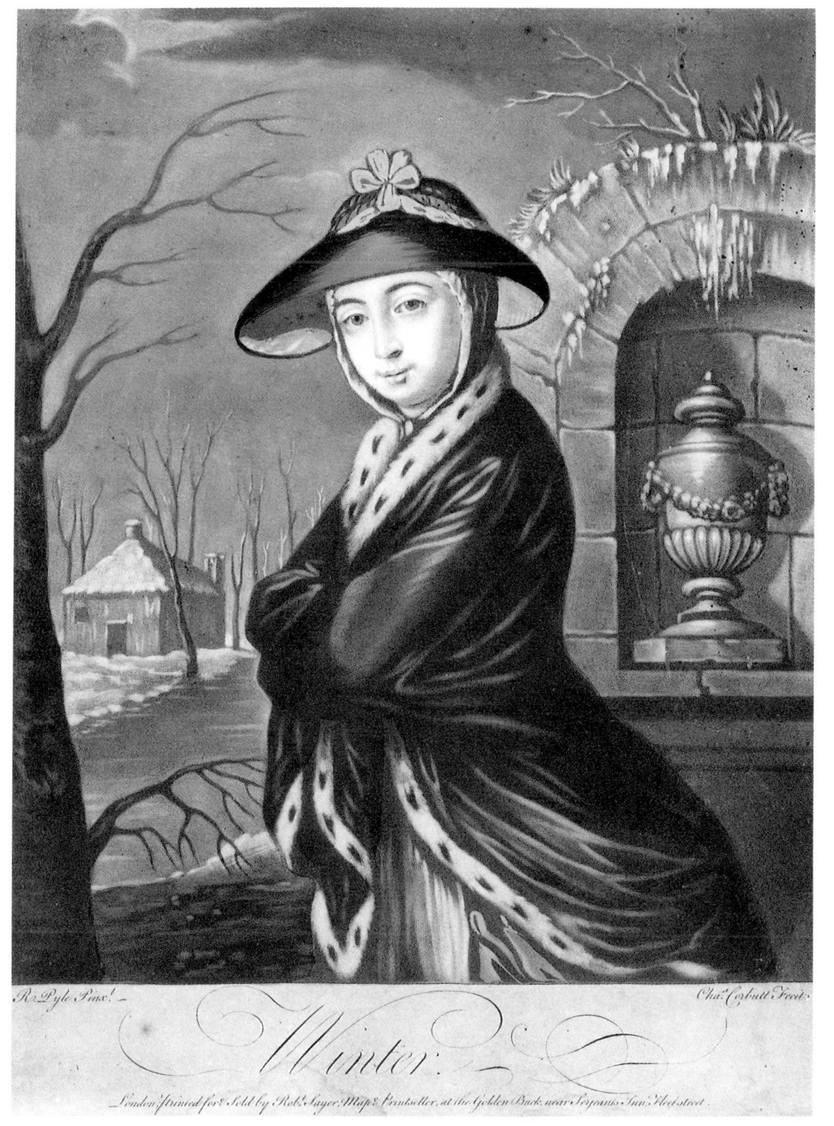
R. Pyle Pinx.
Chas. Corbutt Fecit
Winter.
London Printed for & Sold by Robt. Sayer, Map & Printseller, at the Golden Buck, near Serjeants Inn, Fleet street.

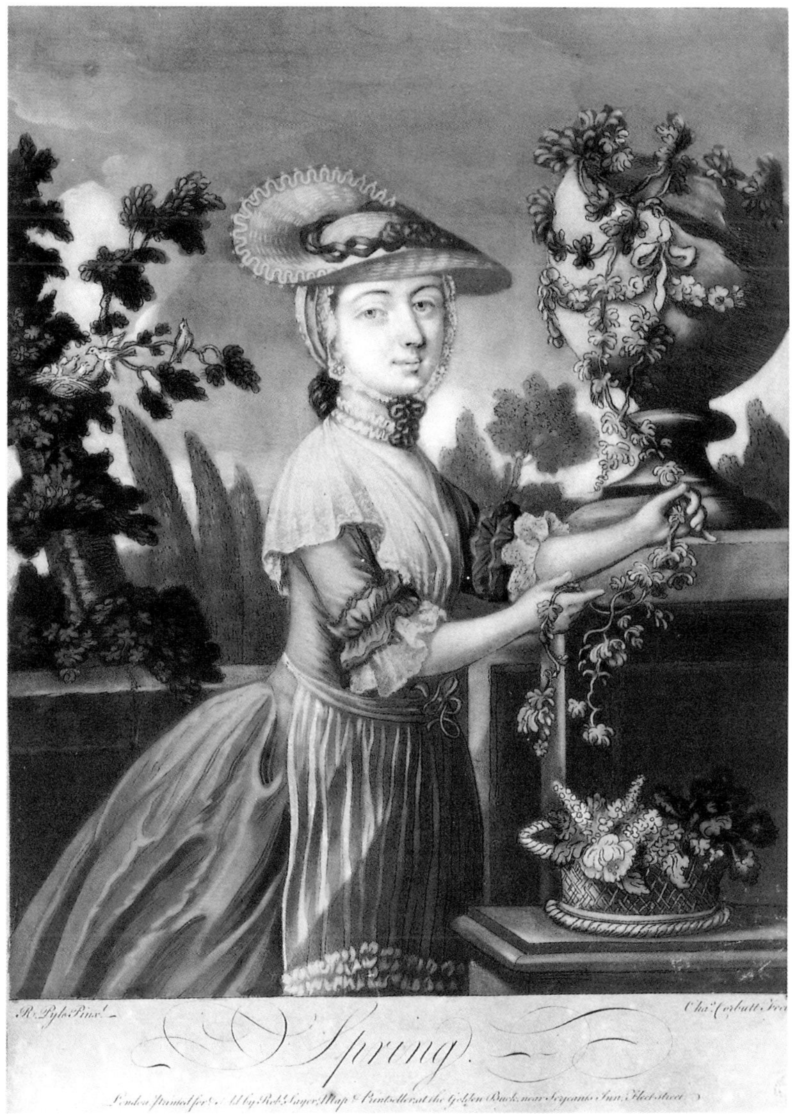
R. Pyle Pinx.
Spring.

76.

Luke Sullivan (1701-1771), delineator and engraver
Thomas Bowles (ac. 1702-d. 1764), John Bowles & Son (firm ac. 1754-ca. 1764), and J. Finney (n.a.), publishers

A View of Cliefden in Buckinghamshire the Seat of the Rt. Honble. the Earl of INCHIQUIN.

London, March 1, 1759
Line etching with burin work
Laid paper

Overall size: 44.0 x 59.9 x 2.19 cm
Platemark: 36.8 x 52.8 cm
Image: 36.1 x 52.5 cm
In original frame

60.86.4

The fashion of fitting up cabinets or smaller rooms with paper printed with bordered reserves that were designed to receive engravings is well documented in eighteenth-century English and American printsellers' advertisements. Sets of views of country seats, country houses, and gardens were considered particularly appropriate decoration for these elaborate walls. Such cabinets or print rooms survive in Britain. None seem to have survived in America, although colonial inventories and account books show that views of English country seats such as Cliveden ("Cliefden") were bought framed and glazed for American households. "Large and Splendid Views of some of the most remarkable places in North-America and of the most magnificent Palaces and Gardens in England" appeared in an advertisement in the *Boston News-Letter* on April 23, 1762.

The frame that surrounds this view by Luke Sullivan is typical of those mentioned in both English and American advertisements as being double carved, gilded, and ebonized.

References: Sayer and Bennett, *Sayer & Bennett's Catalogue of Prints for 1775,* 34; Michael Symes, "The Landscape Park Engravings of Luke Sullivan," *Journal of Garden History* 4, no. 2 (Spring 1984): 179-89; Dow, *Arts and Crafts in New England,* 24.

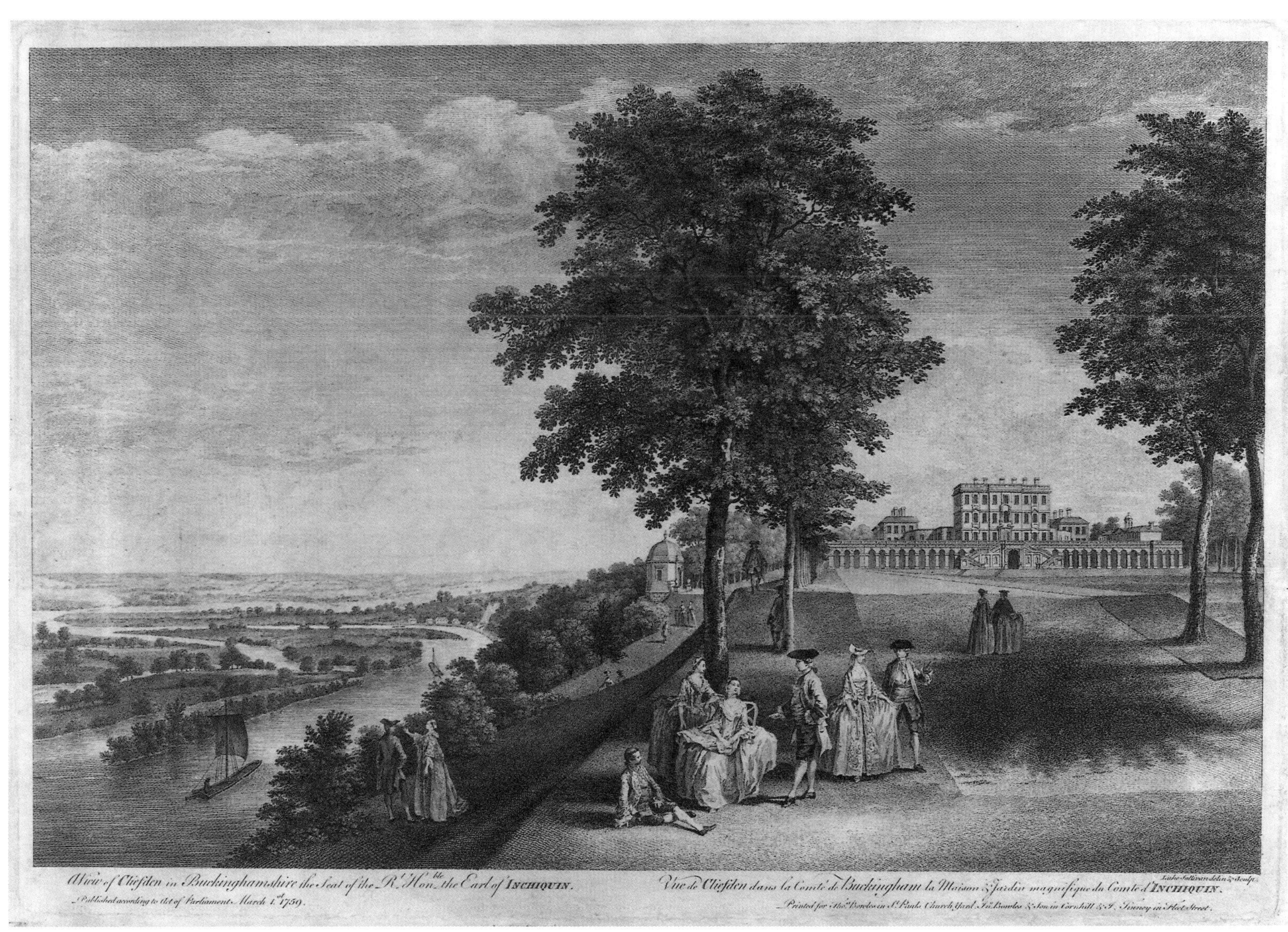
View of Cliefden in Buckinghamshire the Seat of the Rt. Hon.ble the Earl of INCHIQUIN.
Vue de Cliefden dans la Comté de Buckingham la Maison & Jardin magnifique du Comte d'INCHIQUIN.
Published according to Act of Parliament March 1st 1759.

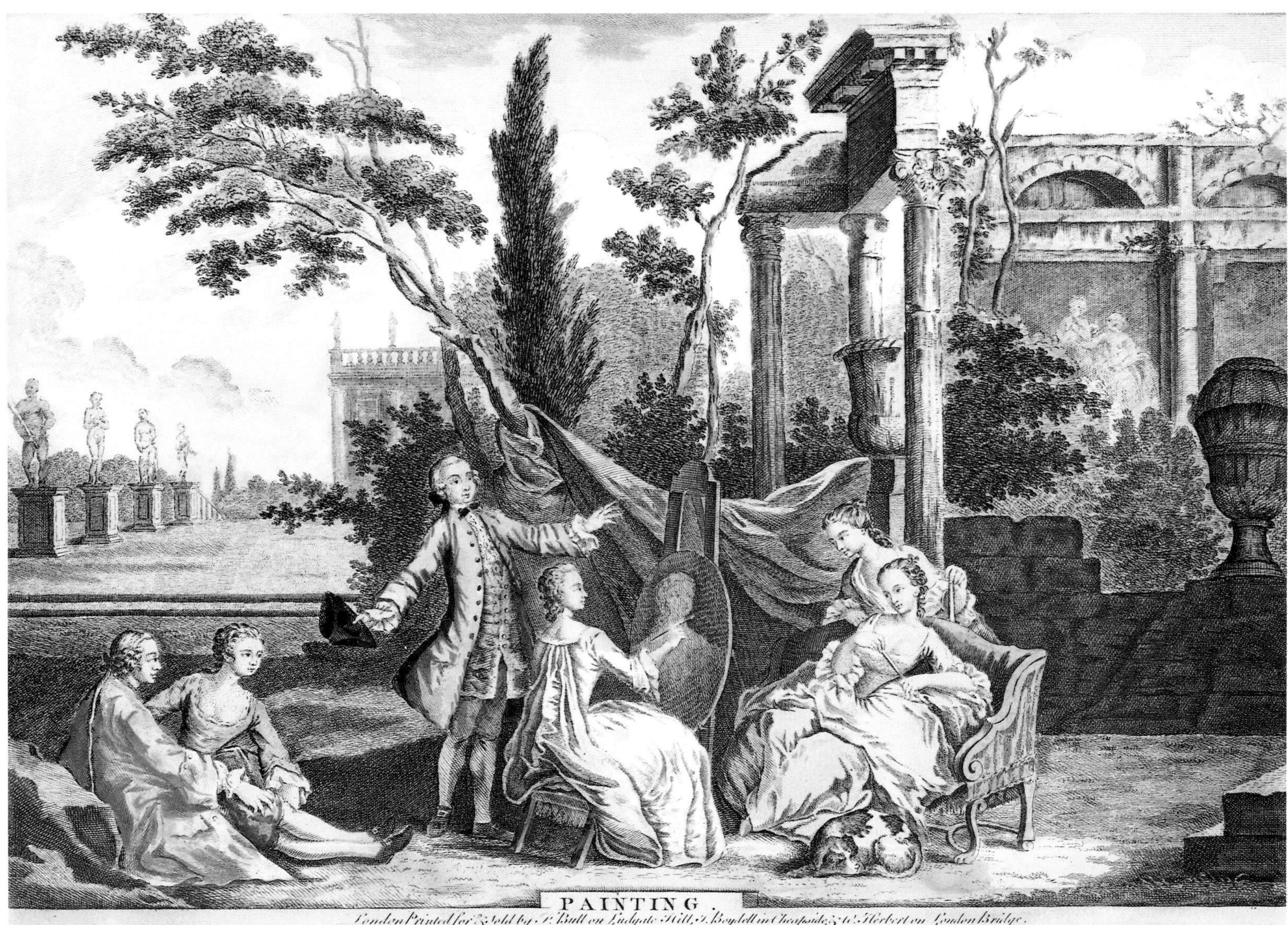
PAINTING.
London Printed for & Sold by T. Bull on Ludgate Hill, J. Boydell in Cheapside, & W. Herbert on London Bridge.

77.

James Amiconi
(1675-1752), artist
John Boydell
(1719-1804), publisher
Mrs. Frances Bull (n.a.),
publisher
William Herbert (n.a.),
publisher

PAINTING

London, 1766-75
Line etching with some burin work, watercolors
Laid paper, watermark of lily and bend with "L V G"

Overall size: 25.5 x 35.6 cm
Platemark: 24.7 x 35.1 cm.
Image: 23.6 x 34.0 cm

57.126.21

78.

James Amiconi (1675-1752), artist
John Boydell (1719-1804), publisher
Mrs. Frances Bull (n.a.), publisher
William Herbert (n.a.), publisher

SCULPTURE.

London, 1766-75
Line etching with some burin work, watercolors
Laid paper, countermark of "IV"

Overall size: 26.2 x 36.6 cm
Platemark: 24.8 x 33.5 cm
Image: 23.5 x 33.5 cm

57.126.23

To please the widest possible audience and particularly to attract more modest householders, eighteenth-century printsellers kept in their inventories a wide variety of sets, smaller in overall size, that could be framed and glazed at a fraction of the cost of the more "elegant" editions. Robert Sayer listed in his catalogue of 1775 no less than twenty-seven sets, ranging from four to twelve plates per set, with each plate being about ten by fourteen inches (25.4 by 35.5 cm) in size. Among these is a set of six prints of the "Sciences," which included painting, astronomy, poetry, architecture, sculpture, and music. Sayer's detailed descriptions of each in both size and subject would apply fully to a set in the Winterthur Museum, with the exception that only two carry Sayer's publication line. The rest, including *Painting* and *Sculpture,* give credit to John Boydell, Mrs. Frances Bull, and W. Herbert, London publishers at the addresses given in 1769. It may not be possible to determine who was responsible for first copying these designs by James Amiconi onto copperplate, but evidence of the popularity of the series or set is that four of London's leading printsellers lent their names to the publication.

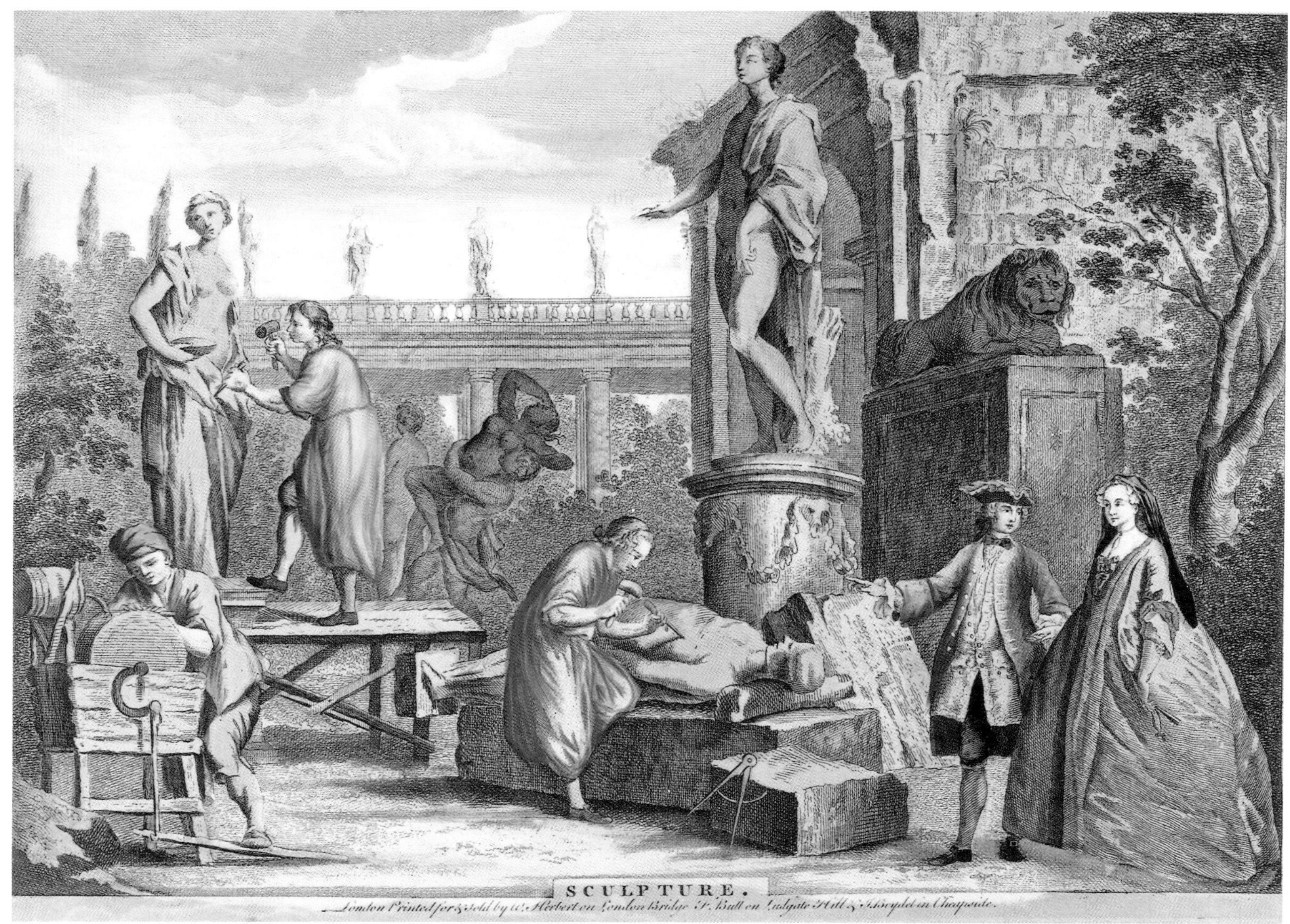
SCULPTURE.
London Printed for & Sold by W. Herbert on London Bridge T. Bull on Ludgate Hill & J. Boydel in Cheapside.

79.

Robert Dighton (1752-1814), artist
Carington Bowles (1724-1793), publisher

FEBRUARY. FEVRIER

London, June 24, 1784
Mezzotint with some burin work
Laid paper, watermark of "PTOMAS FIN DANGOVMOIS"

Overall size: 36.7 x 26.8 cm
Platemark: 35.2 x 25.0 cm
Image: 32.8 x 25.0 cm

64.892.2

80.

Robert Dighton (1752-1814), artist
Carington Bowles (1724-1793), publisher

DECEMBER. DECEMBRE.

London, 1784
Mezzotint with some burin work
Laid paper, watermark of "PTOMAS FIN DANGOVMOIS"

Overall size: 36.9 x 26.8 cm
Platemark: 35.4 x 25.2 cm
Image: 32.8 x 25.1 cm

64.892.12

American printsellers, eager to bring current fashion to colonial cities, at least as it was reflected in prints and engravings, included sets of the months in their inventories from the 1740s and possibly earlier. The *New York Mercury* of April 21, 1760, carried a typical advertise-ment in Garrat Noel's notice that he had for sale "12 Months after a new and Genteel Taste."

Carington Bowles and Robert Dighton combined efforts in 1784 to produce a set of months that explored the topic of how fashionable ladies occupied their time and what costumes were appropriate for each occasion. Indoor activities for *February* and *December* include playing music or cards. These pastimes are set against detailed descriptions of the room furnishings, with clear delineations of contrasting textile patterns, mantel decorations, floral arrangements, and window hangings. In contrast, subjects for warmer months appear out of doors in the landscape, engaged in such activities as supervising summer gardening and harvest, or watching an October fox hunt from a discrete distance.

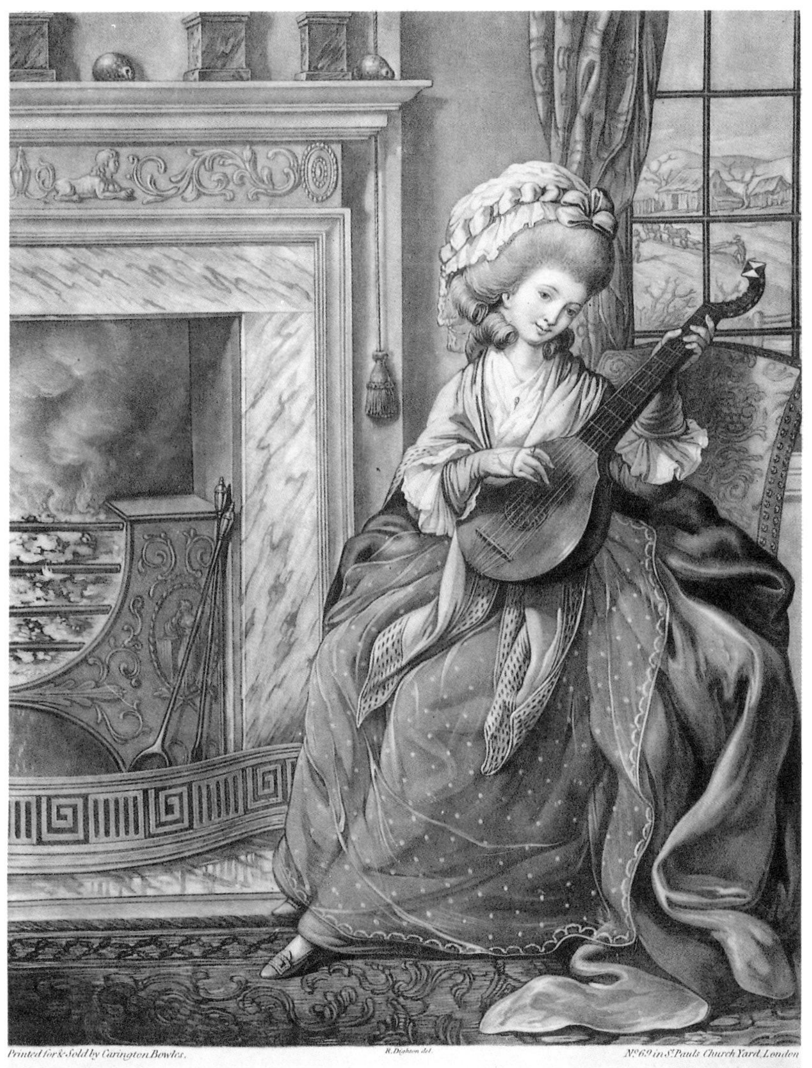

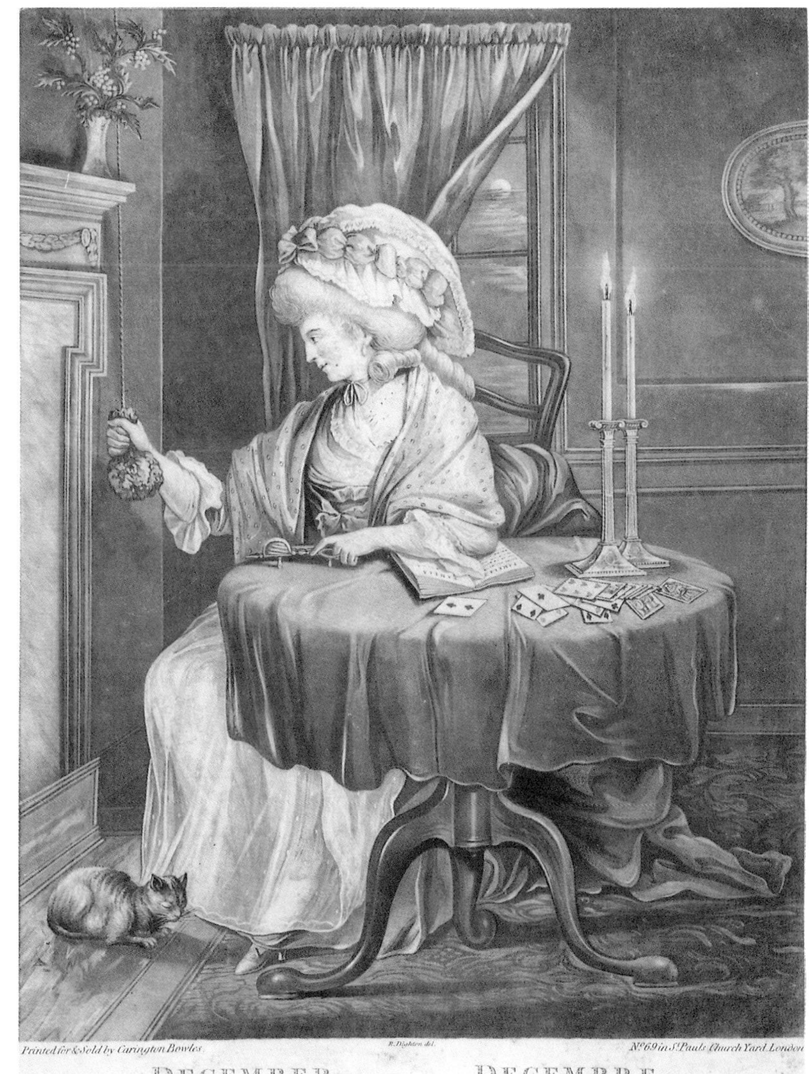

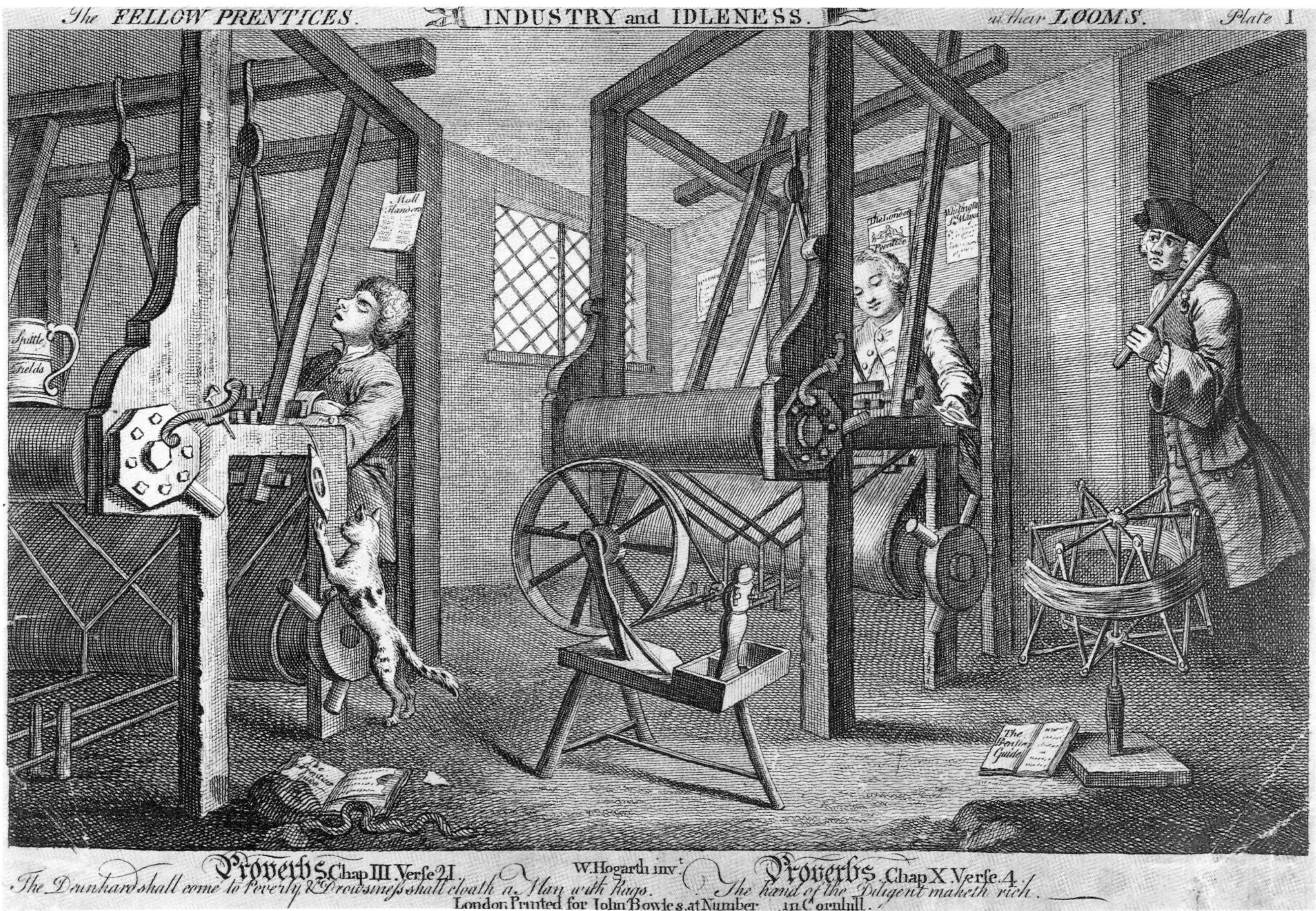
The FELLOW PRENTICES.
INDUSTRY and IDLENESS.
at their LOOMS.
Plate 1
Moll Flanders
The London Prentice
Whittington Ld Mayor
Spittle Fields
The Prentice's Guide
Proverbs Chap III. Verse 21.
The Drunkard shall come to Poverty, & Drowsiness shall cloath a Man with Rags.
W. Hogarth inv.
Proverbs Chap X Verse. 4.
The hand of the Diligent maketh rich.
London Printed for John Bowles, at Number 13 Cornhill.

81.

William Hogarth (1697-1764), artist
John Bowles (1701-1779), publisher

The FELLOW PRENTICES at their LOOMS. Plate 1
Proverbs Chap III, Verse 21.
The Drunkard shall come to Poverty & Drowsiness shall clothe a Man with Rags.
Proverbs, Chap X. Verse 4. The hand of the Diligent maketh rich
W. Hogarth invt. London
Printed for John Bowles. at Number [?] in Cornhill

London, after 1750
Line etching and some burin work
Laid paper, watermark of Strasburg lily with "L V G"

Overall size: 19.9 x 27.9 cm
Platemark: 18.8 x 27.5 cm
Image: 16.6 x 26.5 cm

56.42.8

Engraved pictures especially suitable for children had been advertised in America from the 1740s and included both moral subjects and penmanship sheets. Hogarth's series *Industry and Idleness* was introduced in 1747 and described by the artist as "calculated for the use & instruction of youth." Its popularity continued to the end of the century and beyond. Printsellers in the colonies advertised the series from South Carolina to Boston.

Hogarth used a simple theme: those who are diligent at their work will succeed and prosper; those who are slothful will fall into ruin. He delineated the stages of advancement and decline with sharp, linear characterizations, and he eliminated distracting flourishes of the burin and intricate tonal transitions. In the original edition, Hogarth sharpened his message further by including such devices as manacles and a hangman's rope on one side of the border and the badge of political office and the mace of authority on the other. In spite of copyright laws in effect from 1735, *Industry and Idleness* was copied with only minimal changes in size or in the elimination of the original border designs.

In Plate 1 of the series, the characters are presented in strong contrast. Mr. Goodchild, the industrious one, is neat, clean of face, and busy at work in the bright light of the window. His fellow apprentice, Thomas Idle, sits in the shadows in a state of drowsiness apparently induced by the ale that once filled the large tankard on the spindle of his loom.

Reference: Paulson, *Hogarth's Graphic Works,* 1:194-202, 8-9.

British Museum, *Satires,* 2896

VIEWS FOR THE PERSPECTIVE GLASS AND OTHER AMUSEMENTS

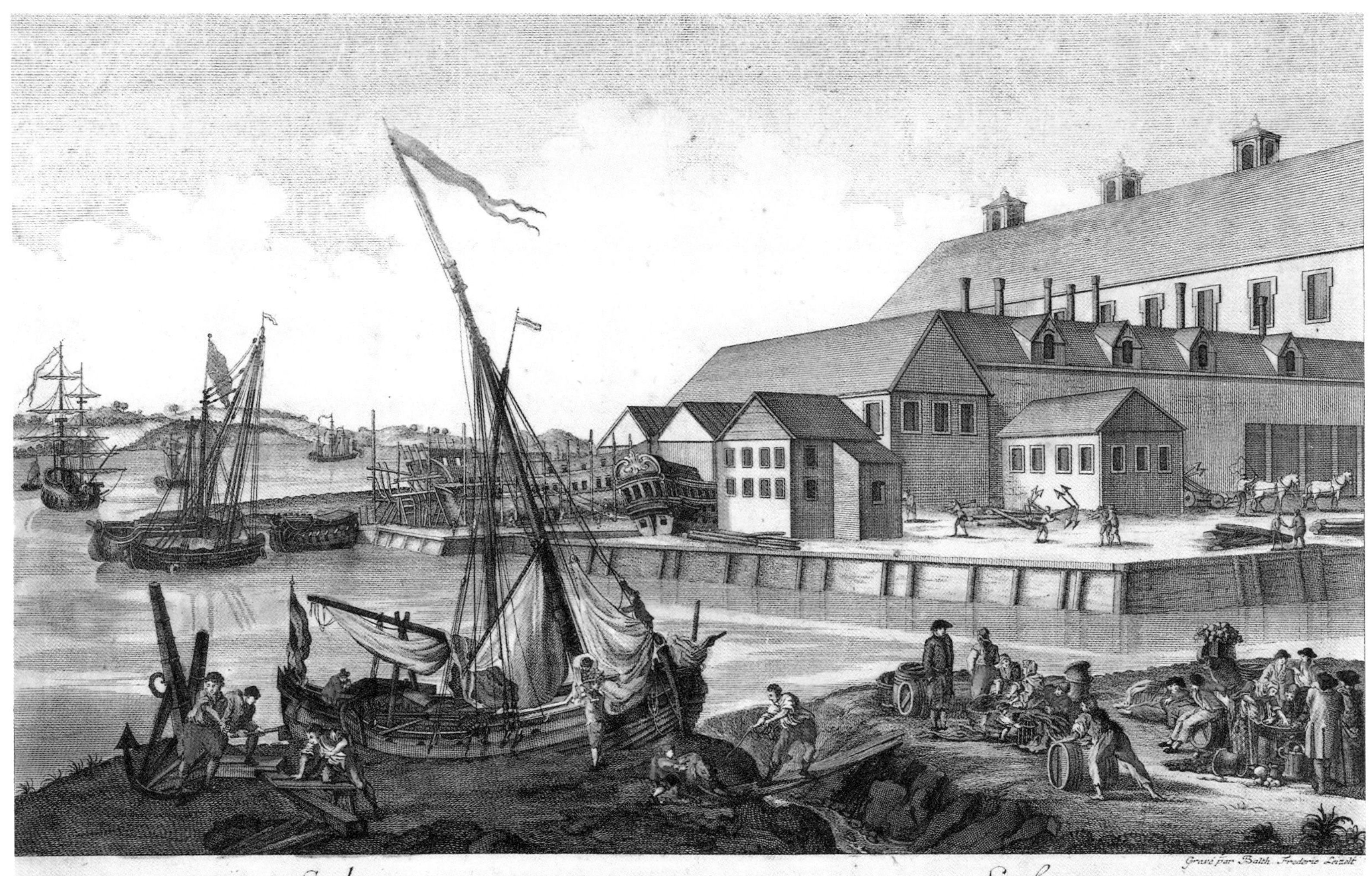

82.

Balthazar Frederick Leizelt (n.a.), engraver
François Xavier Habermann (1721-1796) and Balthazar Frederick Leizelt, publishers

VUE DE SALEM

Augsburg, Germany, ca. 1776
Published in *Collection des Prospects*
Line etching with some burin work, watercolors
Laid paper, watermark of "AD" in heart surmounted by an elongated "4" or Byzantine cross

Overall size: 32.2 x 43.2 cm
Platemark: 31.6 x 42.6 cm
Image: 24.9 x 39.4 cm

56.25

83.

Balthazar Frederick Leizelt (n.a.), engraver
François Xavier Habermann (1721-1796) and Balthazar Frederick Leizelt, publishers

VUE DE PHILADELPHIE

Augsburg, Germany, ca. 1776
Published in *Collection des Prospects*
Line etching with some burin work, watercolors
Laid paper, watermark of "AD" in heart surmounted by an elongated "4" or Byzantine cross

Overall size: 31.2 x 40.9 cm
Image: 25.0 x 39.5 cm

60.357.6

In late March or early April of 1740, a Boston carver by the name of Hubbert received, presumably from England, "a certain machine by which is presented to the sight a Prospect of Landskips, beautiful, Seats, Water Works, Alcoves, Groves, and Sea Pieces." Fourteen views could be seen at Hubbert's shop on Common Street between three and six o'clock in the afternoon. Variously called perspective machines or glasses, or optical machines, these devices depended upon a darkened room, the direct light of a lamp or candle upon a flat image (either a print or a drawing), a reflecting mirror or mirrors, and a magnifying lens to lend a sense of distance and a third dimension.

It has been suggested that the invention of the perspective glass for viewing prints occurred in France, where courtly ladies and gentlemen with diminished sight could enjoy the details of a picture without giving away their handicap. Whatever the original purpose, this portable machine and a stock of pictures of distant locations provided evenings of entertainment for young and old alike. In eighteenth-century America, it was not uncommon for traveling showmen to set up their glasses and invite the public—for a small fee—to enjoy the latest views of England, Rome, Paris, and other places of interest. Printsellers in Boston, New York, and Philadelphia advertised the sale of prints suitable for the perspective glass. Customers could buy professionally colored and mounted views or the supplies to color their own. Although any print could be used, those especially designed for the glass carried titles printed in reverse above the image that were to be left in place for easy identification of the scene when viewed through the machine. The complete title or description below was intended to be cut off and affixed to the back of the mount.

A complete catalogue of views for the perspective glass remains to be researched. It is documented, however, that some individuals in America owned as many as a hundred or more of these prints. Perspective views were published in England and on the continent over much of the eighteenth century, and large quantities of them remain in public collections today. Like these views of Salem and Philadelphia, prepared in Augsburg by an engraver who obviously had not seen either city, some were more fanciful than real. Europeans would not have been surprised by the architecture, although eighteenth-century Bostonians and Philadelphians must have been greatly amused.

References: M. C. Chaldecott, "Zograscopes," *Annals of Science* 9, no. 6 (December 1953): 315-22; Joe Kindig III, "The Perspective Glass," *Antiques* 65, no. 6 (June 1954): 466-68.

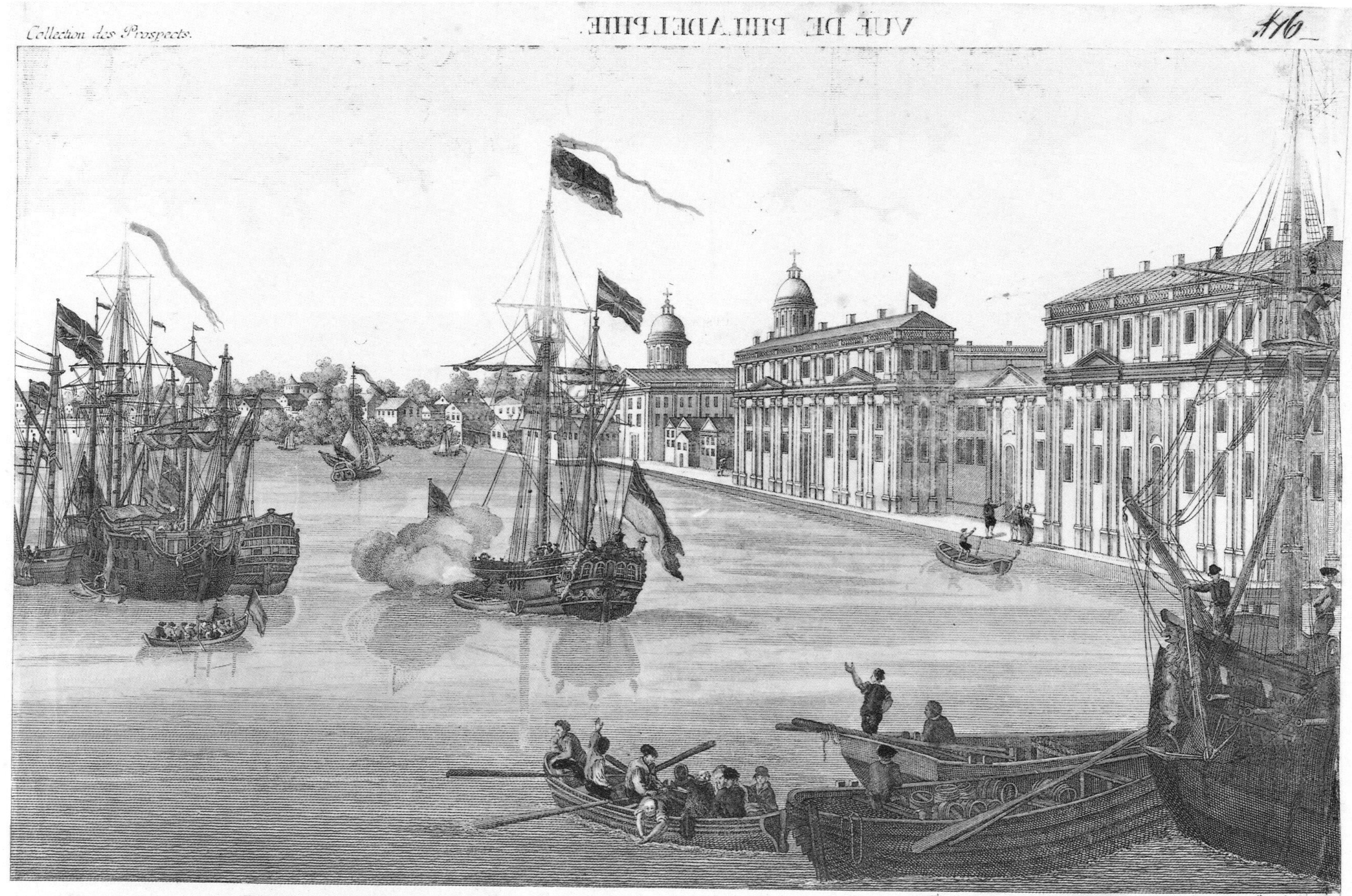

Gravé par Balth. Frederic Leizelt

Philadelphia.

Die Haupt Stadt in der Nord-Americanischen Provinz Pensylvanien, sie ist vom William Penn (dem Caroll II. König in Engelland die ganze Provinz geschencket hatte) im Jahr 1682. zwischen 2. Schiffreichen Flüßen angelegt und deßwegen Philadelphia genennet wordē, weil die Einwohner in Brüderlicher Einigkeit daselbst lebē sollen.

Philadelphie.

La Ville Capitale de Pensylvanie Province Nord-Americaine. William Penn, à qui Charles II. Roi d'Angleterre donna cette Province entière la planta en 1682 entre deux fleuves navigables et l'apella Philadelphie, parceque les habitans y vivoient dans une Harmonie fraternelle.

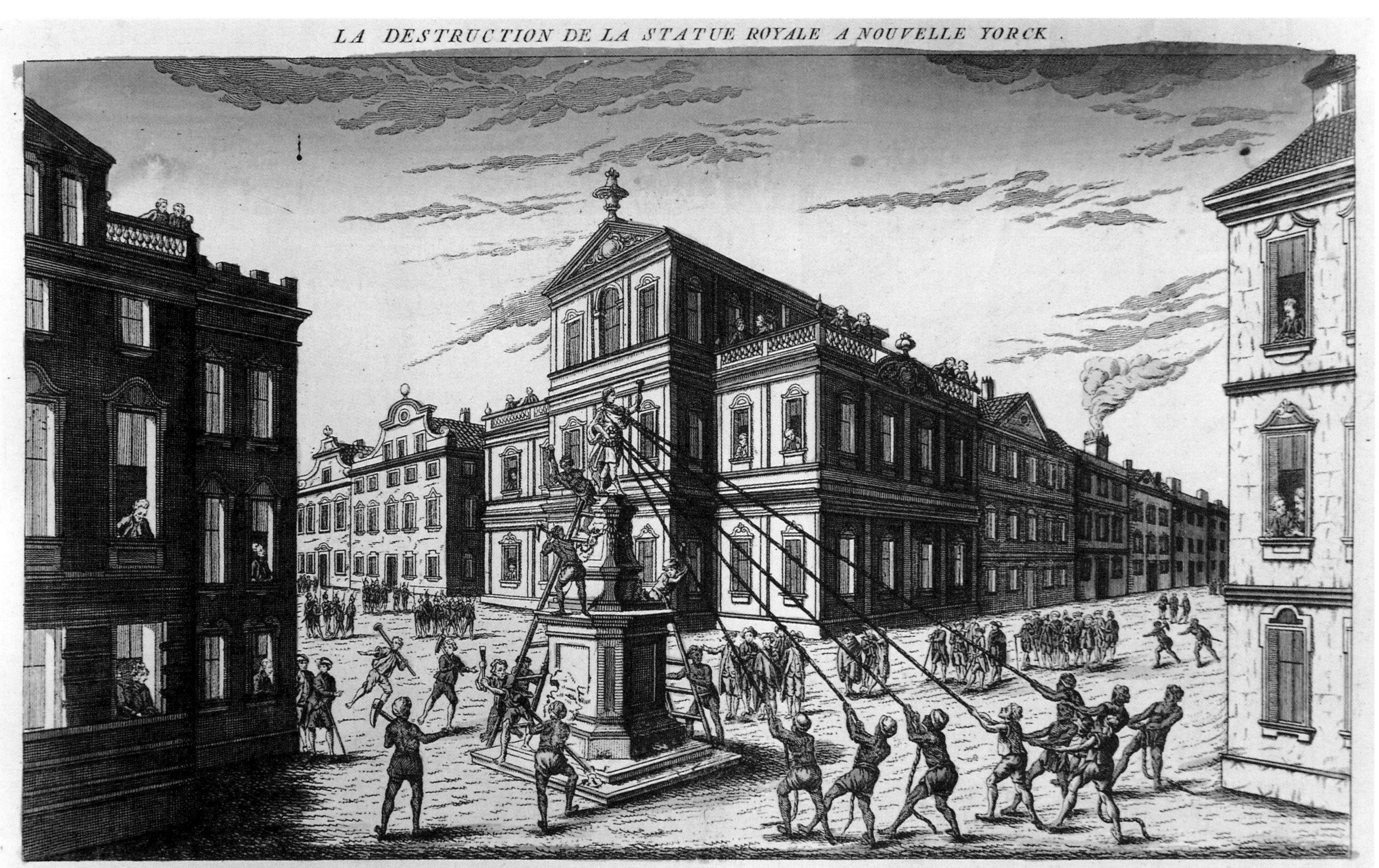

Die Zerstorung der Koniglichen Bild Saule zu Neu Yorck | La Destruction de la Statue royale a Nouvelle Yorck

A Paris chez J. Chereau rue St. Jacques au dessus de la Fontaine St. Severin No. 257

84.

André Basset (ca. 1750-1800), and J. Chereau (n.a.), publishers, after François Xavier Habermann (1721-1796)

Die Zerstorung der Koniglichen Bild Saule zu Neu Yorck La Destruction de la Statue royale a Nouvelle Yorck

Paris, France, ca. 1776-1800
Line etching with minimal burin work, watercolors
Laid paper, watermark of "JAD" with countermark of a hand

Overall size: 33.5 x 48.7 cm
Platemark: 28.0 x 40.5 cm
Image: 23.2 x 38.4 cm

76.227

News of the signing of the Declaration of Independence reached New York on July 10, 1776. In the emotion of the moment a group toppled a statue of George III that had been on Bowling Green at the southern end of Broadway since shortly after the Stamp Act was repealed.

The architectural reality of American cities and towns may have escaped continental publishers of views for the perspective glass, but most, like their immediate customers, were well aware through newspaper accounts of political developments in the colonies. Although the English had long been major customers for French and German engravings, it would appear that this one, on the basis of subject and lack of English subtitle, was not expected to sell well in London.

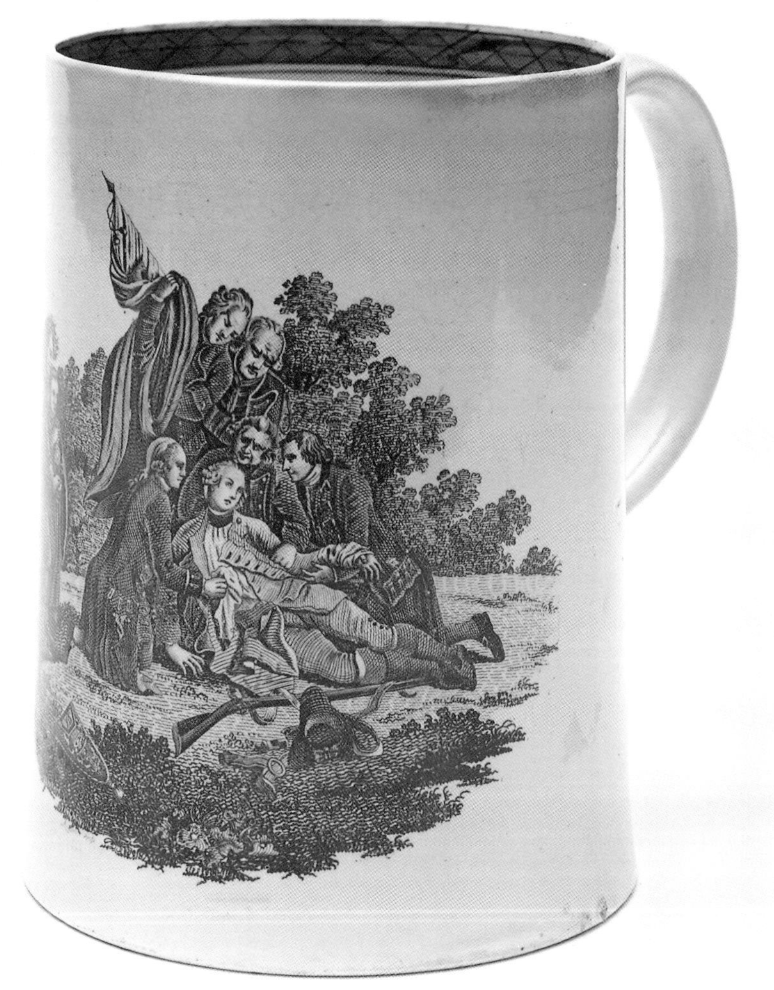

85.

Mug or can

England, 1780-1800
Earthenware, with transfer print in mulberry or purple of "The Death of General Wolfe"

14.9 x 15.6 cm
(5 7/8 x 6 3/8 in.)

75.112
Ex coll. Gordon A. Rust; Funds gift of the Claneil Foundation

From its first exhibition at the Royal Academy in London in 1771, Benjamin West's painting of *The Death of General Wolfe* won international acclaim for its treatment of classical virtues interpreted through modern events. It was engraved for John Boydell by William Woollett and offered for sale at one guinea. The plate was complex, and even as London's leading engraver, Woollett took four years to complete the task. It became the prototype for other engraved history subjects after it was published in 1776. A number of copies were issued in smaller sizes, including those produced in Basel, Paris, and Nuremberg. In addition, the central portion of the scene became a popular design for transfer printing on English earthenware or pearlware.

This late eighteenth-century pearlware mug features the painting's principal scene. General James Wolfe, commander of the British expedition to Canada, falls mortally wounded just at the moment he learns his forces are victorious in routing the French enemy from Quebec. He is surrounded by his officers: Brigadier General Monckton; Colonel Williamson; Major Isaac Barré; Captain Debbieg; Captain Hervey Smythe; Robert Adair, the surgeon; and Colonel George Napier. The engraver and presumably designer of this vignette, Thomas Rothwell, elected to finish the background with an abundance of vegetation rather than the complex details of the original composition.

References: British Museum Catalogue of Engraved English Portraits, comp. Freeman O'Donoghue and Henry M. Hake, vol. 5 of *Catalogue of Political and Personal Satires Preserved in the Department of Prints and Drawings in the British Museum* (London: Trustees of the British Museum, 1922), 8; Bruntjen, *John Boydell,* 35-38, 61-63.

86.

Pitcher

England, ca. 1780
Earthenware, with transfer print in black after "A Picturesque View of the State of the Nation for Feby 1778"

16.8 x 18.0 cm
(6 5/8 x 7 1/16 in.)

58.1201

A copy of the so-called Cow Caricature, or *A Picturesque View of the State of the Nation for February 1778* (see cat. no. 51), as it first appeared in *Westminster Magazine* decorates the verso of this pitcher of the Liverpool type. On the reverse, above the motto Come Box the Compass, is a mariner's compass, in the hub of which is a ship flying the British Union Jack.

In later wares, Liverpool merchants substituted the principal design for an adaptation engraved by American artist James Akin (ca. 1773-1846), who showed a figure representing Thomas Jefferson milking the British cow.

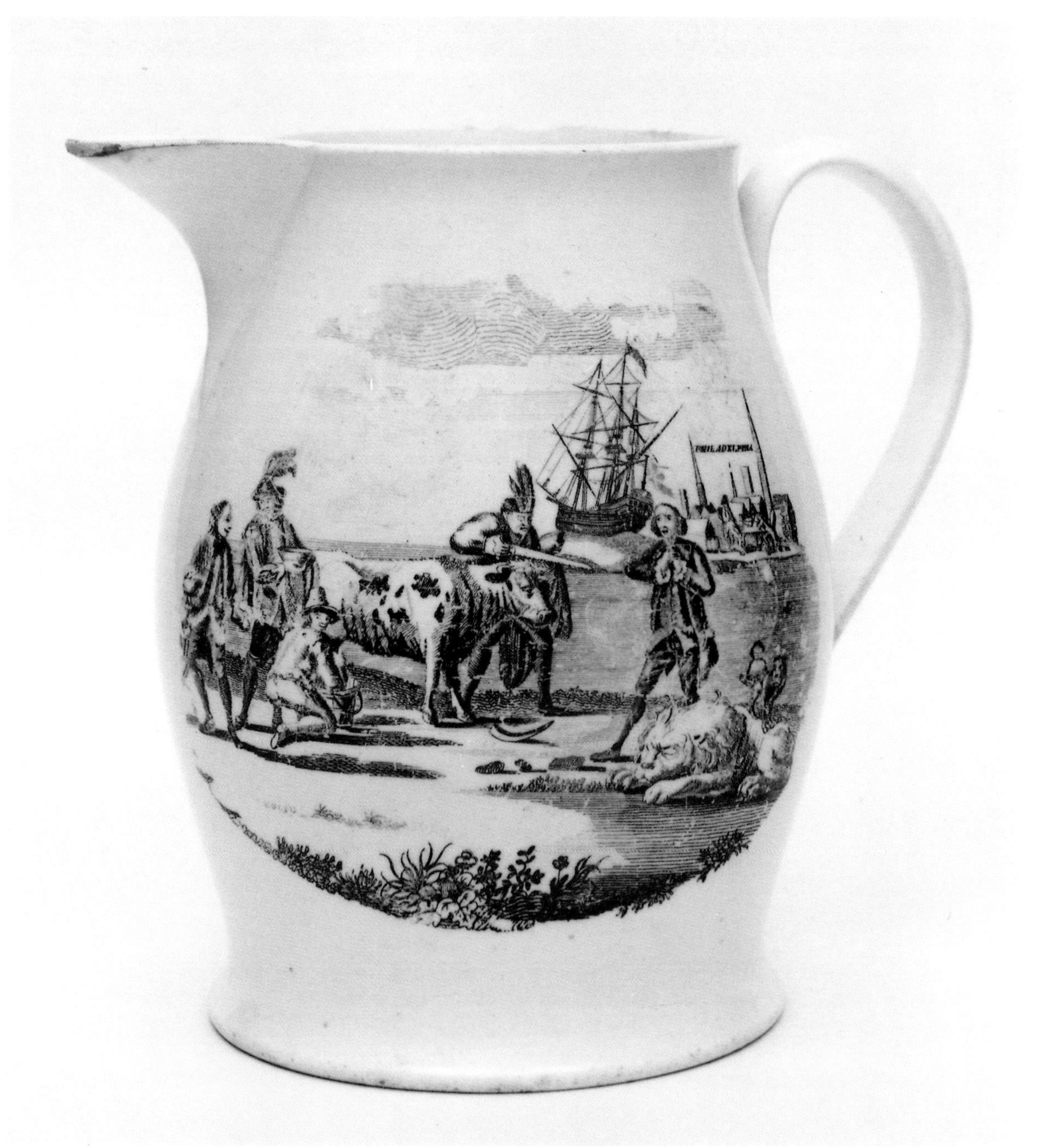
PHILADELPHIA

87.

Punch bowl

China, ca. 1775
Porcelain, hand-painted decoration after William Hogarth's *John Wilkes* and after *Mirth and Friendship* and *Night Amusement* by unidentified engravers

Overall height: 17.5 cm (6 7/8 in.)
Diameter: 28.0 cm (11 in.)

60.503

Like many engraved visages, William Hogarth's portrait of a sneering John Wilkes (see cat. no. 40) was sent to China for translation onto the surfaces of a wide variety of porcelain wares, and it suffered somewhat in the process. Not understanding occidental humor or physiognomy, the Chinese porcelain painters followed their own instincts. In this case that meant giving Wilkes oriental eyes and a tiny mouth fashionably turned up at the corners.

In other reserves around the exterior of this bowl are two scenes from small mezzotints, each being four by six inches (10.1 by 15.2 cm), offered by Sayer and Bennett in their catalogue for 1775 under *Droll and Humorous Subjects:* as no. "149. *Night* amusement, no. 150. *Mirth* and *Friendship*."

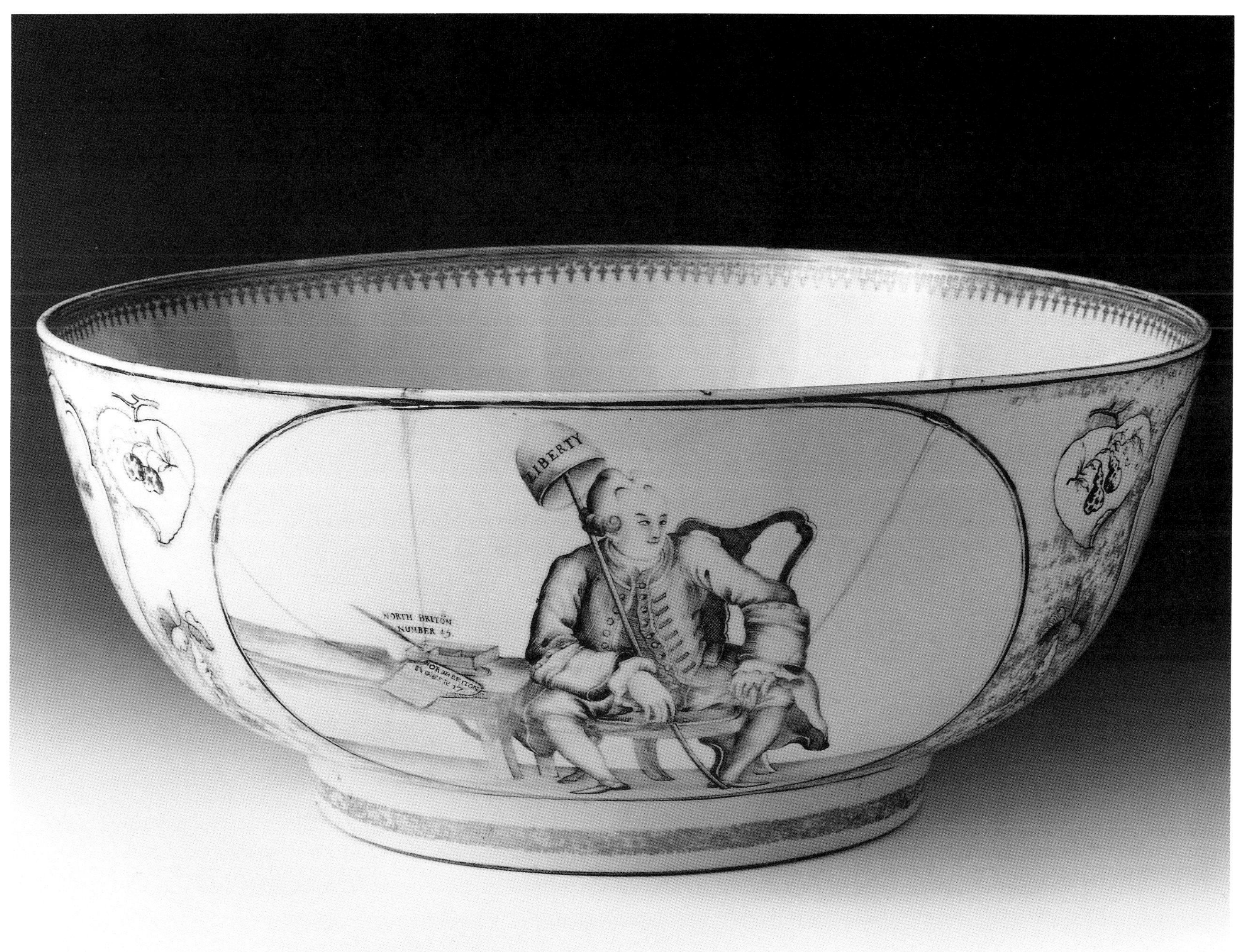
LIBERTY
NORTH BRITON
NUMBER 45.

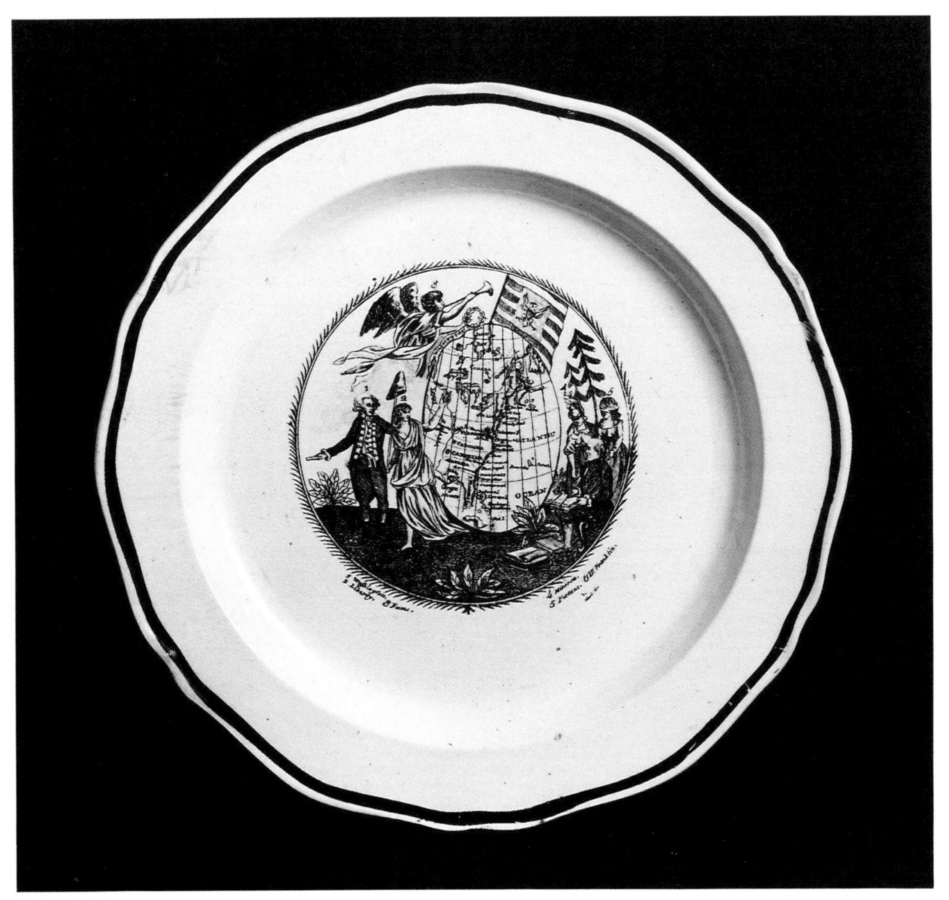

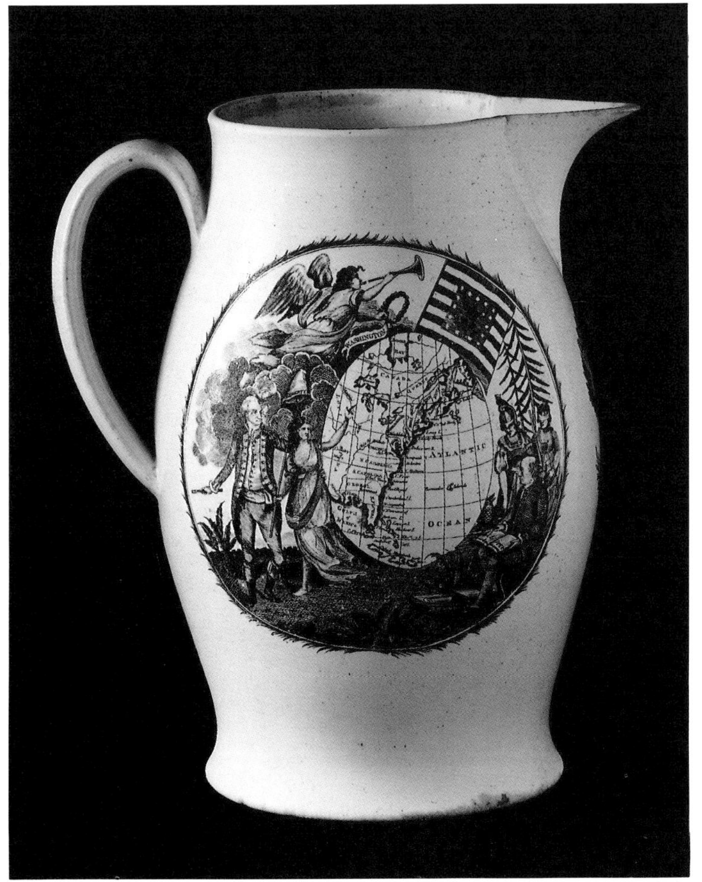
ATLANTIC
OCEAN

88.

Plate

Liverpool, England, possibly Herculaneum Factory, 1790-1820
Earthenware (creamware), transfer-printed design taken from the cartouche of *Map of the United States 1783* by John Wallis

2.2 x 25.1 cm dia.
(7/8 x 9 7/8 in.)

71.189
Gift of Mr. and Mrs. John Mayer

Ceramic factories contracted with independent engravers, many of whom possessed only modest skills, to execute the small copperplates from which images were printed on lightweight transfer papers. These printed images were applied face down onto the ceramic body and lightly rubbed to transfer the design. The paper was removed and the design fixed in firing.

Possibly concerned that a wider market would not readily recognize the figures in the design for this plate, the engraver added a key below the image and outside a wreath border: "1 Washington. 2. Liberty 3. Fame 4. Minerva. 5. Fortune. 6. Dr. Franklin." Still other variations on the cartouche taken from the *Map of the United States 1783* by John Wallis (see cat. no. 3) were engraved for transfer printing onto pitchers. The Winterthur Museum has four examples in small and large sizes.

References: Alan Smith, *The Illustrated Guide to Liverpool Herculaneum Pottery, 1796-1840* (London: Barrel and Jenkins, 1970), pl. 183; Pitchers with similar designs include 64.1284, 58.1193, and 58.1194.

89.

Pitcher

England, 1792-1810
Earthenware, with transfer-printed decoration in black of eagle, cartouche, and vignette from *Map of the United States 1783* by John Wallis and two-masted ship with American flag, partially colored

24.1 x 21.6 cm
(9 1/2 x 8 1/2 in.)

58.1192

90.

Handscreen

Paris, France, ca. 1780
Paper, card, wood, with printed DESCRIPTION DE L'AMERIQUE on reverse

40.0 x 25.0 x 1.5 cm
(15 3/4 x 9 7/8 x 5/8 in.)

65.2116

Handscreens were an eighteenth-century device to protect a sensitive cheek and easily dissolved wax-based cosmetics from the heat of a nearby fireplace or candle. Since paper offered lightweight and effective insulation, it proved useful in the design of these articles. This example features an elegantly bordered map of North America, and for the amusement or enlightenment of the user, a description of the subject on the reverse.

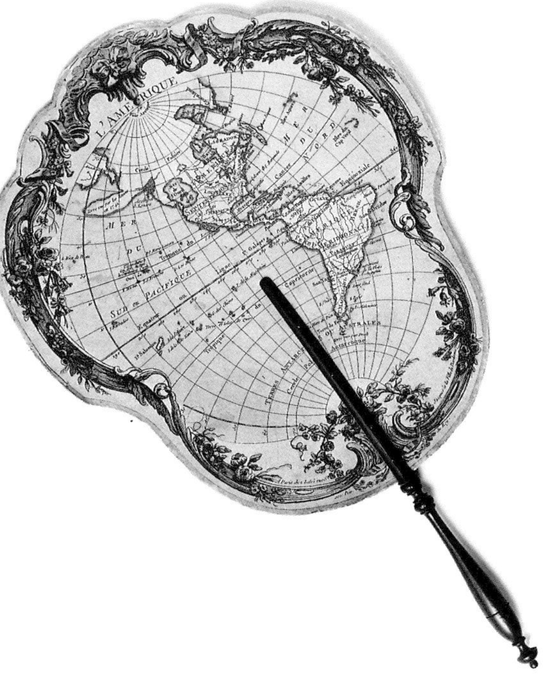

91.

Perspective glass

America or England, 1780-1800
Glass, mahogany with inlay,
brass, ivory

69.95 x 31.1 cm
(27 1/2 x 12 1/4 in.)
22.2 cm dia. of base (8 3/4 in.)

58.2414

Designed to be used on a table top and enjoyed from a seated position, this instrument for viewing engraved images served two purposes in the eighteenth century: it magnified the finer details of the two-dimensional image placed below it, and it created an illusion of greater depth to the image. Intended to be used by all ages, it was particularly useful to those with diminished eyesight.

The principal assembly consists of a frame enclosing a magnifying glass to which a mirror in a frame is attached by means of hinges. The hinges allow the mirror to be adjusted in relation to the magnifier, and the entire assembly can be moved up or down on the supporting shaft with the aid of a wood screw. With a variety of positions possible, the perspective glass could be arranged so a sitter might comfortably view the latest scenes from abroad for an hour or so.

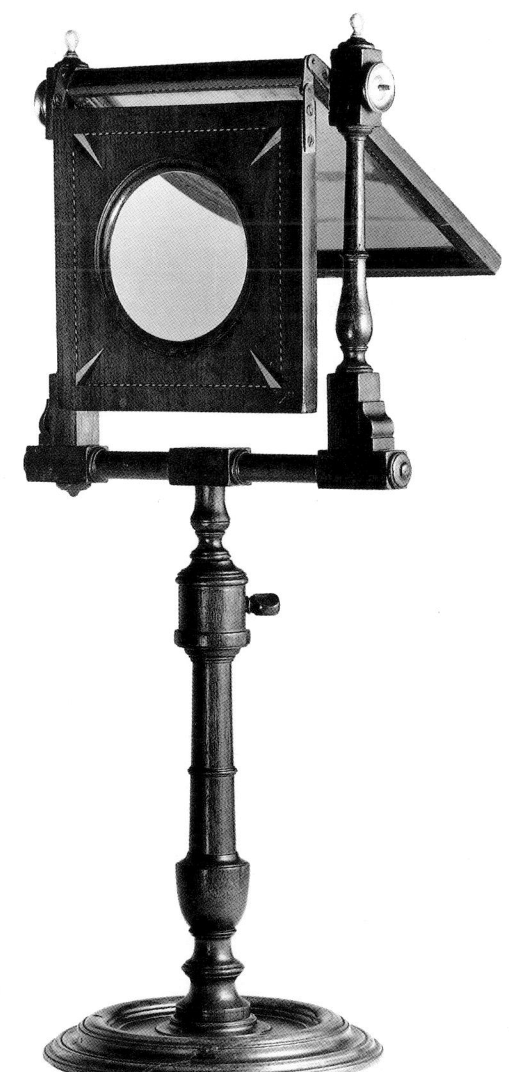

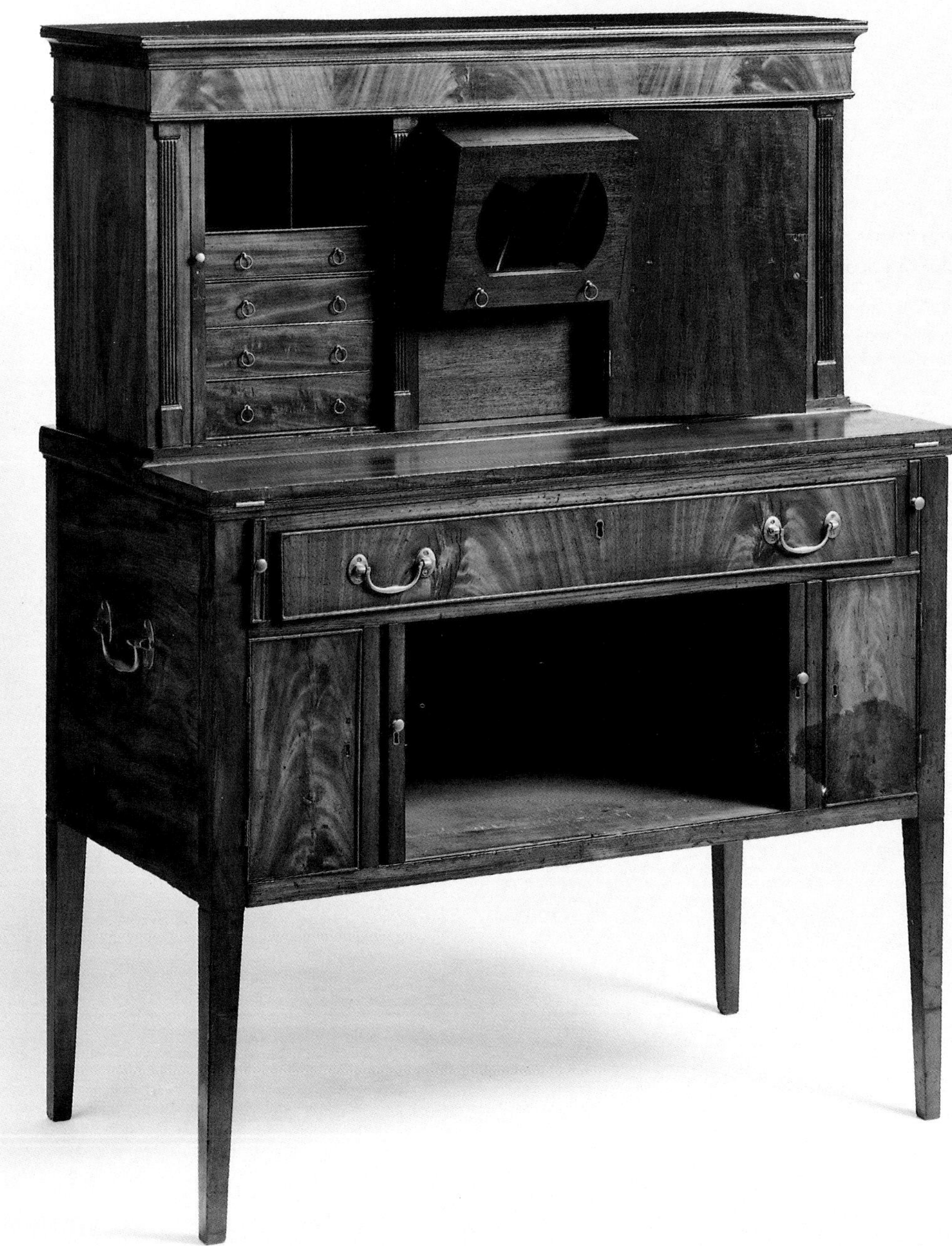

92.

Attributed to Edmund Johnston
(w. 1793-1811)

Tambour desk with perspective glass

Salem, Massachusetts, 1793-1811
Mahogany, white pine as secondary wood

132.1 x 98.4 x 50.8 cm
(52 x 38 3/4 x 20 in.)

55.96.4.1

This desk was first owned by Benjamin Pickman (1763-1843) of Salem, Massachusetts, and passed to his son, Francis Willoughby Pickman (1804-1886), who took it to Nova Scotia. It descended in the Pickman family of Nova Scotia to M. E. L. Lynch. When it was acquired by Winterthur in 1955, thirty-four hand-colored etchings of European views were found in the long top drawer of the lower section.

Not unlike today's multifunctional wall units or space dividers, this is both a writing desk and an entertainment center. A shallow shelf surfaced with green baize is hinged to the top of the lower section. In the upper section tambour doors on either side open to reveal small drawers and pigeonholes to contain writing equipment and papers. A large central panel in the upper section slides to the right to disclose a slightly convex glass similar to those used in early television sets. Two large tambour doors in the lower section open onto a commodious shelf, sufficiently low to accommodate a lighted candle or two with a stack of printed views in the center. The uppermost print is reflected to the viewer through a series of mirrors in the upper case.

With the stack of views easily accessed from the front, an individual could enjoy perusing the views in solitude. An access door from the back of the lower case also allows the front doors to be closed, thus removing the mechanics from the spectator's eye. Eighteenth-century advertisements placed by traveling vendors indicate their willingness to bring collections of the latest perspective views into private homes for the entertainment of a small company. Whether this concealed access to the desk was designed to be operated by some itinerant entertainer with an engaging narrative or by another member of the household, it did complete the illusion.

At least one other of these rather elaborate devices designed for the eighteenth-century *vües d'optique,* or perspective views, is known. Illustrated in Joe Kindig III's article in *Antiques* (June 1954) is a nearly identical desk that bears the label of Edmund Johnston.

References: Charles F. Montgomery, *American Furniture: The Federal Period* (New York: Viking Press, 1966), 99, 231, 233, cat. no. 187; Kindig, "The Perspective Glass," 468.

SELECTED BIBLIOGRAPHY

Barton, William. *Memoirs of the Life of David Rittenhouse.* Philadelphia: Printed by W. Brown for Edward Parker, 1813.

Beardsley, The Reverend William A. "An Old New Haven Engraver and His Work: Amos Doolittle," in *Papers of the New Haven Historical Society* 8 (1914): 132-50.

Belknap, Waldron Phoenix , Jr. *American Colonial Painting: Materials for A History.* Cambridge, Mass.: Belknap Press of Harvard University Press, 1960.

The Diary of William Bentley, D.D. Pastor of the East Church, Salem, Massachusetts.... 4 vols. Salem, Mass.: Essex Institute, 1904-1905.

Berkley, Edmund, and Dorothy Smith Berkley. *Dr. John Mitchell: The Man Who Made the Map.* Chapel Hill: University of North Carolina Press, 1958.

Bond, Richmond P. *Queen Anne's American Kings.* Oxford, England: Clarendon Press, 1952.

Brigham, Clarence S. *Paul Revere's Engravings.* Worcester, Mass.: American Antiquarian Society, 1954.

Brinton, Ellen Start. "Benjamin West's Painting of Penn's Treaty with the Indians," in *Bulletin of Friends' Historical Association* 30 (1941): 99-189.

British Library. *The American War of Independence, 1775-83.* Exhibition organized by the Map Library and Department of Manuscripts. London: British Library, 1975.

British Museum. Department of Prints and Drawings. *Catalogue of Prints and Drawings in the British Museum.* Division 1. *Political and Personal Satires.* London: Printed by Order of the Trustees, 1870-1954. Vols. 1-4 prepared by Frederic George Stephens; vols. 5-11 by Mary Dorothy George. Title changes with vol. 5 to *Catalogue of Political and Personal Satires Preserved in the Department of Prints and Drawings in the British Museum.*

Browne, Alexander. *Ars Pictoria: Or An Academy Treating of Drawing, Painting, Limning, Etching. To which are added XXI Copper Plates Expressing the Choicest, Neatest, and Most Exact Grounds and Rules of Symmetry, Collected out of the most Eminent Italian, German and Netherland Authors.* 2nd ed., corrected and enlarged. London: Arthur Tooker and William Battersby, 1675.

Bruntjen, Sven H. A. *John Boydell, 1719-1804: A Study of Art Patronage and Publishing in Georgian London.* New York and London: Garland Publishing, Inc., 1985.

Bush, Alfred L. *The Life Portraits of Thomas Jefferson.* Charlottesville, Vir.: Thomas Jefferson Memorial Foundation, 1962.

Calloway, Stephen. *English Prints for the Collector.* Guilford and London: Lutterworth Press, and Woodstock, Vt.: Overlook Press, 1981.

Chaldecott, M. C. "Zograscopes," in *Annals of Science* 9, no. 6 (December 1953): 315-22.

Churchill, William Algernon. *Watermarks in Paper in Holland, England, France, etc. in the XVII and XVIII Centuries and Their Interconnection.* Amsterdam: M. Hertzberger & Co., 1935.

Cohen, Hennig. *The South Carolina Gazette.* Columbia: University of South Carolina Press, 1953.

Journal of Nicholas Cresswell, 1774-1777. New York: Lincoln Macveagh, Dial Press, 1924.

Colwill, Stiles Tuttle. *Francis Guy 1760-1820.* Baltimore: Museum and Library of Maryland History, Maryland Historical Society, 1981.

Cumming, William P., and Helen Wallis. *A Map of the British Empire in America with the French and Spanish Settlements Adjacent Thereto by Henry Popple.* Lympne Castle, Kent: Harry Margery, 1972.

Cummings, Abbott Lowell. *Rural Household Inventories Establishing the Names, Uses and Furnishings of Rooms in the Colonial New England Home, 1675-1775.* Boston: Society for the Preservation of New England Antiquities, 1964.

Deák, Gloria-Gilda. *Picturing America, 1497-1890: Prints, Maps, and Drawings Bearing on the New World Discoveries and on the Development of the Territory that is now the United States.* Princeton, N.J.: Princeton University Press, 1988.

___________. *William James Bennett: Master of the Aquatint View.* With introductory essay by Dale Roylance. New York: New York Public Library, 1988.

Dolmetsch, Joan D. "Prints in Colonial America: Supply and Demand in the Mid-Eighteenth Century," in *Prints in and of America to 1850.* Edited by John D. Morse. Charlottesville: University Press of Virginia for the Henry Francis du Pont Winterthur Museum, 1970.

__________. *Rebellion and Reconciliation: Satirical Prints on the Revolution at Williamsburg.* Williamsburg: Colonial Williamsburg Foundation, 1976.

Dow, George Francis. *The Arts & Crafts in New England, 1704-1775: Gleanings from Boston Newspapers.* Topsfield, Mass.: Wayside Press, 1927.

Dunlap, William. *A History of the Rise and Progress of the Arts of Design in the United States.* Compiled by Frank W. Bayley and Charles Goodspeed. Rev. and enl. ed. 3 vols. New York: Benjamin Blom, 1965.

Dunthorne, Gordon. *Flowers and Fruit Prints of the 18th and 19th Centuries.* Washington, D.C.: Published by the author, 1938.

Fairbanks, Jonathan. "Portrait Painting in Seventeenth Century Boston: Its History, Methods, and Materials," in *New England Begins: The Seventeenth Century.* 3 vols. Boston: Museum of Fine Arts, 1982.

Fales, Martha Gandy. "Heraldic and Emblematic Engravers of Colonial Boston," in *Boston Prints and Printmakers, 1670-1775.* Edited by Walter Muir Whitehill and Sinclair H. Hitchings. Boston: Colonial Society of Massachusetts, 1973.

Journal and Letters of Philip Vickers Fithian 1773-1774: A Plantation Tutor of the Old Dominion. Edited by Homer Dickinson Farish. Charlottesville: University Press of Virginia, 1957.

Fowble, E. McSherry. *Two Centuries of Prints in America 1680-1880: A Selective Catalogue of the Winterthur Museum Collection.* Charlottesville: University Press of Virginia for the Henry Francis du Pont Winterthur Museum, 1987.

The Papers of Benjamin Franklin. Edited by Leonard W. Labaree et al. Vol. 3, January 1, 1745, through June 30, 1750. New Haven: Yale University Press, 1961.

Garratt, John A. "The Four Indian Kings," in *History Today* (London) 18, no. 2 (February 1968): 93-101.

Garratt, John A., and Bruce Robertson. *The Four Indian Kings.* Ottawa: Public Archives of Canada, 1985.

Godfrey, Richard T. *Printmaking in Britain.* New York: New York University Press, 1978.

Goodspeed, Charles E. *Yankee Bookseller, Being the Reminiscences of Charles E. Goodspeed.* Boston: Houghton Mifflin Co., and Cambridge, Mass.: Riverside Press, 1937.

Gottesman, Rita Susswein. *The Arts and Crafts in New York 1726-1776: Advertisements and News Items From New York City Newspapers.* New York: New York Historical Society, 1938.

__________. *The Arts and Crafts in New York 1777-1799.* Reprint ed. New York: New-York Historical Society, 1954.

Halsey, R. H. T. *The Boston Port Bill as Pictured by a Contemporary London Cartoonist.* New York: Grolier Club, 1904.

Hamilton, Alexander. *Gentleman's Progress: the Itinerarium of Dr. Alexander Hamilton 1744.* Edited by Carl Bridenbaugh. Chapel Hill: University of North Carolina Press for the Institute of Early American History and Culture Press, 1948.

Hart, Charles Henry. "Charles Willson Peale's Allegory of William Pitt, Earl of Chatham, and the Pitt Statues in Cork, Ireland and Charleston, South Carolina," in *Proceedings of the Massachusetts Historical Society* 48 (1915).

Hitchings, Sinclair H. "Thomas Johnston," in *Boston Prints and Printmakers, 1670-1775.* Edited by Walter Muir Whitehill and Sinclair H. Hitchings. Boston: Colonial Society of Massachusetts, 1973.

Holman, Richard B. "Seventeenth-Century American Prints" in *Prints in and of America to 1850.* Edited by John D. Morse. Charlottesville: University of Virginia Press, 1970.

__________. "William Burgis," in *Boston Prints and Printmakers, 1670-1775.* Edited by Walter Muir Whitehill and Sinclair H. Hitchings. Boston: Colonial Society of Massachusetts, 1973.

Honour, Hugh. *The European Vision of America.* Cleveland, Ohio: Cleveland Museum of Art, 1975.

Hough, Oliver. "Captain Thomas Holme, Surveyor-General of Pennsylvania and Provincial Councillor," in *Pennsylvania Magazine of History and Biography* 38, no. 2 (1913).

Jaffe, Irma B. *John Trumbull: Patriot-Artist of the American Revolution.* Boston: New York Graphic Society, 1975.

Jarrett, Derek. *England in the Age of Hogarth.* New Haven and London: Yale University Press, 1974.

Lambert, Susan. *The Image Multiplied: Five Centuries of Printed Reproductions of Paintings and Drawings.* London: Trefoil Publications, 1987.

Keys, Willard E. "The Cow and the Sleeping Lion," in *Antiques* 39, no.1 (January 1941): 25-27.

Kindig, Joe, III. "The Perspective Glass," in *Antiques* 65, no. 6 (June 1954): 466-68.

Mackay-Smith, Alexander. *The Colonial Quarter Race Horse: America's First Breed of Horses, ...* Richmond, Vir.: Whittet & Shepperson, 1983.

Millar, Oliver. *Van Dyke in England.* London: National Portrait Gallery, 1982.

Miller, Lillian B. *In the Minds and Hearts of the People: Prologue to the American Revolution: 1760-1774.* Greenwich, Conn.: New York Graphic Society, 1974.

Morgan, John Hill, and Mantle Fielding. *The Life Portraits of Washington and their Replicas.* Philadelphia: Privately printed for subscribers, 1931.

John Norton & Sons: Merchants of London and Virginia: Being the Papers from their Counting House for the Years 1750-1795. Edited by Frances Norton Mason. Richmond, Vir.: Deitz Press, 1937.

Olds, Irving S. *Bits and Pieces of American History.* New York: Privately printed, 1951.

Oliver, Andrew. "Peter Pelham (ca. 1697-1751): Sometime Printmaker of Boston," in *Boston Prints and Printmakers, 1670-1775.* Edited by Walter Muir Whitehill and Sinclair H. Hitchings. Boston: Colonial Society of Massachusetts, 1973.

Paulson, Ronald. *Hogarth's Graphic Works.* Rev. ed. 2 vols. New Haven and London: Yale University Press, 1970.

Phillips, P. Lee. *A List of Maps of America in the Library of Congress.* Washington, D.C.: Government Printing Office, 1901.

Pleasants, Jacob Hall. *Four Late Eighteenth Century Anglo-American Landscape Painters.* Worcester, Mass.: American Antiquarian Society, 1943.

Pownall, Thomas. *A Topographical Description of the Dominions of the United States of America.* London, 1776. Edited by Lois Mulkearn. Pittsburgh: University of Pittsburgh Press, 1949.

Prime, Alfred Coxe. *The Arts and Crafts in Philadelphia, Maryland, and South Carolina 1721-1785: Gleanings from Newspapers.* Topsfield, Mass.: Walpole Society, 1929.

__________. *The Arts and Crafts in Philadelphia, Maryland, and South Carolina 1786-1800.* Series 2. Topsfield, Mass: Walpole Society, 1932.

Prown, Jules David. *John Singleton Copley in America, 1738-1774.* Cambridge, Mass.: Harvard University Press for the National Gallery of Art, Washington, D.C., 1960.

Quimby, Ian M. G. "The Doolittle Engravings of the Battle of Lexington and Concord," in *Winterthur Portfolio* 4:83-108.

Richardson, Edgar Preston. "Charles Willson Peale's Engravings in the Year of National Crisis, 1787," in *Winterthur Portfolio One.* Edited by Edgar P. Richardson, John D. Morse, and Milo M. Naeve. Winterthur, Del.: Henry Francis du Pont Winterthur Museum, 1964.

Roylance, Dale. "Aquatint Engraving in England." In Gloria-Gilda Deák, *William James Bennett: Master of the Aquatint View.* New York: New York Public Library, 1988.

Russell, Ronald. *Guide to British Topographical Prints.* London: Newton Abbott, England, and North Pomfret, Vt.: David & Charles, 1979.

Rutledge, Anna Wells. "Charleston's First Artistic Couple." *Antiques* 52, no. 2 (August 1947): 100-102.

Saunders, Richard H., and Ellen G. Miles. *American Colonial Portraits: 1700-1776.* Washington City: Smithsonian Institution Press for The National Portrait Gallery, 1987.

Sayer, Robert, and John Bennett. *Sayer and Bennett's Enlarged Catalogue of New and Valuable Prints in Sets, or Single . . . in Great Variety . . . Where Gentlemen for Furniture, Merchants for Exportation, and Shopkeepers to sell again, May be supplied with the greatest Assort-ment, on the most reasonable Terms. For 1775.* London, 1775; reprint, Townbridge and London: Redwood Press for the Holland Press, 1970.

Schaw, Janet. *Journal of a Lady of Quality, Being a Narrative of a Journey from Scotland to the West Indies, North Carolina, and Portugal in the Years 1774 to 1776.* Edited by Evangeline Walker Andrews and Charles McLean Andrews. New Haven: Yale University Press, 1923.

Sellers, Charles Coleman. *Benjamin Franklin in Portraiture.* New Haven: Yale University Press, 1962.

___________. *Portraits and Miniatures by Charles Willson Peale*, in Transactions of the American Philosophical Society, vol. 42, pt. 1. Philadelphia: American Philosophical Society, 1952.

Shadwell, Wendy J. *American Printmaking: The First 150 Years.* Washington, D.C.: Smithsonian Institution Press for The Museum of Graphic Arts, 1971.

___________. "The Portrait Engravings of Charles Willson Peale." *Eighteenth Century Prints in Colonial America: To Educate and Decorate.* Edited by Joan D. Dolmetsch. Williamsburg: Colonial Williamsburg Foundation, 1979.

Shorter, Alfred H. *Paper Mills and Paper Makers in England 1495-1800.* Vol. 6 of *Monumenta Chartæ Papyraceæ Historium Illustrantia.* Hilversum, Holland: Paper Publications Society, 1958.

Smith, John Chaloner. *British Mezzotinto Portraits: Being a Descriptive Catalogue of These Engravings from the Introduction of the Art to the Early Part of the Present Century.* 4 parts. London: Henry Sotheran & Co., 1884.

Snyder, Martin P. *City of Independence: Views of Philadelphia Before 1800.* New York: Praeger Publishers, 1975.

Sommers, Frank H., III. "Thomas Hollis and the Arts of Dissent," in *Prints in and of America to 1850.* Edited by John D. Morse. Charlottesville: University Press of Virginia for the Henry Francis du Pont Winterthur Museum, 1970.

Stauffer, David McNeely. *American Engravers Upon Copper and Steel.* 2 vols. New York: Grolier Club, 1907.

Stokes, Isaac Newton Phelps. *Iconography of Manhattan Island 1498-1909.* 3 vols. New York: Robert H. Dodd, 1915.

Stokes, I. N. Phelps, and Daniel C. Haskell. *American Historical Prints: Early Views of American Cities, Etc.* New York: New York Public Library, 1932.

Swan, Bradford F. "Prints of the American Indians, 1670-1775," in *Boston Prints and Printmakers, 1670-1775.* Edited by Walter Muir Whitehill and Sinclair H. Hitchings. Boston: Colonial Society of Massachusetts, 1973.

Symes, Michael. "The Landscape Park Engravings of Luke Sullivan," in *Journal of Garden History* 4, no. 2 (Spring 1984): 179-89.

Temple, Sarah B. Gober, and Kenneth Coleman. *Georgia Journeys: Being an Account of the Lives of Georgia's Original Settlers and Many Other Settlers from the Founding of the Colony in 1732 Until the Institutions of Royal Government in 1754.* 3 vols. London, 1920-23; Athens: University of Georgia Press, 1961.

Thorne, Thomas. "Eighteenth Century Painting in the South" in *Antiques* 59, no. 3 (March 1951): 204-206.

Tooley, Ronald Vere. *Tooley's Dictionary of Mapmakers.* With introduction by Helen Wallis. Tring Hertfordshire, England: Map Collector Publications, Limited, 1979.

Wainwright, Nicholas B. *Colonial Grandeur in Philadelphia: The House and Furniture of General John Cadwalader.* Philadelphia, 1964.

___________. "Scull and Heap's East Prospect of Philadelphia," in *Pennsylvania Magazine of History and Biography* 73 (1949): 16-25.

Waite, Emma Forbes. "William Price of Boston: Map Maker, Merchant, Churchman," in *Old-Time New England* 46, no. 2 (October-December 1955): 52-56.

Wick, Wendy C. *George Washington, An American Icon: The Eighteenth Century Portraits.* Washington, D.C.: Smithsonian Institution Traveling Exhibition Service and The National Portrait Gallery, 1982.

Wilder, F. L. *Sporting Prints.* New York: Viking Press, 1974.

Diary of Anna Green Winslow: A Boston School Girl of 1771. Edited by Alice Morse Earle. Boston and New York: Houghton Mifflin & Co., and Cambridge, Mass.: Riverside Press, 1894.

Wittkower, Rudolph. *Art and Architecture in Italy 1650-1750.* Harmondsworth, Middlesex, England, and Baltimore: Penguin Books, 1958.

Editor: Nancy Eickel

Design: Grafik Communications, Ltd.
Alexandria, Virginia

Typeset in Percepta.

Text printed on
Japan New Age Matt Art.

Printed in Hong Kong by
South China Printing Co.

Cover: A View of Part of the Town of Boston in New-England and Brittish Troops of War Landing Their Troops! 1768 *(cat. no. 42)*

Frontispiece: Thomas Jefferson
A Philosopher a Patriote and a Friend
(cat. no. 39)

ISBN 0-88397-098-8